# Reading Is Believing

# Reading Is Believing

The Christian Faith through Literature and Film

## David S. Cunningham

**Brazos Press**

A Division of Baker Book House Co
Grand Rapids, Michigan 49516

© 2002 by David S. Cunningham

Published by Brazos Press
a division of Baker Book House Company
P.O. Box 6287, Grand Rapids, MI 49516-6287

Printed in the United States of America

**Library of Congress Cataloging-in-Publication Data**

Cunningham, David S., 1961–
    Reading is believing : the Christian faith through literature
and film / David S. Cunningham
        p.    cm.
    Includes bibliographical references.
    ISBN 1-58743-044-4 (pbk.)
    1. Religion and literature. 2. Literature, Modern—History
and criticism. I. Title.
PN59 .C86 2002
809′ .933823811—dc21                    2002006207

Scripture is taken from the New Revised Standard Version of the Bible, copyright 1989 by the Division of Christian Education of the National Council of the Churches of Christ in the USA. Used by permission.

For current information about all releases from Brazos Press, visit our web site:
http://www.brazospress.com

To the many students
over the past decade and more
at
Austin College
Sherman, Texas
The University of St. Thomas
St. Paul, Minnesota
and
Seabury-Western Theological Seminary
Evanston, Illinois
who have read, listened to, debated, and struggled with
my theological reflections on fiction, drama, and film:
this book is dedicated
with respect, affection, and gratitude

# Contents

# Preface

In the early 1990s, a well-known scholar of classics and philosophy, Martha Nussbaum, gave a series of lectures at Hamline University in St. Paul, Minnesota. The subject of her lectures was philosophical, but she chose, as one of her primary texts, a novel: Charles Dickens's *Hard Times*. Since she knew that many of her fellow philosophers, at least, might well have found this choice somewhat surprising, she began her first lecture with an *apology* (in that word's ancient meaning of "defense") for giving so much attention to literature. Among other points, Nussbaum emphasized that fiction encourages readers to "get involved" in the story; they are asked to participate, to allow the imaginative world of the work of fiction to become a world that they themselves can inhabit. Moreover, she said, novels point us toward the "ordinary" aspects of human existence; they are not focused only on rare occurrences or on events that will transpire in only a tiny percentage of the lives of those who read them. Novels often help us to focus on the ordinary case—not on the exception to the rule. They therefore encourage us to acknowledge the full humanity of others: their joys and sorrows, their hopes and aspirations.

I was present at Professor Nussbaum's lecture, and it led me to reflect on the relationship between narrative fiction and my own academic discipline of Christian theology. I had already been teaching for several years at that point, and I had made considerable use of novels, short stories, and plays in my classes. I had found these works of fiction to be an extraordinarily helpful teaching tool: for one thing, students always enjoyed reading and discussing them. Moreover, most of my students were able to recognize how the fiction that we were reading exemplified and explicated the Christian beliefs that we were studying. So I had already gathered quite a bit of evidence that Christians could gain a clearer perspective on their own faith by reading literature. But Professor Nussbaum's lecture led me to think more broadly about the relationship between reading literature and believing in the Christian faith. I started to realize that literature could be more than just a useful teaching tool or a reservoir of concrete examples for illustrating theological claims. In short, I came to the conviction that, for Christians, "reading is believing."

Literature—particularly fictional narratives and drama—tends to encourage its readers to acknowledge and attend to the *humanity* of other human beings. Consequently, it seems a particularly appropriate medium for thinking through the claims of Christian theology, since Christianity has, from its beginnings, stressed the importance of such acknowledgment and attention. Most of us, as we work our way through life, tend to focus on *ourselves*. This is certainly understandable to a point, since we all participate in the biological "drive to survive"; but Jesus lived his life focused on the significance of other people, and he taught us to try to do the same. Reading fictional narratives helps to reinforce that lesson, for if we are to enter into the world of the novel (or short story, or film, or play), we have to step out of the limelight ourselves. If I am to enter this fictional world, I will have to accept that I am no longer the main character; in all likelihood, I am not a character at all. At least in their form, even if not always in their content, narratives and drama encourage us to become more other-directed.

Moreover, in order to enter the imaginative world that the author has constructed, we are encouraged to "get to know" the characters, often in a thoroughgoing way. Even if we do not particularly care for a certain character's outlook on life, our intimate knowledge of that person's joys and hopes, as well as sorrows and despairs, can give us a certain appreciation for the circumstances in which fictional characters find themselves. Even the most despicable characters—and we will certainly meet a few of them over the course of this book!—tend to evoke our pity or compassion rather than only our anger and resentment. We are strengthened in our resolve to live better lives rather than merely exulting in our superiority over others, and this strengthening mirrors the traditional teachings of Christianity. In fact, I would suggest that if we can learn to react to the various faults and foibles of real human beings with the same spirit of pity and compassion with which we often react to the faults of fictional characters, we will, most probably, *already* be living more authentically Christian lives.

Finally, by presenting to us a detailed description of a person's life, literature helps us to understand the relationship between our beliefs and our actions. When we begin to discern the entire shape of a person's life, we also begin to understand why a particular belief might or might not be important to that person—and why that belief might lead a person to *act* in particular ways. The circumstances in which many fictional characters find themselves are often similar to the circumstances in which we find ourselves in our day-to-day lives; this similarity can be recognized even if the main characters are talking animals, or the setting is a fantasy world. Whatever takes place in narrative and drama can provide us with fertile soil in which to cultivate a better understanding of the central beliefs of the Christian faith.

Of course, *the Christian story itself* is in the form of narrative and drama: the stories of the Bible, for example, are stories about people we can recognize and relate to, about their encounters with obstacles and their struggles to survive, about their deepest longings and their greatest triumphs. The stories of the people of Israel, the Gospel accounts of Jesus and the disciples, and the lives of the saints are among the most basic building-blocks of the Christian faith. We should also remember that, when Jesus was trying to help his followers to understand a particularly difficult concept, he often did so by telling them *a story*.

None of this is meant to imply that the Christian story is *fiction* (in the sense of "an invented story that never happened"), nor that other stories can *substitute* for the Christian story as it comes to us in the Bible and its interpretation through history. This central narrative of the Christian faith must always remain primary. Rather, I am simply trying to suggest that Christians don't usually need to stretch very far in order to grasp the structure and significance of narrative and drama. We are already well trained by the heavily *storied* nature of our own faith and its *dramatic* enactment in our worship and in our lives. The Christian story has helped to make us who we are. Thus, when we read a story that takes up the themes of our faith—even if only implicitly or tangentially—we will begin to make connections and to develop new perspectives on the Christian life.

My hope is that those who encounter this book will emerge from the experience with a deeper and more profound appreciation for the central beliefs of the Christian faith—beliefs that are meant to be embodied by those of us who claim that faith as our own. It may also lead to a better *understanding* of these beliefs; but it is not intended only, or even primarily, to move the intellect. I also want this book to help us to imagine how these beliefs hang together as a whole, to enter into these beliefs and to inhabit them, and thereby orient our whole lives so that our Christian faith can become our source, our path, and our goal. Regardless of the extent to which it can help others on their pilgrim way, I can at least testify that writing this book has certainly helped me on my own.

Books are written by people who sit alone at a computer and stare at the screen. This can sometimes give the impression that writing is a solitary or individualistic activity, but nothing could be further than the truth. I was able to write this book only because my life is so interwoven with many others who continually provide support, encouragement, and a sounding board for my ideas. These include colleagues and editors who have solicited my reflections on fiction and film over the past decade. Most of this book was written "from scratch," but a few of the chapters incorporate a small amount of material from previously published works; in particular, my comments on the film versions of *The End of the Affair* and *A Pure Formality* appeared in *The Christian Century* (vol. 117, no. 4, 2–9 February 2000, pp. 156–58) and *Sojourners* (vol. 25, no. 1, January–February 1996, pp. 62–64), respectively. Some material on *The Time of the Angels* and *Beloved*, as well as my general reflections on the Christian understanding of God, comes from my book *These Three are One: The Practice of Trinitarian Theology* (Blackwell, 1998). These materials were rewritten when they were incorporated into the present book.

My ability to complete this book—as has been the case with every book I have written—is due primarily to the good graces of my family: my wife, Teresa Hittner, and my daughters, Monica and Emily Hittner-Cunningham. Not only do they let me work when I must; they also remind me, regularly, that good writers need rest and playtime as well, and they make sure that I get plenty of both. The faculty and staff of Seabury-Western Theological Seminary have been thoroughly supportive of my research and writing commitments, even in the midst of the heavy teaching and administrative load that is so much a part of theological education. The people of St. Luke's Episcopal Church in Evanston, Illinois, have provided a wonderfully supportive environment for our whole family. In addition, they—along with members of other churches in the area—have heard and responded to many of my theological reflections on literature in sermons and adult education workshops. Thanks also to the staff at Brazos Press, including Bobbi Jo Heyboer, Rebecca Cooper, and (in particular) Rodney Clapp, whose early and sustained confidence in this project has been instrumental in its completion.

Finally, I want to thank my students. Special credit goes to those who enrolled in the course "Reading is Believing" that I taught here at Seabury-Western, and who provided comments and feedback on many of the earliest drafts of these chapters: Hickman Alexandre, Henry Austin, Anne Cothran, Kristen Fout, Mary Ann Garrett, Kate Guistolise, Melissanne Hughes, Mary Koppel, Diane Markevitch, Jojo Pamatmat, Hilda Sey, Jerry Shigaki, Roma Simons, and Mollie Ward. Thanks also to my student assistants, who have done research, catalogued books and articles, assisted me in the classroom, and taken a number of tasks off my hands so that I could concentrate more fully on this project: Margaret Adam, Jason Fout, Julie Gilbert, Clifton Healy, and Lisa Walters.

All of them have contributed more than they know to this volume and have enlivened my personal and professional life by their very presence in it. They have also been among the hundreds of students in my classes over the years who have endured my theological reflections on litera-ture with patience and grace. To all these students this book is dedicated in the same spirit of affection, friendship, and love that was embodied and encouraged by the great leader of the church whose life and work is celebrated on this day.

The Feast of St. Aelred of Rievaulx
Anno Domini 2002

# Introduction
## "I Believe . . ."

In the very earliest years of the Christian movement, as the community of disciples increased in number and spread over a vast geographical area, the beliefs and practices of its members began to diverge. The followers of Jesus began to differ about some of the most basic assumptions that gave them their identity as Christians. We see evidence of this in some of the earliest writings within the community of faith—for example, in the book of Acts, in Paul's letters, and even in the subtle differences of emphasis among the four Gospels.

In Paul's letter to the Galatians, for example, he remarks that, during the time since he originally preached there, the people of Galatia had begun to follow "other gospels" and "other Christs." It soon became obvious, not only to Paul but to many members of the earliest Christian communities, that if the followers of Jesus were to retain any sense of unity, they would have to come to some agreement about what they believed and what they practiced.

Such agreement as there was in these early days developed by means of letters and face-to-face conversations among the leaders of various Christian communities. In comparison with our contemporary experience of instant communication and easy travel, the world of the earliest Christians was one in which transportation was complicated and difficult, and in which long-distance communication was slow and unreliable. Thus, it was not uncommon for very different assumptions and practices to develop in the far-flung reaches of the known world.

Of course, this diversity was not necessarily a bad thing. From the beginning, Christians understood their faith as something that would need translation and adaptation into differing cultural settings. The story of the sending of the Spirit at Pentecost (Acts 2) makes it very clear that people from a wide variety of nations and cultures were able to hear

15

the message of the Christian faith in their own language. Unlike Judaism and Islam, Christianity did not endow the original language of its revelation with a mystical or sacred status. Rather, the gospel can be presented in a variety of languages, to a variety of cultures, and still retain its original shape. (Of course, Western Christianity did experiment with the notion that its adopted language, Latin, demanded a similar sort of reverence; more recently, however, the faith has embraced a wide variety of local languages.)

On the other hand, this diversity does not imply a complete relativism. If the word "Christianity" is to have any meaning at all, the faith must have a recognizable shape—a general outline of its claims and some degree of agreement about the practices through which it comes to life. Without such agreement, Christians would not really be in communion with one another. For example, if one group understood Jesus to be God, while another group believed him to be simply a highly successful moral teacher, the beliefs and practices of the two groups would likely diverge; eventually, they might find it difficult to recognize one another as identifiably Christian.

Nor would such groups be able to defend themselves against false charges. For instance, in the earliest period of Christian history, the introduction of such language as "eating the body of Christ" and "loving all people" led to a number of misunderstandings about the new faith. Some local Roman officials worried that Christians under their jurisdictions were promoting cannibalism and group sex. Christians could only respond to these charges if they could state precisely what sorts of activities Christians *were* practicing and that the immoral practices of which they were suspected were not, in fact, "what Christians do."

Eventually, the exchanges of letters and the face-to-face conversations among the leaders of Christian communities gave rise to the creation of short statements of belief, often referred to as "credal" statements, or simply "creeds." (The word comes from the Latin word for "I [or we] believe," which was often the first word of these statements.) These creeds were intended to summarize the most important claims of the new faith and to provide some grounding of and explanation for basic Christian practices. Some of these statements of belief were probably used in connection with the rite of baptism. The earliest among these statements were probably very simple; many scholars believe that the phrases described in the New Testament as associated with baptism ("in the name of Jesus" or "in the name of the Father, the Son, and the Holy Spirit") probably reflect the creeds that newly baptized Christians might have been expected to proclaim at their baptisms.

As time went on, these statements of faith became lengthier and more complex. Some of the earliest creeds were incorporated into Christian worship, and many of them retain a place in the liturgical texts of various Christian denominations to this day. However, some of the later "statements of faith" became so complex that their liturgical use was considered inappropriate. (One example is a lengthy creed sometimes attributed to St. Athanasius, which attempts to offer a finely-differentiated account of the relationships among the persons of the Trinity. This creed is printed in the standard worship texts of some denominations, but its minute distinctions would probably seem out of place within a worship service. On the other hand, some people would say the same thing about those creeds that *are* used regularly in worship; more on that point in a moment.)

The latest and lengthiest creed that became thoroughly incorporated into the Western liturgy was the statement finalized at the Council of Constantinople (381). It was based on a similar but shorter version developed at the Council of Nicea, and so is officially known by the somewhat cumbersome label of "the Nicene-Constantinopolitan Creed." Fortunately, everyone seems to have developed the habit of calling it, more simply, the Nicene Creed.

The Nicene Creed is used in the worship of the overwhelming majority of the world's Christians: Roman Catholics, Eastern Orthodox, Anglicans, and many other Protestants as well. The breadth of its usage sometimes comes as a surprise to members of those denominations within which the creeds play little or no role. I grew up in the Christian Church (Disciples of Christ), which uses no creeds at all other than a simple declaration that Jesus is the Christ. My first introduction to the Nicene Creed came, as it comes for many Protestant Christians, when I began to listen to musical settings of the Mass by Bach and Mozart. I thereby became aware that, regardless of my own denomination's use (or, in my case, nonuse) of creeds, the Nicene Creed had made an extraordinary impact on the church through the ages—and indeed, on various forms of art, music, and literature as well. I began to realize that, even as a member of a noncreedal denomination, I would need to get to know, and to wrestle with, this text.

Moreover, some denominations that "officially" endorse the Nicene Creed do not incorporate it into their worship services on a regular basis; still others who have used it in the past have reduced or eliminated its usage (or have replaced it with a very different statement of belief). Consequently, some Christians who grew up saying the Nicene Creed may today find it to be little more than a dim, distant memory. Nevertheless, the fact that the Nicene Creed retains an official (or at least a semi-official) status in many denominations is evidence of its importance. Despite the complexity of some of its language (I will return to this matter), the Nicene Creed has played an enormously important role in the self-understanding of Christians throughout the ages.

All the same, this lengthy, complex creed is not the only statement of the Christian faith that has had a significant status over time. Before the final formulation of the Nicene Creed, a much shorter statement of similar structure was already well known throughout the Christian world. This statement was known as the Apostles' Creed, and was attributed, by legend, to the original twelve apostles. According to this legend, the twelve apostles themselves created the creed shortly after the day of Pentecost. This occurred under the guidance of the Holy Spirit, and was said to have happened in this way: first, Peter said: "I believe in God the Father almighty, maker of heaven and earth," then Andrew said: "and in Jesus Christ his son," and so on. The creed was therefore described as having been composed by the apostles, and as consisting of twelve parts or *articles*.

This story is certainly legendary, but like all legends, it "tells the truth" more adequately (and certainly more interestingly) than would a complicated documentary history of events that attempted to "stick to the facts." In this particular case, the legend emphasizes something that Christians have, throughout history, generally believed—namely, that there are some significant lines of continuity between the creed itself and the beliefs that motivated the original followers of Jesus. Recent scholarship has demonstrated significant connections between the phrases of the Apostles' Creed and the New Testament. Moreover, because of its brevity and its ancient origin, it has come to serve as one of the most clear and concise statements of the essential structure of Christian belief. Even those denominations that do not regularly use (or even officially recognize) the Apostles' Creed have often used it, whether explicitly or implicitly, to structure their ministries of teaching, preaching, and social action.

In sum, then, the Apostles' Creed provides us with a biblically based, historically attested, and frequently used statement of the most basic claims of the Christian faith. Its traditional division into twelve articles, however legendary, is very helpful to us today; it allows us to break down this statement of faith into its component parts, and to consider each one in turn. It also provides a straightforward system for the chapter divisions of books—including this one—that explore the contours of Christian belief.

At the same time, this process of division can be misleading; it can suggest that a creed is simply a checklist or a series of litmus tests of Christian belief. One can imagine someone looking down the list and saying something like, "Let's see, 'I believe in God'—okay, yes, I can agree with that one; then comes 'in Jesus Christ'—yes, fine; now this next one, 'born of the virgin Mary'—I'm not so sure about that," and so on. In practice, however, the creeds have not typically functioned as a checklist. The phrases of the creed are not a series of tests of one's adherence to Christian belief; they are closely interrelated aspects of the whole story of God and our relationship with God. Thus, if we divide up the creed too sharply—thinking of it as nothing more than a checklist of isolated beliefs—we may be missing the point.

Nor should we think of the creeds primarily as tools for helping outsiders understand why the Christian faith is such "Good News." These creeds were never intended to be self-explanatory. We wouldn't normally expect a frantic rush of new seekers into our churches if we hung a big banner outside that read "We believe that Jesus ascended into heaven." While this claim is a key part of the Christian story, and while it encourages us to think deeply and profoundly about certain elements of our faith (see chapter six), it may not have much attraction for those who are unacquainted with the Christian faith.

I find it more useful to think of the creed, first, as a *summary* of the vast narratives of the Christian faith; second, as a *resource* for study and conversation among those who already know those stories well; and finally, as a *goal* that encourages all Christians as they try to *live into* those stories in their worship and in their daily lives. The relationship between the creeds and the Bible is thus not a matter of opposition or competition, but rather a matter of concentration and complementarity. British theologian Nicholas Lash puts the matter like this: "What the Scriptures say at length, the creeds say briefly." Those who are unfamiliar with the Christian faith will come to know it through the primary narratives of the Bible and the liturgy, and through an encounter with the actual lives of Christian believers. The creeds are more useful to those who are already familiar with the stories and practices of Christianity; they help believers understand and summarize their faith.

At the same time, we should note that, not only to those who are unfamiliar with the Christian faith but also to those who are well-acquainted with it, the phrase "I believe" at the beginning of the creed can be misleading. The reasons for this are deeply embedded in our current cultural assumptions and in our most common uses of the word. We use the verb *believe* in a variety of ways, none of which is particularly apt for explaining how the word has traditionally been understood in the creeds. We sometimes use the word to describe an opinion or a fact about which we are uncertain: "I believe that meeting is tomorrow," meaning: I'm not sure, but I think so. We also use the word to describe a tentative or provisional intention on our own part: "I believe I'll take a walk this afternoon," meaning: I've pretty well made up my mind to do this, though I could be dissuaded. Sometimes it's an expression of trust: "I believe you," meaning: I trust that you are telling me the truth. And of course, it can also describe convictions: "I believe in free speech," meaning, I think it's the right thing, I wouldn't have it any other way, and I might even die for its protection. These various meanings of the verb *believe* have led to a certain degree of confusion among speakers of the English language, and are also occasionally a source of humor (as in the T-shirt that reads: "Everyone has to believe in something; I believe I'll have another cookie").

But none of these meanings is really descriptive of the use of the word *believe* in the creeds, or in more general statements that "Christians believe in" particular things. While the word *believe* does carry with it some of the above-mentioned connotations—including a proclamation of trust and a statement of conviction—it ultimately transcends all these elements. Part of this is due to the little word that appears just after the word *believe*—the little unobstrusive word *in*. To recognize the importance of this word, think about the two statements "I believe you" and "I believe *in* you." The first one expresses a willingness to accept what the other says as truthful or accurate; this decision may be based on the person's perceived authority, an external corroboration, or just habit. But the second expression, "I believe *in* you," implies a real relationship and something of a personal investment in the other person. It suggests commitment, trust, acceptance, conviction, and even certainty—something like, "I know you can do it" or "My whole life is wrapped up in you."

This is part of what we mean when we make a claim such as "I believe in God." In doing so, we are announcing an orientation of our whole lives, a direction and a focus that we have come to acknowledge. When we speak about our beliefs, we are describing ourselves as being part of a much larger group—part of the whole company of faithful people, over time and across space. We are aligning ourselves with billions of Christian believers, the living and the dead, who make up the Body of Christ. I might well interpret some aspect of my faith differently from the way a twelfth-century Christian in eastern Europe would have done; but this should not prevent me from accepting that we are both recognizably members of the same Body.

But just how different can our interpretations be before we (and others) begin to have difficulty recognizing our commonality? If we are to hope for any real *content* in a phrase that begins with words "Christians believe in . . . ," then we will need to be continuously about the business of exploring, examining, and discussing the meaning and significance of whatever we claim to believe in. We need to have some inkling of what we are saying when we say that "we believe in the Holy Spirit" or "we believe in life everlasting." We need to think about what these words might refer to, why they have been considered to be so important across all of Christian history, and how they might continue to be meaningful for us today. Working through a basic statement of Christian belief (such as the Apostles' Creed), phrase by phrase, has thus been a favorite procedure for Christian theologians throughout the ages. Even writers in noncreedal traditions often attend to the various elements of belief that are highlighted in the creeds when writing a general text about the shape of Christian faith. (For an example, see the work of the Baptist theologian James McClendon, cited at the end of this chapter.) Choose almost any significant theological writer at random, from the second century to the present day, and you will find—somewhere among that person's works—an exploration of the essential features of Christian belief. More often than not, that exploration will, at least implicitly, be attentive to the form and content of the Apostles' Creed or the Nicene Creed.

Unfortunately, many readers of these accounts find them fairly dry, and often come away from the encounter with more than a few doubts about their relevance to present-day Christian practice. Sometimes these accounts attempt to provide rather more historical detail than most believers care to know—explaining the biblical and traditional origins of a particular phrase, commenting in detail on the problems of translation from the original language, and sometimes describing how particular elements of belief are related to others. Since many of the phrases in the creeds were hammered out in an attempt to settle some very complex theological argument, a fair amount of historical contextualization is often necessary in order to show why and how someone came up with a particular phrase and why that phrase won widespread acceptance. As the centuries passed and the number of theological arguments multiplied, so did the number and complexity of the forms of words invented to address them.

For example, many Christians regularly repeat the phrase in the Nicene Creed in which Jesus Christ is said to be "eternally begotten of the Father." Very few people have the slightest idea what it means. The phrase's origins are deeply buried in an early controversy over the relationship between Jesus and God; some wanted to describe Christ as a *creature*—created (as is the rest of the world) by God. Others wanted to put Christ in the same category as God—uncreated and therefore not having a beginning. Both groups agreed that the Son was generated ("begotten") by the Father, but this seemed to suggest that the Son had a starting point in time—therefore implying that there was a time at which the Son did not yet exist. But for some, it was essential to insist that, although begotten by God, the Son had no starting point in time. Somewhere along the way, someone hit upon the solution of describing the Son as "eternally begotten of the Father."

Now that explanation may seem a bit complex (not to mention dry and irrelevant), but at least it was relatively short, and you will note that I spared you the names, dates, and circumstances involved in each of the arguments! But such details are in fact the mainstay of a great many commentaries on the creed and other accounts of the essential structure of the Christian faith. Such detailed accounts can be extremely important, and I have no desire to malign them in general; indeed, I've written a few of them myself. Such analyses clearly have their place; for example, they are extremely important among academic theologians, whose business it is to discern problems and questions where others might have seen none. Nevertheless, such finely nuanced explications of the basic elements of our faith do little to inspire the typical Christian reader to understand why a particular belief is being held up as so central. Since the argument that was taking place in the fourth century (about the nature of the generation of the Son by the Father) is not an argument that we tend to be much interested in today; we have a hard time seeing the point. Moreover, an academically-oriented commentary (along the lines that I have just described) usually does little to explain just how different the Christian life might look, were a particular belief to be *implemented* and *lived out* in a profound and thoroughgoing way.

These two shortcomings of many traditional explications of Christian belief—their failure to focus on the *relevance* and the *ethical implications* of particular Christian beliefs—need particular attention in our contemporary "post-Christian" context. Even in the majority-Christian culture of the United States, we can no longer expect most people to have "grown up" in the faith or to have absorbed a general outline of the Christian story through the narratives and practices of the wider culture. Even those who have grown up within a church community will not typically have experienced the extensive programs of Christian education and formation that were par for the course for those of previous generations. In order for any statement about Christian belief to serve as a useful claim about Christian identity and to make a difference in the lives of Christian believers, that statement needs to be explicated in detail. Otherwise, it will survive only as an object of rote memorization—reeled off at the designated moment in a worship service or Christian education class, but rarely understood, embraced, cherished, or put into practice.

Precisely because I hope that Christians will want to understand, embrace, cherish, and practice their faith, I have sought to write a book that would help them do so. I want to develop a conversation about Christian belief that helps to explain *why* particular beliefs are important, as well as *what difference* these beliefs make for the Christian life. And I would like this discussion to be accessible to persons who do not necessarily bring a great deal of background in the academic study of theology or the history of Christian thought, and who don't find themselves compelled to investigate those fields of study in much detail.

I have chosen the vehicle of *literature* as a means of underscoring both the relevance and the practical implications of some of the most central beliefs of Christianity. (I will also make a number of comments on the vehicle of *film*, since a fair number of the works that I treat here have been made into films; one chapter focuses exclusively on a film.) I have chosen these particular vehicles because I believe that there are some important resonances between *reading* and *believing*. By "reading," I mean not just the reading of the Bible or of books that are explicitly about the Christian faith; rather, I want to suggest that belief can be inspired by a very wide range of reading material. In fact, I'm trying to use the word *reading* in the broadest sense possible: we can often arrive at a better understanding of our faith by reading novels, plays, short stories, and even works of nonfiction that aren't directly about religion at all. We can even "read" films—by which I mean not just viewing them, not just allowing ourselves to be entertained by them, but thinking carefully about how they are constructed and how they "mean." (In this book, films are treated mostly as a supplement to novels; readers who would like to learn more about "reading" a film are encouraged to consult Bryan Stone's excellent book *Faith and Film*, which offers an explication of the Apostles' Creed through films rather than novels. The book is included in the reading list at the end of this chapter.)

Of course, not just anything that we read will necessarily inspire or explicate belief of any kind, let alone specifically Christian belief. We have to make choices based on the underlying assumptions and effects of a particular piece of writing or film. I'm not trying to suggest that reading *makes* a person into a believer, nor that one can only come to belief through reading. (In fact, most people come to the Christian faith through other people—parents, teachers, pastors, and friends—and often primarily through actions rather than words.) But I do want to suggest that *reading* can frequently lead Christians to a clearer and deeper understanding of their own beliefs, and thereby to a deeper faith. In this sense, then, for Christians, "reading is believing."

In the preface to this book, I suggested that the reading of literature can have a number of positive resonances with the belief and practice of Christian faith. Literature encourages us to get involved with the characters, thereby helping us to recognize the depth of their humanity. It redirects our energy away from an excessive focus on ourselves, lifting up the significance of other people. Literature also helps us see the whole of a human life, in all its breadth and complexity; this in turn can help explain why people think the things they think, and why they do the things they do. Literature therefore helps us understand the relationship between belief and action—which is, of course, a central feature of the Christian faith.

These advantages of the literary form are present, whether the story is long or short, whether it is history-like or fantastical, whether its form is narrative (novels and short stories) or dramatic (plays and films). In each case, an author must offer us some clues about the motives of the characters—if for no other reason than to insure that we can follow, and begin to make sense of, the story. Such clues are even more important when a particular character's actions seem irrational, cruel, or just plain evil. For example, in "real life," we may suddenly meet a person who seems to us extremely angry. We might guess that there are *reasons* for this person's anger; but we are not usually privy to the information that would explain these reasons to us, and we are sometimes too hurt or bewildered by this anger to bother with wondering about the reasons. If the person becomes more than a casual acquaintance, we may eventually find opportunities to inquire about, and perhaps even discover, the reasons for this anger. But in many cases, we see only a snapshot. We do not know enough about the whole, complex course of the person's life—where he is coming from, or where she is going—to understand the attitudes and emotions being displayed.

But in most fiction, a person about whom we only have this snapshot of information will never become a significant or important character in the work. We tend to allow such characters to move onstage and offstage quickly; they do not attract much attention. We attend only to those characters about whom the author or director has given us adequate background information. When we have such information, we have a context within which we can understand the character's actions and thoughts. This context helps us understand why the characters might think and do the kinds of things that they think and do.

I hope that the insights that can be gleaned from narrative fiction will help readers imagine what our beliefs might look like in concrete, real-life circumstances (and, it must be added, some examples of what they should *not* look like). If we are going to continue to say such apparently outlandish things as "Jesus ascended into heaven" or "I believe in the resurrection of the flesh," we ought to be able to say not only what such a claim might mean, but also why or how it might make a difference in the lives of those who claim to believe it—and how you might be able to tell someone who does believe it from someone who doesn't. I hope that this book will be of service in this regard, and that its readers will feel encouraged to seek out additional novels, short stories, plays, and films that might likewise point readers and viewers toward a clearer understanding of the theological relevance and the ethical implications of Christianity.

My confidence in this approach has been reinforced over the past twelve years, as I have taught theology to a wide variety of audiences using fiction, drama, and film. Time and again, I have seen students who thought that they could never understand the basic claims of the Christian faith—as well as students who thought that they couldn't care less!—come to a quite profound understanding of difficult theological concepts by discussing their development within the structures of narrative and dramatic fiction. This process has usually been most successful when students are introduced to the general outline of a particular theological claim, are then asked to read a book or see a film that has been chosen to illustrate it, and are then encouraged to talk about it. Consequently, I have structured the chapters of this book so as to encourage this kind of approach.

Each chapter begins with a brief discussion of the questions or problems associated with a basic element of Christian belief. (The chapter titles are quotations from the Apostles' Creed, but you don't have to use the creed, or even be familiar with it, in order to follow the structure of the book.) The chapter then introduces a work of literature that I have chosen to explicate that element. (Most of these works are contemporary novels; I have also commented on the filmed versions of these works when they exist. I have also included one nineteenth-century novel, as well as one short story, one play, one film that was originally written as a screenplay, and one nonfictional narrative. This, I hope, will encourage readers to adopt the very broad definition of "reading" that I used when thinking about this subject.) In each case, I offer a short summary of the work in question; but of course, in the short space available to me here, I cannot capture all the subtleties and nuances of the work as a whole. Fortunately, many readers will already be familiar with the novel or film in question (many of them have been bestsellers).

Those who are able to do so can begin by reading only the first section of the chapter, and then, when they come to a row of asterisks, like this one,

* * * * *

they can turn to the novel or play or film described. (Most of them are currently in print, and can be expected to remain so; all are widely available at bookstores and libraries. The films are widely available in both VHS and DVD format.) After encountering the work first-hand, readers can return to the relevant chapter and see what they think of my interpretation.

But whether or not you are able to read the novels, attend the plays, and see the films in question, I have provided a plot summary in each case, focusing especially on those elements of the work that I am trying to bring to the forefront. My summaries are necessarily abbreviated and selective, but they may be helpful for those who weren't able to examine the work in question or who finished it a month ago (or a decade ago!) and have forgotten it, or who can't imagine to what elements of a long and convoluted plot they were supposed to have been giving their fullest attention. After the plot summary (and sometimes woven into it as well), readers will find my own theological commentary on the book, and a description of how it might help us better understand whatever element of Christian belief is being examined in that chapter.

I want to stress, however, that my particular perspective on these books and films is only *one* of many possible readings. Part of what makes literature so durable, so ever-new in every age, is its ability to meet every generation of readers in their own place. My perspectives grow out of my experience as a Christian, as a professional theologian, and as a teacher. Obviously, my interpretations are heavily influenced by my decision to use particular texts to illustrate particular elements of Christian belief. In no case am I trying to suggest that my interpretation is necessarily that of the book's author. (Many would probably deny any conscious attention to the themes I'm raising; others might be aghast that I'm suggesting *any* possible connection to the Christian faith; and still others aren't around to defend themselves!) Nor am I denying the existence of different, even sharply contrasting interpretations. I'm simply trying to allow my own background in theology and ethics to come to the forefront as I discuss the work in question.

Readers who have the opportunity to do so are encouraged to work through this book with others, allowing for the possibility of discussion and conversation about each chapter. This conversation could take place in a university or seminary classroom, a church-based discussion group, an informal book group, or even over the Internet. This is not to suggest, of course, that the individual reader cannot also put the book to good use. In any case, we all carry around within ourselves a thousand conversations and encounters amassed over the years and brought back to mind by new encounters with a text. Because the works of literature and film discussed in this book are particularly rich and pregnant with meaning, readers usually find themselves offering interpretations or making connections that are different from those offered in this book and from those that might be offered by other readers. Such variations are, I think, all to the good; I have already denied any claim to offer a definitive or ultimately authoritative interpretation (whatever that would be) of these rich and multilayered works of literature and art. On the other hand, precisely because of this richness of these texts, I can't guarantee that everything that my readers might see or feel when encountering them will necessarily lead to sound theological conclusions! I hope that readers will find some pointers in that direction in my own commentaries, and that they will find other conversation partners with whom they can discover more.

At the end of each chapter, I have listed a few discussion questions; many people will find these wholly unnecessary, since these chapters tend to provoke conversation and discussion automatically. But for those looking for a place to begin, and for those who must work through the text in relative isolation from others, the questions may be of some use. In each chapter, the list of discussion questions is followed by two brief lists of suggestions for further reading. The first of these points to some of the more useful and accessible books or articles examining the element of Christian belief that is discussed in the chapter, or the particular work used to illustrate it. It also includes those books that I have cited (by quoting or paraphrasing) within the chapter, so that those who want to learn more can do so without wading through footnotes. Books in this list are designated as introductory, advanced (requiring a little more background in theology or literary criticism for a full appreciation of its contents), and specialized (more technical works, many of which have influenced my own thinking on the subject at hand). Split designations denote the border regions between these categories. The list appearing at the very end of all chapters (except this one) suggests some other novels and films that might provide further raw material for discussion of the same topic. At the end of the present introductory chapter, this list is replaced by an English translation of the Apostles' Creed, which also shows how it is parsed into the twelve chapters that follow.

This book is meant only to provide the overall structure for a discussion of some of the essential beliefs and practices of Christians. It cannot hope to nuance every argument or provide every scrap of detail that might possibly be included. My plot summaries and my theological reflections are only meant to be provide a springboard to a much wider conversation and exploration of Christian belief. The word *reading* in the title of the book you're now holding does not refer primarily to the reading of *this* book. My confidence in the claim that, for Christians, "reading is believing" is derived from the enthusiasm, the joy, and the life-changing experiences reported by those who have read the twelve brilliant authors discussed within these pages, and many other great works of fiction and drama. By encountering their works, may you also become convinced that, for Christians, *reading is believing.*

## Questions For Discussion

1. Most people tend to think that works of fiction and drama are easier (or more fun) to read than other forms of writing. Why do you suppose this is?

2. What makes a work of literature relevant to faith? Does it need to make explicit reference to God, Jesus, or the church? If not, what elements would you expect to be present for a work of literature to have relevance for Christian faith?

3. Of the various senses of the verb *to believe* that are discussed in this chapter, which do you find yourself most frequently intending? Do you think that your everyday uses of the word have any effect on what you mean by "belief" in the context of Christian faith?

4. Expand upon this chapter's discussion of the relationship between literature (particularly narratives and drama) and the Christian faith. In what other ways does reading such stories have the potential to build up our faith?

5. What are your own expectations for undertaking the readings suggested in this book? What are your hopes (and fears) associated with this enterprise?

## For Further Reading

Fackre, Gabriel. *The Christian Story: A Narrative Interpretation of Basic Christian Doctrine.* 3rd ed. Grand Rapids: Eerdmans, 1996. (Advanced)

Frei, Hans W. *The Eclipse of the Biblical Narrative: A Study in Eighteenth and Nineteenth Century Hermeneutics.* New Haven: Yale University Press, 1974. (Specialized)

Lash, Nicholas. *Believing Three Ways In One God: A Reading of the Apostles' Creed.* Notre Dame, Ind.: University of Notre Dame Press, 1992. (Introductory/Advanced)

Lochman, Jan Milic. *The Faith We Confess: An Ecumenical Dogmatics.* Philadelphia: Fortress Press, 1984. (Advanced)

McClendon, James Wm., Jr. *Systematic Theology.* Vol. 2, *Doctrine.* Nashville: Abingdon Press, 1994. (Advanced)

McIntosh, Mark. *Mysteries of Faith.* Boston: Cowley Publications, 2000. (Introductory)

Nussbaum, Martha C. *Love's Knowledge: Essays on Philosophy and Literature.* New York: Oxford University Press, 1990. (Advanced/Specialized)

Placher, William C. *Narratives of a Vulnerable God: Christ, Theology, and Scripture.* Louisville: Westminster/John Knox Press, 1994. (Introductory/Advanced)

Stone, Bryan F. *Faith and Film: Theological Themes at the Cinema.* St. Louis: Chalice Press, 2000. (Introductory)

## An English Translation of the Apostles' Creed

(in twelve articles, each indicating who was legendarily responsible for its creation)

[Peter:] I believe in God, the Father almighty, creator of heaven and earth

[Andrew:] And in Jesus Christ, God's only son, our Lord,

[James:] Who was conceived by the Holy Spirit, born of the Virgin Mary,

[John:] Suffered under Pontius Pilate, was crucified, died, and buried,

[Thomas:] Descended into hell, on the third day rose again from the dead,

[James:] Ascended to heaven, sits at the right hand of God the Father almighty,

[Philip:] From there he will come to judge the living and the dead;

[Bartholomew:] I believe in the Holy Spirit,

[Matthew:] The holy catholic Church, the communion of saints

[Simon:] the forgiveness of sins,

[Thaddeus:] the resurrection of the flesh,

[Matthias:] and the life everlasting.

# one

# "God, the Father Almighty, Creator of Heaven and Earth"

One might be tempted, at first glance, to regard the opening clause of the creed as the least controversial of its elements. In North American society at least, the claim that one believes in God is, in itself, unlikely to raise many eyebrows. In most circumstances, it is a socially acceptable and rather mundane claim—rather like espousing a belief in free trade or admitting a fondness for artichokes. Belief in God is implied rather pervasively: the motto "In God We Trust" appears on our coins and currency, and Presidents like to end their speeches with the phrase "God Bless America." Consequently, the claim "I believe in God" seems unlikely even to catch the attention of most audiences. That, I would like to suggest, is precisely the problem.

References to *God* in the public discourse of the United States (and, for that matter, of most of the Western world) tend to be very nonspecific. Only when someone attempts to articulate the *specific character-istics* of this God in whom we claim to place our trust (or who is asked to "bless America") does widespread disagreement begin to emerge. The god named on dollar bills and in campaign speeches can only be a generic god, a "higher power" whose traits and characteristics are defined by each hearer as that person sees fit. As a result, the word *God* becomes a mere placeholder, endowed with specific content only in the mind of the individual (or, perhaps more often, left without much specific content). This represents a serious shift in the traditional usage of the word *God*.

At one time, this generic notion of god would have seemed very odd indeed. In a culture in which belief in some form of deity was nearly universal and taken rather more seriously, the word *god* was only relevant if one could specify the particular god or gods in whom one believed.

31

Without such specification, the claim "I believe in God" was about as useful as "I am breathing" or "I am a human being." In fact, until the modern era, the word *atheism* did not typically designate someone who believed that there were no gods; rather, it was used to label those who believed in a different god or gods than did the dominant culture. So Akhenaten and Socrates were denounced as atheists, not because they denied the existence of God, but because they believed in only *one* God— in defiance of the polytheistic cultures that surrounded them (ancient Egypt and ancient Greece, respectively).

Only in the modern era do we witness a widespread willingness to deny the existence of *any* god or gods; and thus, this is the era in which human beings develop the general categories of *theism,* "belief in some god(s)," and atheism, "belief in no god(s)." Consequently, only in the modern era does anyone take an interest in the generic notion of belief in god; previously, the statement "I believe in God" would have usually provoked the scoffing reply: "Well of course you do! But just *who is* this God in whom you believe?"

Today, we like to think that the widespread popularity of the generic notion of god is a sign that everyone believes in the same divine being or person or force. But as even the most casual student of culture will observe, the various gods (in whom human beings have, from time to time, believed) differ considerably from one another. Some are angry and isolated; some are conniving and deceitful; some are joyous and tolerant. These gods differ not only in their "inner being," but also in their relationship with the world and in their ethical demands. So it is never enough to say, simply, "I believe in God"; one must also specify the character of the God in whom one believes.

The importance of such specificity would be more obvious to a person who was convinced that the god(s) exercise an extraordinary degree of power and control over one's life. In our culture, God has a rather marginalized status; we are too busy with so many other aspects of our lives to dwell very much on our belief in God. At one time, however, God (or the gods) had more status. One's gods were responsible for one's creation and preservation, and at any moment they might bring about the end of one's life (whether for a good reason, a bad reason, or no reason at all). Such gods were believed to be powerful and demanding of allegiance; they did not necessarily curse what we would like to have cursed or bless what we would like to have blessed. Because of the authority and power imputed to such gods, people tended to work rather hard to understand them, to discern their will, and to obey.

This strong sense of the power of the gods (and the allegiance that people owe to them) has led us to develop another, even less specific sense of the word *god*: a person's god is whatever being (or person, or force) that the person holds in highest regard—that which is placed above all other competitors for that person's allegiance. If you want to know what someone's god is, pay close attention to whatever that person allots the most time and energy. Most of us have known people who have worshiped the gods of money, food, alcohol, sex, fame, career, or family.

Of course, when people in the United States repeat phrases like "in God we trust," they are not consciously placing their trust in money, food, sex, or any of the other common candidates for divine status in our culture. That is the beauty of the generic usage of the word *God*—it does not ask us to be specific, and does not encourage us to understand the nature of our god or gods. Taking on such a task would require us to think about who controls our lives and our destiny, and about where we place our strongest allegiances. For most of us, that would not be a pretty picture. We're not particularly proud of the material goods and self-possessed thoughts that get most of our attention. So we are much more content with the generic god, whose particular features are always determined by the individual, and who therefore rarely demands that we do anything other than whatever we were already planning to do.

The Christian faith has never been comfortable with such generic notions of God. The God in whom Christians believe is a very specific God—is, in fact, the only God—and is therefore worthy of our complete worship and allegiance. The Christian God is not one god among many, not just a particular instance of a more general category entitled "Gods, Higher Powers, and Miscellaneous Deities." The Nicene Creed accents this element of Christian belief by inserting the word *one:* "We believe in one God." The Apostles' Creed does not use that word; but most Christians recognize the importance of the claim, at least on a theoretical level. If asked whether they believed in one God or many, they would undoubtedly respond, "one." That, at any rate, is the theory; in practice, it is rather easy for us to lapse into the worship of a variety of people and objects. Although these people and objects are not gods, we allow them to take the role of god in our lives.

If we recall some of the comments made in the introductory chapter of this book concerning the verb *believe,* we will recognize that believing in God involves placing our trust in God, coming into a relationship with God, knowing and loving God, and making God the object of our heart's desire. To believe in God is to orient one's whole life toward God, to proclaim that God alone is worthy of worship. But how many of us, when we say "I believe in God," are thinking about this kind of whole-life orientation?

I suspect that most Christians would prefer to think that, when they speak of God, they are naming one of the very many elements in which they invest their lives. When we say "I believe in God," we may simply be starting a checklist of beliefs that includes a long list of statements such as "I believe in the free market," "I believe in my friends," and even "I believe that this is the best pasta salad I have ever had." We hold a very large number of beliefs, from the monumental to the trivial, but we think of these beliefs as all being members of the same category or kind. Many Christians would probably say that their belief in God was one of the more significant of their many beliefs. But because of the widespread acceptance of the generic notion of God, this claim doesn't necessarily carry much freight. It doesn't cost much, in our culture, to go along with the crowd. Everyone else seems to believe in God; surely it wouldn't hurt to do the same.

But the Christian faith ought not to be very satisfied with this rather leisurely acknowledgment of the existence of God. For one thing, if belief in God really does connote a kind of whole-life orientation, then one's "belief in God" cannot remain on a par with one's beliefs in various political institutions, personal associations, and artistic judgments. If one's God is the one in whom one places one's "ultimate concern" (to use Paul Tillich's phrase), the claim that "I believe in God" is not simply one belief among many. When we say "we believe in God," we are saying that we have embarked upon a path in which God is the overriding concern, the ultimate power, and the only one to whom our allegiance is properly due.

Consequently, the *character* of this God is of absolute significance. This is why the Apostles' Creed goes on to specify the God in whom we believe: the Father Almighty, Creator of heaven and earth. (The Nicene Creed goes on to provide a bit more detail about this Creator: God is "the maker of all that is, seen and unseen.") God is thereby designated as the greatest power in the universe and the source of all that is. This designation reinforces the inadequacy of a generic portrait of God. A God who simply inherits a universe that was already in place, or who merely intervenes arbitrarily in its activities from time to time, is emphatically *not* the God in whom Christians believe.

In addition, the Christian God is here designated as "Father." This term has become troublesome in recent decades, and for good reason. While our everyday use of the word almost always designates a male, Christian theologians from as early as the third century were arguing vehemently that the categories of sex and gender do not apply to God. In other words: God is not male, but one of the most frequently used names for God is a word that, in almost all its other uses, names a male. In recent decades, Christians have become more and more sensitized to the grammatically male language that has often been used to refer to God, and are rightly trying to think and speak of God beyond the categories of sex and gender.

I cannot address this question in detail here, but at the end of this chapter I have included some useful resources for this process of expanding our language about God. For the present, I want to try to step back from the male and masculine connotations of the word *father,* and to think instead about its *relational* qualities. (The following reflections will work just as well if you substitute another relational word for *father:* you could use *mother* or *grandmother* or, for that matter, a relational term that doesn't usually refer to human persons, such as *source* or *destiny.*) The word *father* (or *mother* or *source*) implies a relation; you can't be a father by yourself. You can only be the father (or mother, or brother, daughter, source, goal) *of* someone. So to speak of someone using one or more of these relational terms implies an *other* with whom that one is in relation. In this way, the use of the word *father* in the creed propels us forward to the question: *father of whom?*

The Christian faith has given two answers to this question: God is the father of Jesus Christ, who is therefore called the Son of God. We will take up the question of Jesus and his relationship to God in the following two chapters; for now, suffice it to say that the father-son language implies a significant degree of continuity between the two, such that there is a sense in which, when we look at Jesus, we see God. Similarly, when Jesus is sent into the world, the one who comes is not just a prophet or a messenger, but (again, in some sense) God's own self.

But God is father (mother, source) in another sense as well: through Christ, we are adopted into the same kind of relationship with God that Jesus has with God, becoming daughters and sons of God as well. We are taught to pray to God as "our Father in heaven" and to understand ourselves as children of God. So, to return to our original question, God is the father of Jesus—and, by adoption, of us as well.

To speak of God as both Father and Son (parent and child, source and wellspring) is to imply that God is an internally differentiated being. While we continue to believe in one God, we believe that this God is complex and internally relational. Moreover, this is not just a simple, two-way relationship between individuals; later in the Creed, we will be introduced to the Holy Spirit, whom Christians also designate as God, and who further complexifies God's internal relationality.

Thus, the God of Christian faith, though one, is also three. This is not a completely unimaginable concept for us: when we come to know a friend very well, we know that he or she is just *one* person, but we recognize the complex internal interactions of that person's mind, body, and spirit. Or, to take a very different example: we know that a spring of water consists of a source (which is typically hidden from our view), a wellspring (which rises up out of the ground), and flowing water (which moves out away from the source). In most cases, however, it would be difficult for us to specify just where one part began and another ended.

This complex, internal relationality of the one God is referred to by Christians as the *Trinity:* the one God who is also, in some sense, three (but is not three gods). The traditional Christian claims about the Trinity are mind-bogglingly complex, and I will not attempt to explicate them here. (I have already written a very long book about these claims, and that's enough for now!) Again, I have included some resources at the end of this chapter for those who would like to pursue the question further. For now, I would only want to emphasize that the Trinity is not just a matter of esoteric speculation on the part of theologians. This claim about God arose from the fact that the earliest Christians experienced three very different ways of believing in God: first, in the transcendent source who had no source, whom they had known in the Jewish faith; second, in Jesus of Nazareth, begotten of God and present among them; and finally, in the descent of the Holy Spirit at Pentecost, who was also present among them—no longer in a single individual, but in the corporate body of the church. These three experiences of God, three *ways of believing* in God, were sufficiently different from one another that they eventually became embodied in the Christian claim that the one God is the Triune God, the Trinity.

We are now a very long way indeed from the generic, watered-down version of God that appears in national slogans and nonspecific prayers. As it turns out, Christians have at their disposal an extraordinarily rich set of resources for describing and specifying the God in whom they believe. Unfortunately, however, having lived through a couple of centuries' worth of invocations of the most generic, unspecified, and disinterested god imaginable, Christians have nearly forgotten the rich detail, the profound depths, and the active care of the specific God in whom they believe.

How might we go about learning, or perhaps relearning, the significance of our belief in the only true God, the Trinity, who is (or at least should be) the focus and orienting power of our entire life? One of the best ways to do this is by comparison: to examine, alongside our own lives, the lives of persons who do not believe in God at all, as well as persons who believe in a God who is recognizably *not* the triune God of Christian faith. By making these comparisons, we will discover differences between such persons and ourselves; somewhat more painfully, we may also discover a number of similarities.

These are precisely the sorts of comparisons that we are encouraged to undertake when we encounter the various characters in Iris Murdoch's novel *The Time of the Angels*. The book whisks us away to an obscure, fog-bound location in London, where all is not well inside the rectory. There we meet a number of carefully constructed, memorable characters whose relationships with one another provide wonderful illustrations of the practice—and malpractice—of faith in God.

\* \* \* \* \*

I chose this novel to illustrate the first phrase of the Apostles' Creed because it offers us a number of perspectives on belief in God. Some characters do not believe in God at all (or claim not to); others have a very bizarre understanding of God; still others attempt to substitute an intellectual ideal or a general faith in humanity for a belief in God. These differences allow us to examine the relationships between the characters' attitudes toward God on the one hand, and the lives they live on the other. In addition, the novel offers a subtle portrait of the God of the Christian faith—but we will have to be careful observers if we hope to spy it out.

One of the first things we notice about the South London rectory in which this novel is set is that the church building to which it was once attached no longer exists; it was bombed out in the Blitz, and all that remains is the bell tower. The rector, Carel Fisher, was installed in this parish-without-parishioners because it seemed a relatively safe place for him. He had been behaving in an increasingly eccentric manner, scandalizing his flock with his atheistic speculations on the nature of the universe. He spends most of his time in his darkened study, and has instructed the housekeeper—a woman of mixed Irish and Jamaican descent named Pattie—to turn away all visitors. The rectory, usually enveloped in a dense fog, soon takes on the aura of a fortress—isolated, self-sufficient, impregnable. The rectory's other inhabitants include Carel's daughter Muriel, her invalid cousin Elizabeth, the porter Eugene Peshkov (a refugee from Russia), and Eugene's son Leo (a self-styled anarchist). The rectory's isolation, together with Carel's general suspicion of the outside world, leave these characters little choice but to depend on one another; but in fact, they each seem isolated from one another, and more so as the novel progresses.

We soon learn that Carel has taken Pattie as his lover—indeed, that he had done so even before the death of his wife—and that Pattie has submitted herself to his control in a thoroughly pathological way. She thus becomes the target of scorn and abuse from Muriel, who blames her for the death of her mother and for her deteriorating relationship with her father, whom she now fears. Muriel sees him rarely; their conversations are businesslike, almost contractual. At one point he simply tells her that she needs to move out and get a job—as though he were speaking to an employee.

Given this kind of treatment from her father, it is no surprise that Muriel avoids him as much as possible. She would have probably left home long ago had it not been for her friendship with her cousin Elizabeth. The two women spend most of their time together—reading Greek poetry, doing jigsaw puzzles, and smoking cigars. Muriel has become something of a full-time nurse to Elizabeth, whose ailment, never precisely specified, is severe enough to confine her to her room. This confinement is a source of constant anxiety to her legal guardian, Marcus (one of the few characters in the book who lives outside the rectory). Marcus is Elizabeth's uncle; he is also Carel's brother, and is concerned about the latter's obvious isolation and eccentricity. But it is not just Elizabeth who draws Marcus to make regular visits to the rectory; his real enthusiasm is for Leo. Marcus is a teacher, and he would like to impart to Leo the wisdom of the ages. But perhaps what Marcus really wants is someone who will look up to him, appreciate his intellectual passions, and love him.

But Leo is not interested in Marcus; he is interested in Muriel. In fact, one of the novel's most recurrent themes is the nonreciprocal nature of the relationships: every character is desired by another, but is unable or unwilling to return the affection, directing it at someone else instead. So Muriel, sought out by Leo, instead pursues Leo's father, Eugene; he finds her advances incomprehensible and keeps her at a great distance. Instead, he becomes involved in a romantic relationship with Pattie (one of the few mutual and potentially positive relationships in the novel). But Muriel, jealous and angry for having been romantically displaced by (of all people) the same person who came between her parents, destroys their affair by telling Eugene about Pattie's former relationship with Carel.

Meanwhile, Leo—having been rejected by Muriel—develops a fascination for the inaccessible Elizabeth. Muriel takes him to a closet so that they can observe her through a crack in the wall. But when she looks into the room, she sees Elizabeth in bed with . . . Carel. In her haste to usher Leo out of the linen closet, Muriel trips over him and they fall to the floor of the closet entangled in an embrace just as the door is opened by Marcus, with Pattie at his shoulder. And as though Carel's incestuous relationship with his niece were not bad enough, Muriel soon discovers that Elizabeth is not actually her cousin at all, but her half-sister—which is to say, she is actually Carel's *daughter*. By the end of the book, all the characters are even more isolated and alienated from one another than they were at the beginning.

What to make of all these happenings? At first glance, the novel appears to be little more than a mixed bag of oddball characters entangled in complex and ultimately fruitless relationships. Indeed, one might well feel some sympathy with the flummoxed reviewer who could only manage to describe the plot of this novel as one in which "Marcus loves Leo, who loves Muriel, who loves Eugene, who loves Pattie, who loves Carel, who loves Elizabeth." And at a certain level, it is just that. But I want to suggest that these characters provide us with a number of models for various types of "belief in God." By comparing them with one another, we may come to understand both the importance of that belief and the necessity of specifying the God in whom we believe.

The first example, and perhaps the most obvious one in the novel, is the rector, Carel Fisher. The jacket cover of my copy of *The Time of the Angels* declares it to be "a novel about a priest who hates God," but that seems obviously wrong: Carel doesn't believe in God at all. He cannot even believe in the Good; he is convinced that the philosophers were wrong who thought that God, or the Good, was "one, single, and unitary" (p. 172). In conversation with his brother, he argues that "There is only power and the marvel of power, there is only chance and the terror of chance. And if there is only this there is no God, and the single Good of the philosophers is an illusion and a fake" (p. 172).

Carel has substituted, in place of an idea of God, a very different understanding of the universe. In his world, chaotic multiplicity reigns supreme; and this, he believes, is the essence of evil:

> There are principalities and powers. Angels are the thoughts of God. Now he has been dissolved into his thoughts which are beyond our conceptions in their nature and their multiplicity and their power. God was at least the name of something we thought was good. Now even the name has gone and the spiritual world is scattered. There is nothing any more to prevent the magnetism of many spirits (p. 173).

These are the only choices for Carel: either the unity of the Good, in which he can no longer believe; or the multiplicity of many spirits, the terrible angels who push and pull us wherever they will.

Note that Carel's beliefs allow him to justify his behavior. His controlling relationships with Pattie, Elizabeth, and even Muriel can all be understood as the forces of the malignant spirits upon him. He is not beholden to any particular understanding of God, or even of goodness. He is completely beyond morality, and this insulates him from whatever criticisms are directed at him from his brother, his daughter, or his employees.

Few of us would ever be tempted to imitate Carel's behavior, nor is his vision of the terrible angels particularly compelling. But he provides a good example of the connection between belief and behavior: those who deny the existence of the Good (whether as God or as a nontheistic principle of some sort) can automatically justify anything that they do. Moreover, if we recall our discussion of "god" as a term that designates that to which a person is most firmly dedicated, we could say that Carel's "god" is *himself*. His physical pleasures, his relationships with others (under his own control, of course), and his desire to shut out the rest of the world are the objects of his worship. When we see how a person can make these things his god, we can more easily recognize the extraordinary importance of specifying the characteristics of the *true* God in whom we believe.

A very different form of belief in God is illustrated by Carel's brother, Marcus. His perspective is neither that of a typical rote religious belief nor that of his brother's cosmic speculations. Instead, he has secularized the idea of God so that it becomes the idea of the Good. This idea, he believes, has the potential for sustaining the moral universe that, as Carel believes, has become fragmented and chaotic. He can't bring himself to believe in God, but he still yearns for a moral force that will hold his world together. The novelist gives us access to Marcus's inner thoughts on the matter:

> Deprived of myth, religion might die, but morals must be made to live. A religion without God . . . represented nothing in itself but the half-conscious realization that the era of superstition was over. It was its too possible consequence, a morality without Good, which was the real serious danger. Marcus's intention was to rescue the idea of an Absolute in morals by showing it to be implied in the unavoidable human activity of moral evaluation at its most unsophisticated level (pp. 71–72).

Marcus would be happy to get along without God, but he fears the moral consequences. And in some sense, Marcus is closest to the novelist's own perspective. Iris Murdoch was both an artist and a philosopher, and her own trenchant statement of this theme can be found in her book *The Sovereignty of Good*. But unlike Marcus, Murdoch knew that stepping away from religious faith was not so simple a matter, and she continued to wrestle with theological questions all her life. Marcus, on the other hand, assumes that he can simply ignore them. This, in fact, may be a key part of his inability to communicate with most of the other characters in the story, many of whom hold a residual (though often very distorted) form of faith.

Marcus's easy confidence that the Good will triumph in the absence of God is particularly damaged by his encounter with Leo. Here, Marcus encounters someone who shares his lack of interest in any conception of God, but who sees no reason to replace this with a secular equivalent. Murdoch has already alerted us to Leo's amoralism by describing him as a sort of chummy, middle-class version of Dostoevsky's famous character in *Crime and Punishment*, Raskolnikov, who kills his landlady just to prove to himself that he can act outside the usual constraints of morality. Leo is a much shallower person, with much less strength of will; but his moral compass is similarly without direction. "I want to train myself in immorality," he says, "really get those old conventions out of my system, so whenever I have a chance to tell a lie I do so. Values are only relative anyway, there are no absolute values" (p. 68). In response to this disdain for morality, Marcus's appeal to "the Good" has no more persuasive power than does an appeal to God.

We could look to other characters for illustrations of belief in God (or in some kind of gods). Pattie, for example, is filled with a rather superstitious faith that makes her easy prey for Carel; she is a sympathetic character, for whom we feel genuine pity. In the end, however, she comes to realize what most of the other characters miss: that the shape of her life has much to do with the nature of her god. When she discovers that she has been worshiping a false God (Carel), she is able to develop the resoluteness of will to make a change. One of the novel's minor characters, a friend of Marcus and part-time advisor to Muriel named Nora, has no discernible belief in God, but instead a profound faith in common sense. This makes her hospitable and caring, and for this reason she is a very likeable character. On the other hand, she is not a very profound character, since the people she meets and the acts that she witnesses are too easily swept into two mutually exclusive containers marked "common sense" and "nonsense."

All of the novel's characters attempt to make a god out of something that is obviously not God. They orient their lives toward lesser gods; these variously take the form of angelic chaos, philosophical abstraction, common sense, or some particular human being. In the end, most of them come to realize the inadequacy, and in some cases the absurdity, of treating such banalities as the object of one's heart's desire. In doing so they help us understand the importance of being clear about the *character* of the God whom we worship.

The few critics who have offered truly theological interpretations of Murdoch's novel have tended to see it as a negative commentary, a remark on the ease with which we construct our own portraits of God and then worship these constructions. What most critics did not notice, however, was that the novel also offers, in a very subtle way, a point of severe contrast to the various self-serving relationships to God among its various characters. Its subtlety is due to the fact that this alternative is offered not through human character at all, but rather an *icon*.

And not just any icon: it is a copy of Rublev's fifteenth-century masterpiece, "The Holy Trinity." It depicts the three messengers of God, visiting Abraham and enjoying a bit of table-fellowship by the oaks of Mamre. In the text of Genesis 18, these three are also identified as "the Lord"; this passage thus became, for many Christian interpreters, a reference to the Trinity. In the novel, the icon comes into contact with almost all the people in the story, and in doing so, reveals the true character of their relationships. Consider, for a moment, a retelling of the story from the point of view of the icon itself.

The icon is owned by Eugene. Early in the story, it is stolen and pawned by Eugene's son, Leo. But it is of such value to Eugene that Muriel tries to convince Leo that he should recover it. The story of the icon's loss is told by Leo to Marcus, who sees this as an opportunity to befriend and impress the young man. The icon is then purchased from the pawn shop by Marcus, providing him with an excuse to enter the often-barricaded rectory in order to return it to Leo and encourage him to make restitution for stealing and pawning it. But before it can reach its intended recipient, both the icon and its bearer are intercepted by Carel; the icon is thus present during the novel's most sustained discussion of the nature and existence of God. At the end of that discussion, Marcus is too mesmerized to think about the icon, so it remains in the study. It is taken from the study by Muriel, who hopes that she will win Eugene's affections by returning it to him. But Muriel is intercepted by Leo, who announces that he is in love with her. The icon is placed on a side-table, while Muriel dispatches Leo. There it is discovered by Pattie, who returns it to Eugene.

Of course, *The Time of the Angels* is not told from the point of view of Rublev's icon. Most critics assumed that the icon was nothing more than an archaic item of religious devotion—the equivalent of an unused rosary or a relic that is known to be fabricated. These critics, like the iconoclasts of Christian history, failed to treat the icon as an *icon:* they saw its surface, but were unable to look "through" it to the reality beyond. Murdoch set them up for it, of course, by having one character describe the icon as "three angels confabulating around a table." Its role thus seemed primarily illustrative—of the book's title and of Carel's cosmology, in which "the death of God has set the angels free. And they are terrible" (p. 173).

About the best the critics managed was to see the icon as a symbol for God, both graphically and metaphorically, and thus see its haphazard sojourn as an indicator of God's low cultural status. But this assumes that the icon simply represents God *in the abstract,* rather than God in the concrete specificity of God's threeness-in-unity. For the reader who, while reading, keeps in mind the traditional Christian claims about the nature of the Triune God, the icon becomes the central focus of the story: not simply a scrap of wood being casually tossed about, but rather the only fixed point of reference in the story. It reveals the nature of the characters by the ways in which they treat it, describe it, and relate to it. The icon points to the quiet desperation of the characters because it embodies what they all lack: peaceful, mutual communion. For Christians, the internal communion of the Trinity is both the source and the goal of our communal relationships on earth.

Interestingly, when Carel first sees the icon (at the end of the scene discussed above), he is stopped for a moment by its power. He first murmurs a single word that has been used throughout the novel to emphasize power: the word *tall.* Then he speculates: "They would be so tall." When Marcus points out that the icon represents the Trinity, Carel is yanked back into his version of reality. He quickly dismisses both his brother and the doctrine of the Trinity with the assurance of a logician: "How can those three be one? As I told you. Please go now, Marcus" (p. 173). Carel's inability to make sense of the internal communion of God is reflective of his own inability to live in communion with members of his own household.

Many art historians and theologians have commented on the theological depths of Rublev's icon. Dan-Ilie Ciobotea and William H. Lazareth provide a noteworthy sample: "Similarity and difference, rest and movement, youth and maturity, joy and compassion, restraint and pity, eternity and history, these all come together. There is no separation or confusion or subordination of the Persons."

But the icon of the Trinity is not simply a glimpse of the inner life of God. If we are to take seriously the Christian doctrine that we are created in the image of God, then this icon must also be a portrait of humanity, or at least its true end. Rublev's "image of the divine Trinity rules out all egotism—whether individual or collective—all life-destroying separation, any subordination or leveling of persons. It invites all humanity to make this world a permanent eucharist of love, a feast of life. Created in God's image (Gen. 1:26), humanity is called to live in the image of the divine life and to share its daily bread together."

This powerful description of the icon trades heavily on the Christian image of the Eucharist. In stark contrast, the characters that inhabit the novel practice a sort of anti-Eucharist: they all live in separate rooms somewhere in the darkened rectory; they often even eat their meals there, alone; the walls that divide them become a towering symbol of isolation, as often in Murdoch's novels. (Sally Cunneen notes, for example, that in Murdoch's novel *The Sea, The Sea,* one of the character's "vaguely sinister house with its windowless inner rooms reflects his lack of self-understanding.") The characters of *The Time of the Angels* are ultimately still isolated individuals, even in the midst of their relationships. Such is life in the modern world, and most critics have read this novel as symptomatic of the individualistic era in which we live.

Nevertheless, there is a glimmer of hope. The Holy Trinity clearly offers another possibility, drawing our attention to the possibility of true mutual participation and self-giving communion. Note that, in the novel, the icon does not attempt to offer what some people might consider to be the only real alternative to our modern individualism; it does not portray a monolithic uniformity in which all distinctions are ultimately meaningless. Instead, the icon is able to offer the possibility of true mutual participation that somehow does not allow the Three to be eclipsed by the One, but calls us to rejoice in their perfect and glorious communion.

This fully developed portrait of God provides a sharp contrast to the banal and marginalized images of god in the minds of the various characters in the novel. It provides an even sharper contrast to the generic conceptions of god that have come to dominate the modern landscape. It thereby helps us understand the necessity of specifying the God in whom we believe, as well as the necessity that God be worthy of our belief. The novel helps us to recognize the importance of claiming not just that God exists, but also that, as Christians, we are willing to orient our entire lives toward God—and that the God in whom we believe is worthy of such allegiance.

## Questions For Discussion

1. What are some of the images of God that might be invoked by generic references to god (as in phrases such as "In God We Trust")? In order to develop a wide range of references, try to think of images that might be important among a very diverse group of people (in terms of race, culture, gender, socio-economic status, educational background, and other differences).

2. List some of the character traits that you have usually associated with the God in whom you believe. Where do these assumptions come from? Bible stories? The language of worship? The lives of the saints? Popular culture? Friends and relatives? Elsewhere?

3. Discuss your own experience of the word *Father* as a name for God. Then consider the experience of someone who views the word

differently from you. What are some of the possible causes of this difference? What similarities can you find in your reactions to this word despite your differences?

4. What images or metaphors have most helped you to understand the Christian belief that God is Trinity? Do you think that this belief has had a significant impact on your worship practices, your conception of God, and/or your day-to-day life?

5. Think about how God is understood by some of the other characters in *The Time of the Angels* (in addition to those discussed in this chapter). How do you understand the relationship between each character's conception of God and that same character's understanding of himself or herself?

6. Did your reading of this novel lead you to want to be more specific about the character of the God in whom you believe? Imagine that you have met someone who knows very little about Christianity, but who has read the novel and is not very enthusiastic about any of the characters' understandings of God. How would you explain to such a person how your understanding of God differs from that of the characters in the novel?

## For Further Reading

Cunningham, David S. *These Three Are One: The Practice of Trinitarian Theology.* Oxford and Cambridge: Basil Blackwell, 1998. (Advanced)

Duck, Ruth C., and Patricia Wilson-Kastner. *Praising God: The Trinity in Christian Worship.* Louisville: Westminster/John Knox Press, 1999. (Introductory/Advanced)

Geitz, Elizabeth Rankin. *Gender and the Nicene Creed.* Harrisburg, Pa.: Morehouse Publishing, 1995. (Introductory)

Lash, Nicholas. *Believing Three Ways In One God: A Reading of the Apostles' Creed.* Notre Dame, Ind.: University of Notre Dame Press, 1992. (Introductory/Advanced)

McIntosh, Mark A. *Mysteries of Faith.* The New Church's Teaching Series, vol. 8. Cambridge, Mass.: Cowley Publications, 2000. (Introductory)

Murdoch, Iris. *The Sovereighty of Good.* London: Routledge and Keegan Paul, 1970. (Advanced)

Placher, William C. *The Domestication of Transcendence: How Modern Thinking About God Went Wrong.* Louisville: Westminster/John Knox Press, 1996. (Advanced)

Williams, Rowan. *A Ray of Darkness: Sermons and Reflections*. Cambridge, Mass.: Cowley Publications, 1995. (Introductory)

Williams, Rowan. *Lost Icons: Reflections on Cultural Bereavement*. Edinburgh: T & T Clark, 2000. (Introductory/Advanced)

## Other Works Cited in This Chapter

Dan-Ilie Ciobotea and William H. Lazareth, "The Triune God: The Supreme Source of Life. Thoughts Inspired by Rublev's Icon of the Trinity," in *Icons: Windows on Eternity: Theology and Spirituality in Colour*, ed. Gennadios Limouris (Geneva: WWC Publications, 1990), 202–03.

Sally Cunneen, "What Iris Murdoch Doesn't Know," *Commonweal* (9 November 1979): 623.

Anastasia Leech, review of *The Time of the Angels*, in *The Tablet*, September 24, 1966: 1074.

## Other Literary Works Exploring God, Divine Fatherhood, and/or the Trinity

Jean Anouilh, *Becket, or, The Honor of God*

Fyodor Dostoyevsky, *The Brothers Karamazov*

David Hare, *Racing Demon*

Barbara Kingsolver, *The Poisonwood Bible*

Toni Morrison, *Paradise*

William Shakespeare, *King Lear*

Alice Walker, *The Color Purple*

# two

# "Jesus Christ, God's Only Son, Our Lord"

Although it was somewhat controversial when it was first published, Nikos Kazantzakis's *The Last Temptation of Christ* sat sleepily on bookstore shelves for many years. It was not until the release of the film version, directed by Martin Scorcese, that people seemed suddenly to become aware of this book's existence. The film, of course, generated great controversy: there were boycotts, angry Letters to the Editor, and protests of various sorts. Apparently, these critics had not been particularly offended at the existence of the *book;* I don't recall many campaigns to remove it from bookstores and libraries. It was the film—which of course brought the story to a wider audience—that provoked the wrath of so many.

It goes without saying that any fictional depiction of the life of Jesus is going to create some controversy. Christian believers are likely to have, at least in their mind's eye, a fairly specific picture of the person of Jesus: his appearance, his demeanor, and his words and actions are already fixed in our minds (even though we have, of course, no unmediated access to these aspects of Jesus' life). Consequently, anyone who attempts to depict Jesus—whether in a text, a film, or any other work of art—will most likely cause offense. In this sense, the anxiety felt by many religious folk over the depiction of Jesus in Scorcese's film is wholly unremarkable. Similar responses met the producers and directors of *Jesus Christ Superstar, Godspell, Jesus of Montreal,* and even highly "traditionalist" depictions of Jesus in films such as *King of Kings* and Franco Zeffirelli's *Jesus of Nazareth.*

But the controversy surrounding *The Last Temptation of Christ* was different, in that the charge was led not so much by ordinary religious people whose sensibilities had been offended, but by pastors and theologians—often across denominational lines—who found the film to be blasphemous or heretical. These critics, whom one might have expected to have been well-informed about the matter, often complained that the film depicted Jesus as manifesting various weaknesses: he is, at various moments, nervous, angry, frustrated, and frightened. He describes himself as fighting against God, as unable to tell the truth, and as nervous about his own pride. He is shown not only being tempted, but vividly considering in his mind the possibility of giving in to the temptation.

In short, Jesus is shown as fully human. And this is precisely why the objections lodged by Christian pastors and theologians seemed, to me at least, so thoroughly out of place. Indeed, these objections gave me pause about the adequacy of theological education and even basic Christian catechesis in our present culture. One of the most fundamental claims that Christians make about Jesus is that *he was fully human.* This was affirmed at the Council of Chalcedon (451), which declared that Jesus Christ was "one person in two natures, fully divine and fully human." This was simply a more detailed and strongly worded elaboration of the claim enshrined in the Nicene and Apostles' Creeds that "We believe in Jesus Christ, God's only Son, our Lord." We believe that he was a human being, Jesus of Nazareth *and* that he was so intimately related to God that he is worthy of the worship that is due to God alone. Strangely enough, the film of *The Last Temptation of Christ*, as well as the book on which it was based, were suddenly being indicted—by people who should know better—for having depicted one of the most basic claims of the Christian faith.

Perhaps the most charitable explanation for this reaction is that, in viewing the film, people had become convinced that Jesus was being portrayed not just as *human* but also as *sinful.* I don't believe that this is the case; despite his self-doubt, self-chastisement, and active mental consideration of the path that leads away from God, the Jesus of Kazantzakis's novel does not actually sin. But as it turned out, the line between Jesus' sinfulness and his humanity was exceedingly difficult to draw. I will return to this point in a moment; for now, suffice it to say that the protest over the film was not only about whether it depicted a *sinful* Jesus, but also about its depiction of a *human* Jesus: one who laughed, danced, wept, hesitated, doubted, and dreamed.

It is worth pausing to ask *why* these elements of Jesus' character are so difficult for us to accept. The answer, I think, is quite simple: the standard picture of Christ held by many Christians is *not* the classical claim of Chalcedon, "one person in two natures, fully human and fully divine." This claim, expressing the standard belief of Christians for some sixteen centuries, has not been very popular in the modern age. In its place, we have moved closer than we would like to admit to the views of an ancient splinter group known to history as the *Docetists*. They believed that Christ was fully divine, but that he only *seemed* to be human (the label derives from the Greek verb *dokeō*, which means "to seem"). The Docetists believed that human existence was necessarily base, corrupt, and unworthy of God. In fact, they often took a very low view of the created order in general, believing it not to be the creation of God at all, but the product of some weak or mischievous demigod who had been playing around with a heavenly chemistry set without parental authorization. They thus believed that the true God could not possibly allow the perfect divine nature to be soiled and corrupted by any contact with fragile, ugly, error-prone human flesh.

This ancient belief, later declared by Christians to be an inadequate understanding of the faith, seems to have been a particular target of the author of the Gospel of John. John strongly affirms God to be the creator of the world (the book's first words, "In the beginning," clearly echo the first chapter of Genesis). This Gospel also proclaims that God's "Word" has come directly into the world. This Word was with God in the beginning, and can even be identified with God ("the Word was God," John 1:1). Indeed, "the Word became flesh and lived among us" (1:14)— a statement that would have made the Docetists shudder. How dare we proclaim that God would become sullied with human flesh? But the message is insistent; at the end of the Gospel, John emphasizes the wounds of Christ were true wounds of a true human body (John 20:27).

Why are some modern Christians so uncomfortable with the picture of Jesus as fully divine and fully human, as the Gospel of John and traditional Christian belief have insisted? Why do modern-day accounts of Jesus tend toward the perspective of the ancient Docetists? The answers to these questions are complex, but we might say this much: European Christianity, particularly as it took root in North America, has always been impatient with some of the more complex and apparently paradoxical elements of the faith. We are more enthusiastic about simple and straightforward depictions. We have developed a fairly short attention span and a desire to have all loose ends tied up at the end of the story. We are therefore uncomfortable with the complex notion that the seemingly irreconcilable opposites of humanity and divinity might somehow be held together in tension with each other, with no neat and tidy solution to the paradox. We are similarly uncomfortable with other tension-producing oppositions: we see love and justice as working against one another (in, for example, issues surrounding criminal justice). We can only think of freedom as the absence of constraint, so we can't imagine how to accept outside authority except as a compromise to our freedom. Plurality is in unpleasant tension with unity (in spite of the motto *E pluribus unum!*). In the United States, in particular, many of our most vociferous debates over the morality of public policy have developed this "either/or" character (think about capital punishment, abortion, gun laws, and diversity education).

Another outcropping of our discomfort with apparent opposites is our treatment of the distinction between *flesh* and *spirit*—a matter that has reared its ugly head relatively often in the history of Christianity. The precise reasons for the Euro-American enthusiasm for this particular form of dualism are, again, complex; however, three significant points should be noted. First, the United States has been the site of some of the most legalistic and moralistic interpretations of Christianity; Puritanism, conservative Catholicism, and fundamentalism are all examples of this tendency. These outlooks are appropriately orthodox in their insistence on the grace of God; but they insist that the only clear sign of a believer's true acceptance of this grace is an unwavering adherence to a very specific moral code. Ironically, this perspective can also turn to the Gospel of John for support: "the spirit is willing but the flesh is weak" (John 6). It adds to this, however, that the weak flesh must be subdued and punished for its weakness.

Second, the United States (and, in its wake, much of the industrialized West) is a highly materialistic culture and is very enthusiastic about gratifying certain desires of the flesh. This also tends to make us very *nervous* about the flesh, since we know how tempting it is to gratify its many desires! Thus, sociologists and psychologists are fascinated by America's love-hate relationship with sex. We enjoy sex immensely, and marketing it is a huge industry; but we're convinced that there's something almost inherently bad about it, so we're ashamed of our enjoyment. Sex is associated with secrecy and privacy; yet our secretiveness about it insulates us from accountability, and we regularly succumb to its power over us in the form of abuse, hypocrisy, and addiction. The same could be said for other material pleasures, such as food, drink, shelter, clothing, and entertainment. All are enjoyable, guilt-provoking, privatized, commodified, and subjected to extraordinary abuse—so we assume that God couldn't possibly have anything to do with them.

This leads to a final point about our inadequate wrestling with the supposed opposition of spirit and flesh: our privatization of religious belief. Most inhabitants of the modern industrialized West tend to think of religion as a largely private matter, based on the relationships between individuals and their god(s). This means that we are tempted toward a highly spiritualized version of the faith that does not need to be manifested in any specific, physical, public way. As long as it remains a *spiritual* or *supernatural* matter, we need not worry about being called to any accountability—at least not in this world.

Given our tendency to think of spirit and flesh as irreconcilable opposites, we often find ourselves in the company of the ancient Docetists.
We can't imagine God, a perfect spirit, actually experiencing this tragic,
troubled world of the flesh. Yet this is precisely what the Christian story
proclaims. In order to recall that story in our contemporary circumstances, we need to enter into an imaginative world that emphasizes the
full humanity of Christ. That is precisely what happens when we read
*The Last Temptation of Christ*—though the book is not without its own
complexities on matters of "flesh" and "spirit." You may have seen the
film; or perhaps, from everything you've heard about the film, you
decided not to see it. Unfortunately, much of what was said in the public press about the film was misleading—partly, I think, because the
pundits that rendered their verdicts had not read Nikos Kazantzakis's
complex, long, and beautifully written novel. The book offers subtleties
and nuances that no film could ever capture, but both the novel and the
film provide an opportunity for some careful reflection on the humanity and divinity of Christ.

* * * * *

The full humanity of Jesus is evident from the opening pages of the
novel, in which he is portrayed as haunted, confused, pursued, and
uncertain. He hears footsteps behind him as he walks; he dreams of
demons (or are they angels?) that chase him relentlessly; and above all,
he senses the constant presence of an eagle-headed, bronze-armored
figure, to whom he refers as "the Curse." (However, with hindsight, her
ability to help Jesus keep on the proper path means that she also resembles the Holy Spirit.) She offers him protection, but rather in the same
sense that the Mob offers protection! She dogs his every step, and when
he begins to stray from the path, she digs her ten sharp talons into the
back of his neck. From the very beginning, Jesus' humanity is leading
him in one direction while his divinity seems to be demanding a different path. Must these two paths ultimately diverge? If they do, he's eventually going to have to choose. After all, he's only one person.

Those closest to Jesus can't figure him out. His mother knows that
he is not like the others, but that is no comfort; "woe betide the mother
who bears a son unlike all the rest," she says (p. 63). His compatriot
Judas suspects that Jesus may have a special role to play in the liberation of Israel, but that doesn't explain why this son of Mary uses his carpentry skills to build crosses for the Romans to crucify his fellow Jews.
But the person most injured by Jesus' inner struggles is Mary Magdalene—she who played with him as a child and fell in love with him; she
whom he was about to choose as his bride when the Curse dug her talons

into him; she who turned to a life of prostitution to drown her sorrows and to shake her fist at the God who took her Jesus away and broke her heart (p. 89).

Jesus does not fully understand the feeling of being hunted, nor the talons that dig into his body, nor his decision to employ his carpentry skills to make the ghastly wooden product currently in such great demand. He senses that he is being called to some special task, but he does not know whether he should accept this call. Its demands are so very different from what is being asked of all the young men around him: they are learning a trade, getting married, having children, and enjoying the fruits of the land and the sea. Why can't he just live a normal, domestic life? Such a life is frequently described in the novel as the "obvious" choice, and yet also so obviously inadequate—one rabbi worries that people might "all rot away in a bog of security and easy living" (p. 64); a successful businessman is told, "Easy living has driven you mad" (p. 166). Why is Jesus being tortured by this demand toward a higher calling and a harder life? He suspects the answer but does not want to admit it. The same answer is also suspected by Mary Magdalene, by Judas, and by his mother (p. 30):

> The rabbi shook his head. "Mary, your boy isn't being tormented by a devil; it's not a devil, it's God—so what can I do?"
> "Is there no cure?" the wretched mother asked.
> "It's God, I tell you. No, there is no cure."
> "Why does he torment him?"
> "Because he loves him," the old rabbi finally replied.

If Jesus and the others are not sure, we (the readers) are: this is God, calling out to Jesus, reminding him of the path that he is called to choose. It is the ongoing struggle between his humanity and his divinity.

Peter gives voice to this struggle in the early pages of the novel: no "Rock" as of yet, Peter is nicknamed "weathercock" or "windmill" for his willingness to be blown about by the wind. His good heart is drawn toward whatever object of pity has most recently been presented to him, because he can see how heavily the everyday burdens of life weigh people down. Looking upon Jesus the cross-maker, he thinks, "The God of Israel had mercilessly chosen him, the son of Mary, to build crosses so that the prophets could be crucified. . . . [God] might have picked me, Peter reflected with a shudder. . . . Suddenly Peter's roused heart grew calm, and all at once he felt deeply grateful to the son of Mary, who had taken the sin and lifted it to his shoulders" (p. 44). Note that Peter does not regard Jesus' role in the death of the prophets as a sin; indeed, it is a necessary part of the fulfillment of the divine plan. More significant is this scene's foreshadowing of Jesus' role in bearing the sins of others; and this is certainly not the only place in the novel where Kazantzakis will make this point. Indeed, this novel could just as easily be used to illustrate the significance of the creedal phrase, *suffered under Pontius Pilate;* this suffering is integrally related to Christ's work of redemption, his salvation of the world.

The inner struggle becomes sufficiently intense for Jesus to break away from his cross-making life and to head toward the desert, where he hopes to wrestle with God more directly. Along the way he is tempted by the lures of the city; he resists them, but has little choice but to enter one city, Magdala, in order to make his peace with the woman whose ruined life is, he believes, his own responsibility. Mary Magdalene is portrayed as a prostitute (indeed, so common are such fictional portrayals that many people are astounded to discover the complete absence of any biblical evidence for it). Jesus observes the abused life that she lives and takes pity on her. In fact, he would like to stay with her, to rescue her from this life—believing that, whether or not he can save the world, he can at least save her. He eventually leaves, as chaste as when he arrived; but the reader knows that the reality and the beauty of physical sexual intimacy has been held clearly before his eyes.

For Kazantzakis, as for much of modern culture, sexual struggles become something of an archetype for all sorts of wrestlings of, let us say, the "soul" or "spirit" against the "body" or the "flesh." (There are some nuanced distinctions among these four words, but examining them in detail will have to wait for a later chapter.) As I have already observed, such dualisms have been a constant struggle for Christians. They certainly lie behind the docetic tendency to emphasize Jesus' divinity to the exclusion of his humanity, and they have other troublesome ramifications as well; I will return to this point in a moment. Kazantzakis repeatedly emphasizes this struggle between flesh and spirit—both in sexual terms and in more general terms of materiality and worldliness. For example, Judas consistently argues that physical liberation must precede spiritual liberation, because the body is the "foundation"; Jesus insists that the foundation is the soul (p. 204 and elsewhere). This dualism is clearly embedded in the life of the ascetic monks of the desert, into whose lives Jesus is about to enter. Can these dualistic oppositions be overcome?

In the monastery, others seem to recognize that Jesus is "the One who is to come." The dying abbot seems to fight to remain alive just long enough to meet him; other monks come to believe that he has arrived in the desert for a special ritual of purification. In any case, he is struggling; he gives voice to this struggle in his conversations with his uncle, a rabbi named Simeon (based on the Simeon of Luke's gospel who pronounces the prayer that has found a permanent place in the daily office of prayer as the *nunc dimittis*). Simeon has been called to the monastery in an effort to save the life of the dying abbot; but he is really there to become a sort of spiritual director for Jesus. In a key passage (pp. 142–48), the rabbi questions Jesus, urges him to listen to himself, and attempts to draw from him his truest thoughts. Jesus admits to a whole range of temptations—sexual, spiritual, theological—but despite his own self-deprecation, the reader can tell (with only the slightest need to read between the lines) that he hasn't actually fallen into the traps that have been set for him. This is what makes Kazantzakis's Jesus such a formidable character: he has resisted temptation, not because he is somehow divinely insulated against it, but because he takes it seriously, wrestles with it, and overcomes it.

This ability to overcome temptation is, in the end, a much more powerfully persuasive aspect of Jesus' character than is the message that he proclaims. Many commentators have criticized Kazantzakis's portrait of Jesus as one that simply would not inspire confidence and devotion on the part of his followers. How could this struggling, uncertain, haunted figure attract so many people to himself? In response, we could make two arguments: first, many of history's most charismatic figures have been hunted and haunted, and struggled against inner demons. Indeed, this struggle may be part of what makes them so attractive—think of Anthony the Hermit, wrestling with the demons in the desert. (Nor is this limited to saintly figures: recall the fascination aroused by Hitler's autobiography, which was entitled *Mein Kampf [My Struggle]*.) But second, and more important, it is not (ultimately) Jesus' message and teachings that are the most important things about him. They are important, yes, but by themselves they are only the wise sayings of a great man, to be placed along other wise sayings of other great people and argued for or against by people through the ages. Directly augmenting the importance of the teachings is Jesus' status as the Son of God; this is what draws people to him. The creeds themselves reinforce this by not making the essence of Jesus' teachings a part of the structure of the creed. (I was always a bit miffed by this omission; Jesus' ethical demands always seemed to me to be the best thing about him! But the creeds do not deny these teachings; they simply tell us *why* we ought to pay such close attention to them.)

And what is this teaching that Jesus offers? It is the message of *love*. In the novel, Jesus bears an extraordinary love for all people: not just for Mary Magdalene, not just for his fellow Jews, but for all human beings—indeed, for all the creatures of the world (animals, plants, insects, even rocks). He loves them all and wants to relieve their suffering. Jesus reflects: "if only one man could be found to approach [God], fall at his feet and succeed, before being reduced to ashes, in telling him of man's suffering, and of the suffering of the earth and of the green leaf!" (p. 140). And yet, somehow, this philosophy of love and compassion is able to "awaken so much hatred in the hearts of men" (p. 126). Jesus is intolerable to others precisely because of his unbounded love. If anything, Kazantzakis radicalizes Jesus' message of love and forgiveness, altering his parables of Lazarus and the Rich Man (p. 202), and of the wise and foolish virgins (p. 217), such that even those who are unmerciful or unprepared, and who appear to be condemned in the canonical versions of the parables, are given a second chance.

Jesus leaves the desert and begins to preach, but his message—"Love one another"—is met with laughter and derision. When an occasional follower does turn up, it isn't because Jesus' "message" seems innately appealing. Rather, there is just "something about" Jesus that draws people to him: a depth of Spirit, a connectedness to God, or simply a puzzle worth deciphering. The most obvious example of this magnetic attraction, almost against one's own will, is the figure of Judas. He doesn't like Jesus' methods, is deeply impatient with his refusal to speak out against the Roman occupation of Israel, and threatens more than once to kill Jesus for standing in the way of revolution. But he waits and stays with Jesus because he harbors a real suspicion that this might be the One. And so with the others: John had sought out the monastery; James (Jacob, in the translation) planned to take over his father's fishing business; Matthew was doing well collecting tolls for Rome. All are inexorably *drawn* to Jesus for reasons that they can't quite specify.

The gathered followers go with Jesus to Jerusalem and then down to the river Jordan, where they will encounter the Baptist. Judas and Jesus expect this encounter to offer some kind of final, definitive sign about Jesus' identity. Is he truly the Messiah? How will he know? How can he be sure? Throughout the book, he has wrestled with the paradoxical problem of not being able to affirm his own special status. His divinity allows him to imagine himself to be God, but his humanity catches him up short, reminding him of the blasphemous character of such a claim. (The irony is not lost on the reader, who recognizes that, for Jesus alone, this claim is actually *not* blasphemy.) Jesus needs someone else to make it clear to him, to corroborate his suspicions. But even the Baptist's clear affirmation of his messiahship is difficult for him to accept at face value, so he returns to the desert—this time, alone—in order to become truly convinced of his identity.

The book's account of Jesus' three temptations in the wilderness is a beautiful filling-out of the highly compressed narrative in the Gospels (forty days in a dozen or so verses leaves a lot of room for speculation!). The first temptation is not just about physical hunger, but concerns all bodily desire; and in this book, that means wrestling with sex. The tempter takes the form of a snake-woman, drawing him toward married life and domesticity. The second temptation, in the form of a lion, urges him to claim power and dominion over the kingdoms of this world. The final temptation, in the form of an archangel, encourages him to claim the fullness of his divine glory. In each case, the temptation is extended through time and presented in great detail, allowing us to see Jesus actually struggling with these exquisite offers of pleasure, rather than just brushing them aside as though they were nothing. He must actually discern their source: Are they from God or from the devil? If the answer were as easy as looking around for a forked tail and a pitchfork or a halo and some wings, we probably wouldn't be very impressed by Jesus' accomplishment!

When he returns from the desert, Jesus' message seems to have changed: perhaps love is not enough. His new symbol is the axe, which must be taken to the root of the tree: the slate must be wiped clean in order to start anew. Judas likes the new version; it smells to him of the blood of Roman soldiers. But this is not what Jesus means. When he is spurned in his own hometown, and his followers resort to violence to defend him, he rebukes them. Once again, notions that appear oppositional to us are somehow reconcilable in Jesus' mind: love and justice, flesh and spirit, God and humanity. But he doesn't yet know how best to communicate this inner reconciliation to others. And no surprise—for unlike him, they are human only, and not divine.

Jesus continues to attract new followers, but they are a very mixed bag. Like the Gospel writers themselves, Kazantzakis portrays them as a bit slow on the uptake, lacking complete confidence in their mission, and ready to run when things get difficult. Some are resolute; Judas is a model in this regard, as are some of the women who follow him (in several cases, they throw away their own housekeys before joining the entourage, whereas several of the male disciples keep their own keys hidden away, just in case!). Matthew is a particularly interesting disciple, always scribbling notes for the story that he will write, and occasionally provoking arguments about "whether things really happened that way."

Throughout this section of the book, three themes recur regularly. The first is that of grace. Jesus is able to see and be thankful for the gifts of God in the most ordinary moments of human life: the sighting of a butterfly, the onset of a beautiful night. Where others become annoyed or dejected or angry, Jesus sees beauty and gift. Second is the theme of nourishment: food, too, is a gift of God, and one for which Jesus always seems profoundly thankful. Often this thankfulness moves in a specifically eucharistic direction: the work of human hands is changed into true nourishment for others. (Peter receives a different kind of renaming: this ever-changing "windmill" will eventually "grind the wheat into bread so that men may eat" [p. 303].) The third theme has already been mentioned, that of bearing the sins of others. Several times, Jesus encounters the male goat that is symbolically laden with the sins of the people and sent into the wilderness to die (a ritual from which we derive the word "scapegoat"). Increasingly, Jesus comes to understand himself more in these terms: he is the One who—because he reconciles the apparent opposites of humanity and divinity, flesh and spirit, love and justice—can somehow bear the sins of all.

After Jesus' triumphal entry into Jerusalem, things happen very quickly. There seems to be an inverse relationship between Kazantzakis's novel and the canonical Gospels: when the Gospels mention something only briefly, the novel elaborates it in much detail (giving us a full portrait, for example, of Simon the Cyrene, who seems not to care much for the disciples' devotion to Jesus—and yet it is he, and not they, who shoulders Jesus' cross). Conversely, when the Gospels provide more detail, concerning (for example) the actual events leading up to Jesus' crucifixion, the novel moves at a brisk pace. The author seems to count on the reader's detailed knowledge of the Gospels in order to fill in the appropriate bits and to make sense of the hundreds of biblical allusions (some of them quite clever) made throughout the book. This gives the lie to the many spurious accusations that Kazantzakis (or Scorcese, who also relies on this background knowledge among his viewers) is somehow attacking the core of Christianity. On the contrary: only the Christian can really understand just how thoroughly faithful the author's struggle must have been.

Finally, there is the "last temptation" from which the book draws its title. Between the time that Jesus says the words "Eli, Eli" and the words "lama sabacthani"—a "split second," as the author says (p. 496)—Jesus undergoes one final temptation. It is an elaboration of a temptation that occurs in the Bible itself (Matt. 27:42), in which Jesus is entreated to come down from the cross. In the novel, Jesus is tempted to walk away from his crucifixion, get married, suffer the normal woes and joys of domestic life, rear many children, live and work as a carpenter, grow old, and die. What would such a life be like? To bring the question closer to home, how would *we* react to the choice that he was given? If we had the power to relieve ourselves of pain, suffering, and premature death, and to enter into a more "normal" life, would we even pause to *consider* whether doing so would be attentive to the will of God, or would we just take the path of least resistance?

The "last temptation" is extended over a good fifty pages (about a tenth of the book), so readers have trouble imagining it taking place in a split second. The film version is even more extreme; the "last tempta-tion" sequence takes up a third of the film, and it's very, very vivid. (On the other hand, we could say the same thing about dreams; scientists assure us that many of our dreams take place in a fleeting moment, even though they seem to us to be extended over a long period of time.) Many people who have read the book (and even more who have seen the film) have been "fooled" by this part of the story, thinking that they are watch-ing Jesus actually get married, have sex, rear children, and grow old. That's a strange thing to think, of course, since we all know what really happens, what *must* happen eventually if the novel is to have any cred-ibility at all: Jesus must die on the cross, of course! Such is the power of fiction: even when depicting a thought, a temptation, or a dream—something that the readers all *know* to be contrary to reality—we are encouraged to take these events into the "real world" and to endow them with a sort of reality. And rightly so, for a temptation that we cannot *imagine* actually taking place is not really much of a temptation.

Throughout the "last temptation," things occasionally go wrong, and Jesus appears ready to shake off the tempter's power. Such moments remind us of those times when we begin to realize that we're dreaming and try to wake up, but find ourselves overcome by sleep (or the sheer comfort of the bed), and suddenly we're in dreamland again. In the novel, Jesus experiences several such moments. First, Mary Magdalene, his new bride, is set upon by zealous enforcers of the ritual law and brutally killed. Jesus is overcome by grief and wonders whether it's all worthwhile. Later, Simon of Cyrene stops by his house to question him about his actions and remind him of what he once was. Jesus is taken back into his memory, questioning whether this could possibly be the right path. Occasionally he falls into deep contemplation, wondering what it might be like to die without hope of eternal life. In all of these encounters, he manages to "stay in his dream" through the intercessions of the "guardian angel" who first offered him the opportunity to descend from the cross (a small "Negro boy" in the novel; a white female child in the film version).

Most famously, Jesus encounters one Paul of Tarsus, who travels about preaching that Jesus Christ was crucified and rose again! This leads to an interesting debate between Jesus and Paul on the truth or falsity of such a message, but it would be misleading to suggest that this is the main point we should draw from the encounter. It is, more impor-tantly, a debate on the nature of salvation. In the midst of their heated conversation, Paul reminds Jesus of the call that he is (dreaming about) forgetting:

> If the world is to be saved, it is necessary—do you hear—absolutely nec-essary for you to be crucified and I shall crucify you, like it or not; it is

necessary for you to be resurrected, and I shall resurrect you, like it or not. . . . The whole works is now part of the machinery of salvation—everything is indispensable (p. 477).

But a Jesus who gets married, settles down, has kids, grows old—how can he save the world? Paul poses a series of painful questions to this "domestic" Jesus: "What uplifted example do you offer the world to make it follow you? With you, will it surpass its own nature, will its soul sprout wings?" (p. 478). Jesus feels the sting of the questions and bursts into tears; only with the help of his ever-present "guardian angel" is he able to resist Paul's effort to wake him from his dream.

What *does* eventually wake him is the reappearance of his disciples when Jesus is on his deathbed. They express their brokenheartedness; they had given up everything for him, and he had abandoned them. Most angry of all is Judas—the one who took on the hardest job of all, betraying his master so that Isaiah's prophecy could be fulfilled. Judas reminds Jesus of everything he had said in his life, of his desire to liberate people from their slavery, of his reconciling of (what appear to be) opposites: love and justice, freedom and peace, humanity and God. It is also Judas who reveals to Jesus that the "guardian angel" who accompanied him throughout this dream-life is actually Satan, the prince of lies. As with his earlier temptations in the desert, once Jesus is able to identify the tempter, he is able to overcome the temptation. He is able to complete the cry that he had begun—"lama sabacthani" ("Why have you abandoned me?"). He is thereby able to achieve clarity about his own identity; and because he now knows who he really is, he can cry out: "It is accomplished."

Thus, Kazantzakis presents to us a portrait of Jesus Christ as not *merely* fully divine (as in the docetic heresy), but also fully human. Human beings are not always certain about how they feel or about what they should do. Consequently, neither is Jesus at all certain about these things. He is not certain that God is calling him to be the Messiah. He doubts his own ability to speak on God's behalf (much like Moses, who, according to Exodus 4:10, worried about his own lack of eloquence). In fact, Jesus fights against his vocation, hoping that he can get married, or become a monk, or do just about *anything* rather than undertake the path of humiliation and suffering and death that God seems to be preparing for him. Wouldn't you?

Indeed, I think that this is how we should *want* Jesus to react; he wouldn't seem very human if he didn't. It is, in fact, how he *must* react if we are to take seriously his full humanity. What would we think of a human being who, upon dreaming a strange dream or hearing a strange voice, immediately devoted her life to its call? Wouldn't we consider that a bit compulsive, perhaps even pathological? What would we say to a person who claimed to feel a bird's talons digging into the back of his skull? Indeed, what would we say to someone who told us of a still, small voice saying "you are God"? A "normal" human reaction to these events would surely be to question them, to worry about them, to wonder where they came from, to demand external corroboration. If someone had these experiences and immediately concluded that she or he was the Messiah, most of us would consider such a reaction not merely abnormal, but possibly indicative of mental illness! On the other hand, if Jesus had had some secret knowledge that enabled him to distinguish the voice of God from a voice pretending to be God's, then he would hardly be fully human. Yet if he *cannot* discern the source of the voice, can he really be fully divine? The tensions are nearly overwhelming.

In the creed, we say that we believe in "Jesus Christ." We declare him to be the Son of God and our Lord. In doing so, we are claiming that he is, like us, a human being; yet, in some real sense, he is also God. We usually tend to think of humanity and divinity as irreconcilable opposites; but Jesus Christ is clear evidence that they are not *completely* irreconcilable. This further suggests other things that we have *considered* irreconcilable may have more to do with each other than we had thought: love and justice, spirit and flesh, doubt and certitude. If such overcoming seems unimaginable, we have only to remember Kazantzakis's reminder that "Great things happen when God mixes with humanity" (p. 281). And if we are worried that such "mixing" must require some kind of inappropriate change on God's part, we need only remember that sometimes a change in ourselves appears to be a change in God. In the novel, when John asks whether God changes, Jesus replies: "No, beloved. But the human heart widens and is able to contain more of God's will" (p. 347).

The novel asks us to think seriously about the relationship between humanity and divinity through the category of "temptation." What does it mean to be tempted? Surely it means being able to imagine—that is, seriously to consider in one's mind—the real possibility of at least two different paths. If I am on a low-fat diet, and I tell you that I am "tempted" to eat a large dish of high-fat ice cream (in violation of my diet), then you would naturally assume that I was currently considering, or had recently considered, *actually eating* the ice cream. If I had not even *thought* about eating ice cream, or if I had some secret inner power that always prevented me from doing so, you would rightly think it odd of me to say that I had been "tempted" in any meaningful sense of the word. And yet, when we read the biblical account of the three temptations of Jesus, we seem to have considerable difficulty imagining that *he actually considered choosing* what he was being offered by the devil. Instead, we imagine him as fully in charge, barely affected by his forty days without food, wittily parrying the devil's taunts, and throwing in a few Old Testament quotations for good measure. And once again, we have come under the spell of the Docetists.

If the temptations of Jesus are truly temptations, and if Jesus is fully human, then we must imagine him *actually considering* turning those stones into bread. We must imagine his fully human hunger, and we must imagine his recognition that he did indeed have the power to turn the stones into bread, eat, and be satisfied. We must imagine him envisioning in his own mind what it would be like to do this—how easily the stones would change, how good the bread would taste. Of course, we must also imagine him considering the negative ramifications of giving in to this temptation; for example, that in doing so, he would be putting his own physical needs above his love of God, and that he would be accepting the popular assumption that being well-fed is more important than just about anything else. Only if we can imagine him actually thinking through and considering these two possibilities and *then* choosing rightly can we really imagine an actual temptation, as opposed to a mere game. Only if one doesn't know in advance which commands come to us from God and which ones from someone pretending to be God—only then is temptation *real*.

But of course, the three temptations described at the beginning of the gospels of Matthew and Luke are only pale reflections of what must have been one of the greatest temptations of all for Jesus: the temptation not to follow the call of God, a call that would inevitably lead to profound heartache, excruciating pain, and death. For if he was fully human, then Jesus also possessed free will; and that will, like our own, must have been capable—at least in theory—of choosing either for God or against God. We rarely attend to how difficult it must have been for Jesus to give up all the ordinary pleasures of his time and his place—rewarding work, marriage, a family—and instead to preach a message that he knew full well would bring down upon his head the wrath of the political and religious leaders of his day. If he had not chosen as he did, we would not be able to understand him as fully divine. But if he had not actually considered the options and weighed the consequences, then he would not seem fully human.

In the early church, some writers emphasized the importance of the claim that "what is not assumed is not saved." With this rather cryptic phrase they were attempting to suggest that, in order for our *full humanity* to be saved by God, God had to take on *all aspects* of that humanity: its fragile, fleshly existence; its doubts, anxieties, and despairs; its free and often divided will (see Romans 7!); and of course, the fact that it must eventually suffer and die. Jesus saves us, in the fullness of our humanity, by *assuming* the fullness of our humanity. In Christ, God takes on everything that human beings can be: male and female, joyful and sorrowful, flesh and spirit, doubting and assured, living and dying. And yes, God even takes on our ability to be tempted, our ability *seriously to consider* turning away from and against God—to *envision* it, to hold it in our mind's eye. If this essential part of our human nature were not assumed by God, then our full humanity would not be saved.

The importance of the full humanity of Christ seems to have been lost on those who found Martin Scorcese's film version of *The Last Temptation of Christ* to be so offensive. Perhaps it was similarly lost on those who were offended by Nikos Kazantzakis's novel when it was first published. That offense is a clear testimony to the impoverished theological education of many Christians. Still, I find this offense rather hard to understand, given that Kazantzakis explains the problem quite clearly in the very first lines of the novel, and given that Scorcese places the same lines at the very beginning of his film:

> The dual substance of Christ—the yearning, so human, so superhuman, of man to attain God or, more exactly, to return to God and identify himself with him—has always been a deep inscrutable mystery to me. . . . My principal anguish and the source of all my joys and sorrows from my youth onward has been the incessant, merciless battle between the spirit and the flesh.

This problem has haunted Christian theology from the beginning: how to hold together the full humanity and full divinity of Christ. The words of the creed—"Jesus Christ, God's only Son, our Lord"—offers us a statement that emphasizes the importance of holding these two elements together. However, it does not explain to us how we are to accomplish this rather monumental task. So we will always be in need of works such as *The Last Temptation of Christ* to remind us of just how difficult this task is—and how important it is that we attend to it, again and again, in every age.

## Questions For Discussion

1. Do you remember particular events that surrounded the release of the film version of *The Last Temptation of Christ?* Did you know people or organizations that protested the film, and if so, what were their reasons?

2. What other factors, besides those discussed in this chapter, might contribute to our tendency to be more comfortable with Jesus' divinity than with his humanity?

3. Think of some additional examples of pairs of terms that are usually thought to be irreconcilable opposites. (This chapter uses examples such as humanity/divinity, flesh/spirit, doubt/faith; you will undoubtedly be able to think of others). Are these pairs really irreconcilable? Pick one pair as an example and consider how we might rethink or re-envision the terms such that they interpenetrate one another rather than standing in necessary opposition.

4. Some critics have suggested that Kazantzakis's novel (and, more frequently, that Scorcese's film) pushes the pendulum too far in the other direction, making Jesus seem *too* human or inadequately divine. How might the author and the director respond to this charge? What changes might have helped to deflect this charge without allowing the pendulum to swing too far back in the other direction?

5. Consider the novel's account of the widely varying perspectives on Jesus among those who encountered him directly: Peter, John, Judas, Mary Magdalene, Mary and Martha, Lazarus, Pilate, Paul. Do these differences make it easier to understand the variety of responses that Jesus evokes among contemporary Christians?

## For Further Reading

Bonhoeffer, Dietrich. *Christ the Center.* Translated by Edwin H. Robertson. San Francisco: Harper and Row, 1978. (Advanced)

Iannone, Carol. "The Last Temptation Reconsidered." *First Things* 60 (Fall 1996): 50–54. (Introductory)

Johnson, Luke Timothy. *The Real Jesus: The Misguided Quest for the Historical Jesus and the Truth of the Traditional Gospels.* San Francisco: HarperCollins, 1996. (Introductory/Advanced)

Kähler, Martin. *The So-Called Historical Jesus and the Historic, Biblical Christ.* Translated by Carl E. Braaten. Philadelphia: Fortress Press, 1964. (Advanced/Specialized)

Middleton, Darren J. N. "Nikos Kazantzakis and *The Last Temptation of Christ.*" *Christianity and the Arts* 3 (Winter 1996): 26–28. (Introductory)

Wright, N. T. *Jesus and the Victory of God*. Christian Origins and the Question of God, vol. 2. Minneapolis: Fortress Press, 1996. (Advanced/Specialized)

Wright, N. T. *Who Was Jesus?* Grand Rapids: Eerdmans, 1992. (Introductory)

## Other Literary Works Exploring "Jesus Christ Our Lord"

Denys Arcand, *Jesus of Montreal* (film)
Georges Bernanos, *Diary of a Country Priest*
Don Miguel de Cervantes, *Don Quixote de la Mancha*
Graham Greene, *The Power and the Glory*
Fyodor Dostoyevsky, *The Idiot*
Victor Hugo, *Les Misérables*
John Irving, *A Prayer for Owen Meany*
Anita Mason, *The Illusionist*
Herman Melville, *Billy Budd, Sailor*
Flannery O'Connor, *"Parker's Back"*
William Shakespeare, *Hamlet, Prince of Denmark*

# three

# "Conceived by the Holy Spirit, Born of the Virgin Mary"

We now reach the point in the creed where a great many people find themselves drawn up short. Given some of our explorations through the last two chapters, we could probably say that those claims, too, might now give many of us pause—once their meaning and significance become clear. For example, when we pause to consider how many of our most firmly held beliefs are called into question when we say "I believe in God," its significance is emphasized. And when we recognize how difficult it can be to hold humanity and divinity together in one person, we become more aware of the sheer audacity of the name "Jesus Christ"—the name that *embodies* this union of humanity and divinity. But although it takes some time and effort to recognize the controversial claims embedded in the words "I believe in God . . . and in Jesus Christ," few people would have any difficulty recognizing the controversy inherent in the claim that Jesus was "born of a virgin."

Our modern understanding of pregnancy and childbirth creates certain expectations in our minds about what it means for a child to be conceived and born, and these expectations can exercise a very firm hold on our imaginations. We expect new life to be produced from two individual cells—male and female, sperm and egg. In most cases, this union is a product of some form of sexual intimacy between male and female. These physical and biological realities have such overwhelming significance for us that we find it hard to imagine words like "conceived" and "born" to refer to anything other than the physical and the biological. For us, these terms fall under the expertise of modern medicine; they seem to belong more within the purview of the obstetrician or the gynecologist than that of the theologian.

65

But in the era in which the Scriptures and the creeds were written, and throughout much of Christian history since that time, this supposedly "obvious" connection between birth and biology was anything but obvious. For the ancient writers, conception and childbirth were understood much less biologically and much more relationally. We see a dramatic example of this in the opening of Matthew's Gospel, which traces the generations from Abraham to Jesus. But it does not do this as we would: it does not actually demonstrate a direct "blood relationship" between Jesus and those who preceded him. It begins logically enough with "Abraham was the father of Isaac, and Isaac the father of Jacob, and Jacob the father of Judah and his brothers," and so on; each son is described as being, in turn, the father of the next generation. But when Matthew reaches the end of his list of generations, he dispenses with the biological bloodline and describes Jacob as "the father of Joseph the husband of Mary, of whom Jesus was born" (1:15–16). In other words, after tracing the generations from Abraham down to Joseph through father-son relationships, he points out that Jesus has no blood relationship to these "ancestors." In fact, in the next few verses, Matthew will make it very explicit that Joseph is *not* the biological father of Jesus. Luke's version of the genealogy has a similar gap in the bloodline; Jesus is there described as "the son (as was thought) of Joseph, son of Heli. . . ." So why do the Gospel writers go on and on, regaling us with all those unpronounceable Hebrew names, all for the purpose of tracing a lengthy bloodline that Jesus does not ultimately share?

We find their thinking difficult to understand because, in the modern era, biology rules the world: "biology is destiny," as Freud almost said, and we believed him. If we want to "prove" that John is the father of Becky, we look for physiological resemblance, or ask the mother about the sexual union that resulted in conception, or, today, perform a DNA test. This last option was not, of course, available in the ancient world; but even if it had been, it would have seemed to many people a very odd way of establishing a parent-child relationship. For the ancients, these relationships were established by membership in a particular tribe and by the lineage of the household—not by biological details. In Hebrew culture, slaves and servants from foreign lands could become part of the "house and lineage" of a particular tribe without any biological connection. In this cultural world, writers have no difficulty demonstrating that Jesus is of the house and lineage of David, while at the same time denying a direct biological connection between Jesus and the rest of the tribe of Judah.

We could make some similar observations concerning the meaning of the claim that Jesus is "born of a virgin." For us, this statement seems to be nothing more than the assertion of a medical impossibility. We are trained to think about such matters biologically, and our minds immediately gravitate in that direction when claims about childbirth and virginity are made. In the ancient world, such claims were rather more common—and their focus was not exclusively medical. They provided a way of making assertions about a person's ultimate origins and significance. The claim that Jesus was "conceived by the Holy Spirit and born of the Virgin Mary" is an attempt to express the child's extraordinary relationship to God. At the same time, this claim denies that Jesus is a "typical" human being (if by that we mean the sort of human beings with whom we interact every day). On the one hand, the Gospels show us that Jesus has experienced the human condition as we experience it—with all of its dependence, displacements, sorrows, and death. On the other hand, the story of Jesus' miraculous birth is a way of saying that Jesus' *origins* are significantly different from ours—specifically, he entered this world without the exercise of human initiative.

This last point would have been more obvious in the ancient world as well. According to ancient biology, pregnancy was understood not as the union of two cells, but as the growth of the single seed (supplied by the male) planted in an adequate vessel (supplied by the female). According to this perspective, only the male supplies the substance of new life; the female was thought to provide only the "space" within which the substance matures. Consequently, in order to express the extraordinary nature of a person (or a god), people told of births that came about without the work of a human male: Athena sprung from the head of Zeus, the first human being formed from the dust of the earth, a child conceived by a virgin. These stories tell of individuals who were so significant, so extraordinary, that their conception was beyond the power of men. Someone else was responsible for their generation—someone outside the mundane world of experience. Anyone who was generated through such extraordinary means was capable of bringing into the world not just new life, but new *meaning*.

This is not to say that these new beings would have to be understood as alien, inhuman creatures. But their humanity would have resulted from a "taking on" of human form, or of being endowed with that form, by some power external to (and, typically, much greater than) human beings. These stories offer a way of stressing the extraordinary importance of a particular individual and a way of suggesting that the new creature deserves a higher degree of attention.

Thus, when we claim that we believe that Jesus was "conceived by the Holy Spirit and born of the Virgin Mary," we are, first of all, declaring that he has a special status. He is a human being, but not "just another" human being. His birth marks the intersection of time and eternity; in him, something beyond us, something that we cannot fully imagine, has become present. This new presence is not simply the result of human planning, nor of a complicated scheme that we invented in order to draw these two realms more closely together. Jesus' birth is out of our hands—almost out of human hands altogether. Nevertheless, it does require human consent. In the Christian story, that consent is present in Mary's willingness to say "yes" to God's initiative: "let it be with me according to your word" (Luke 1:38). But in this moment of the making of new meaning on earth, we human beings are the receivers and the nurturers rather than the designers and the engineers.

Mary's acceptance of this divine initiative brings out another aspect of virginity that is not often emphasized today. We tend to concentrate on its medical and sexual implications, but in the ancient world (and through much of Christian history), a person might voluntarily choose a life of celibacy as a sign of particular dedication and devotion to God. In this sense, a *virgin* is rarely naive or sheltered (common connotations of the word today); instead, a virgin is someone who understands her or his commitment to God as a priority outranking all others, including the biological urges toward procreation and physical sexual pleasure. Paul speaks of the superiority of the single life in his letters; those who are married, he says, have divided interests, while the unmarried need only be anxious about the affairs of the Lord (1 Cor. 7:32–34). Of course, this is not a perfect analogy, because although she is a virgin, Mary is betrothed (and, we assume, eventually married) to Joseph. Nevertheless, the Gospel writers do tend to emphasize her devotion to God; this is particularly the case in the first few chapters of the Luke's Gospel. Perhaps we are being asked to understand Mary's virginity not as a judgment about physical sexual intimacy but as an affirmation of her devotion to God. Rather than seeing Mary as a symbol of the subordination or exploitation of women, perhaps we should see the story of the virgin birth as a reminder that sometimes great things happen without any need for men!

The belief in Mary's willing acceptance of God's initiative and of Jesus' miraculous birth is a way of emphasizing Jesus' divine origins and his extraordinary significance. Because of his unique relationship to God, his presence on the earth will make all the difference. The world will, quite literally, become a different place—a "new creation"—as a result of his birth. In this moment, God demonstrates a willingness to enter directly into the world, to take on the human condition and all that goes with it (including, as we will see in the next chapter, suffering and death). This divine initiative implies that God has something of monumental significance in store for us. This unprecedented fusion of humanity and divinity announces to us that here, everything is at stake; the fate of the earth, and particularly of human life upon the earth, hangs in the balance.

Of course, there were many other ways of conveying Jesus' significance. Indeed, in the previous chapter, we discussed how this is emphasized by the title "Christ" and by more general claims about Jesus' divinity. Why, then, do we need the language of the virgin birth, when it is so easily misunderstood—and so much more likely, today, to evoke either absolute skepticism or a blind leap of faith?

We can offer a number of possible answers. For one thing, stories about pregnancy and childbirth are powerful; even in a world of cynicism and doubt, a new birth can still evoke wonder and awe. The keenest skeptic can still refer to "the miracle of new life." Second, the story of Jesus' birth helps us to focus on the importance of "women's work" in a story that is otherwise heavily dominated by men and by masculine imagery. It emphasizes that Jesus was born through the willing response of a faithful young woman, and that he was nursed and nourished and raised in a domestic environment that would have been largely the space of women (despite all the pious images of Jesus in Joseph's carpentry shop!). And finally, our continued attention to the story of Jesus' birth— as well as our continued attention to other parts of the narrative of Jesus—helps maintain the lines of continuity between our present-day belief and the beliefs of those who have gone before us. They too were Christians, and even though their understandings of medicine, biology, and divine intervention may have differed radically from ours, it would be unwise to treat them as poor souls who could never rise to our level of enlightenment. The Christian faith is justifiably proud of the way that it has endured over time and across cultural, racial, and political boundaries. What a shame it would be if modern Christians were to relegate their predecessors to a sort of second-class faith because of differences in their biological assumptions.

In the ancient world, and through much of Christian history, the story of his divine conception was a very forceful and successful means of conveying the uniqueness and importance of Jesus, as well as his intimate relationship to God. The categories and assumptions that made such a story persuasive were widespread and well-known. So, too, were the rebuttals to such stories; the idea that Jesus was the illegitimate son of a Roman solider is not a new accusation, but circulated in the earliest days of Christian history. In the ancient world, such rebuttals would have been seen as damaging, not so much for the sexual scandal they imply (as we tend to assume today), but because they questioned the intimacy of the relationship between Jesus and God, and questioned his extraordinary, world-changing significance. This helps to reveal the sheer wrong-headedness of the present-day enthusiasm (particularly among Christians!) for denying the belief in the virgin birth. In doing so, writers such as John Spong elevate the medical or biological aspects of this belief to the rank of first importance while ignoring its significance in portraying Jesus' extraordinary relationship to God. Such denials, far from making the faith more accessible, end up making it less worthy of belief: Jesus becomes just an ordinary individual who happened to say a few memorable things, some of which are accepted by some people. Why in the world would people devote their lives to that?

Modern-day criticisms of the belief in the virgin birth are right in one sense, however. If we have *reduced* the belief in Jesus' conception and birth to the assertion of a biological or medical factoid, then we have surely missed the point. What is needed is a way of reappropriating the ideas that Jesus is an extraordinary person, that his birth into the world makes all the difference, and that Mary's single-minded dedication to God is ultimately more important than the state of her bodily tissues. How can we, today, convey the uniqueness and extraordinary significance of these events? How can we help one another understand that the fate of the earth turns upon God's birth into the human world?

The challenge is a difficult one. Today, we are so aware of the significance of social, cultural, political, and economic structures—so cognizant of how these structures fundamentally form our lives—that we can hardly imagine how the birth of one child could make all the difference. Nor do we find it easy to imagine someone who lives in full and complete communion with God. And yet, that is precisely the story that is told by the Christian faith. In order to bring that story to life again today, we need to enter the imaginative world of fiction and create a setting in which the conception and birth of the single child is intimately bound to the salvation of the world. This is precisely what the British writer P. D. James has done in her extraordinary novel *The Children of Men.*

The novel certainly ranks among other great works of dystopic fiction. A "dystopia" is like a "utopia"—a vision of the future—but instead of being picture-perfect in all respects, it is perfectly repugnant. James sets her dystopia in the not-too-distant future, when all human beings have become sterile. All the combined energies of scientists, biochemists, and genetic engineers have failed to discover either a cause or a cure for this startling situation. Now, the human race has little more to do than to find some way of keeping the lights on—and coping with the loneliness—until the bitter end. Here indeed is a world in which the conception and birth of a single child could make all the difference.

\* \* \* \* \*

In the figure of Theodore Faron, James provides us with an excellent vantage point for surveying this bleak future world. Through Theo's diary, we are able to experience his own poignant reflections on the discontent, fear, and boredom that sets in when people live without hope. Through the narrative chapters, we watch his life, hitherto lived within the safety and security of Oxford academia, drawn into a series of events and relationships that he cannot understand. Several aspects of Theo's character are worthy of note: his effort to live out the last half of his life without illusion and self-deception; his ongoing willingness to wrestle with the pain and regret brought about by a mostly unhappy childhood, a failed marriage, and the death of his only child; and his ambivalent attitude toward religious faith—he is unconvinced by many of its claims, yet unwilling (and perhaps unable) to dismiss it altogether.

The first half of the book provides James with the opportunity to describe this frightening future world. It has been twenty-five years since the last human being was born, and very few people harbor any hope for future of the race. Human activity continues, but at a slower pace and with considerably reduced enthusiasm. The author's vivid descriptions conjure up nothing so much as the vision of a ghost town: unoccupied buildings, playgrounds with no purpose, fewer and fewer people to inhabit more and more available space. Nothing for the universities to do but to become adult education centers; nothing for would-be parents to do but to create elaborate child-substitutes by adopting pets and robotic dolls.

And nothing for the very old to do but to try to die with dignity; mass suicide rituals, spontaneous at first, have now been institutionalized in the chilling (but wholly believable) Quietus. (The Latin word suggests a state of rest, sleep, being at peace and free from trouble; but these images, in turn, conjure up that of death. Think of Hamlet's line, to which James alludes in passing: "Who would not his own quietus make with a bare bodkin?") In this brave new world, the greatest challenge is to find a reason to care; the population as a whole has fallen into "almost universal negativism, what the French named *ennui universel*"—a profound and pervasive listlessness. A few people find comfort in religious belief, but most of it is either the individualistic rationalism to which most of institutional Christianity has succumbed, or an emotionalistic pietism in which "all you need is love." Very few people show up in the Magdalen College Chapel for the traditional Evensong service; many of those who do have come with purely aesthetic motives, to listen to taped reproductions of the music of boys' choirs. But some, at least, are there for the same reason that Theo is: to try to give themselves some reason to care. "Feel, he told himself, feel, feel, feel. Even if what you feel is pain, only let yourself feel" (p. 39).

The hopelessness that has descended upon England since human childbirth came to an end has made it ripe for dictatorship, and a man with the exotic name of Xan Lyppiatt has risen to the challenge. (He also happens to be Theodore Faron's cousin—another factor contributing to Theo's success as a narrator.) Xan's rule as Warden of England is rather benevolent compared to the images of autocratic state power in dystopic novels such as George Orwell's *1984* or Margaret Atwood's *The Handmaid's Tale*. Nevertheless, when any dissent arises, the State Security Police appear without delay. The government has dealt with the problem of crime by sending all offenders into exile on the Isle of Man and there allowing them to fend for themselves. Many of these prisoners are dying of brutal violence and of starvation; the island has become a place in which the living envy the dead. But through this policy—along with the Quietus, the state-sponsored pornography and massage, and the self-destruction of any "official" Christian faith worthy of the name—the ruling Council has given people what they want. "The system has the merit of simplicity and gives the illusion of democracy to people who no longer have the energy to care how or by whom they are governed as long as they get what the Warden has promised: freedom from fear, freedom from want, freedom from boredom" (p. 89).

But P. D. James is a wise enough author to recognize that, even in the world such as this, the true Christian faith will not vanish entirely. The strength and resilience that the faith has shown over the centuries will not be easily abolished, even when the task is undertaken by its own adherents. In this sense, James's dystopia differs considerably from others of that genre, in which Christianity tends to be either irrelevant (Orwell's *1984*, or Aldous Huxley's *Brave New World*) or corrupted into the service of state power (Atwood's *Handmaid's Tale*, or Golding's *Lord of the Flies*). By contrast, in *The Children of Men*, many of the characters experience a continuing awareness of the Christian resonances that still inhabit this dying world: the music, the symbols, the ethical structures. Many of the book's chapters, including those cast as diary entries, end with a wry (and frequently accurate) comment on the Christian faith. For example, concerning a popular American televangelist's elimination of "the Second Person of the Trinity together with His cross," Theo comments: "the change was immediately popular. Even to unbelievers like myself, the cross, stigma of the barbarism of officialdom and of man's ineluctable cruelty, has never been a comfortable symbol" (p. 50).

Then into Theo's narrowly drawn world enters Julian, a woman who does seem to have found reasons to feel and to care. And, significantly, she believes—in the face of all evidence to the contrary—in a God who feels and cares: she is a devout Christian. She is also part of a ragtag group of dissidents who are distressed by the way the country is being run. They have taken on the rather fruitless task of attempting to bring about change in a country that is being ruled with an iron fist. The dissenters are outraged by conditions on the Isle of Man penal colony. They believe that many elderly people are being forced to participate in the Quietus against their will. They are also distressed about the abusive treatment of the "Sojourner" class (immigrants allowed into England to do the work that no one else will do, and then unceremoniously exiled again at age sixty—a vision that strikes all too close to home for current-day residents of the industrialized West). In short, the members of this small cell believe that Xan has ruled the country undemocratically for far too long, and that some fundamental changes need to be made.

They call themselves The Five Fishes, and the Christian resonances of the name are too loud to escape comment. (They try to nourish and feed others; they seek to be agents of transformation; most of them ultimately die in the process.) But they are not a purified group of holier-than-thou types; this is a decidedly mixed body. (For more on the necessarily mixed nature of the fellowship of believers, see chapter 9 on the church!) Although all the members of the group have different reasons for their involvement, they all seem to have been able to achieve three things that so much of this dying world's population has been unable to achieve: they understand themselves as a community rather than as lonely, isolated individuals; they care about something other than themselves; and they love one another.

After Evensong at Magdalen Chapel, Julian approaches Theo to ask him to meet with their group and to intercede on their behalf with his cousin Xan. He is extremely reluctant to get involved, but he finally agrees to meet with them—partly out of curiosity and partly out of his attraction to Julian. When they describe their demands, he rejects each one with a pragmatic response, and he stresses the futility of their protest. But after witnessing a Quietus in which at least one person (indeed, a person known to him) was clearly not participating voluntarily, he decides to speak with his cousin.

His arguments get him nowhere—except possibly to implicate him in the dissenters' plot against the government. He returns to Oxford, meets with Julian, and attempts to persuade her against further involvement, but she believes that she must continue to work for change "because God wants me to." Theo responds in frustration:

> "If you believe He exists, then presumably you believe that He gave you your mind, your intelligence. Use it. I thought you would have been too proud to make such a fool of yourself."

> But she was impervious to such facile blandishments. She said: "the world is changed not by the self-regarding, but by men and women prepared to make fools of themselves" (p. 110).

Soon after that encounter, a small leaflet with a list of dissident demands begins to circulate throughout the town. Theo is briefly questioned about these documents, but the State Security Police do not seem to be clamping down too hard at this point. Theo decides to spend the summer roaming around Europe, visiting the vast monuments to the creativity and genius of humankind—monuments that will soon be abandoned to decay. But even as he goes, he is aware of his own complicity, standing "a little way off to watch the crosses on the hill" (p. 127).

Thinking back on that summer trip, Theo offers the novel's first direct allusion to the conception and birth of Jesus. In this section, the author develops a heartbreaking contrast between the present sterile world—in desperate need of a child to save it—and the Virgin Mary, whose child actually does save the world:

> His keenest memory was of Rome, standing before the Michaelangelo *Pietà* in St. Peter's, of the rows of spluttering candles, the kneeling women, rich and poor, young and old, fixing their eyes on the Virgin's face with an intensity of longing almost too painful to witness. He remembered their outstretched arms, their palms pressed against the glass protective shield, the low continual mutter of their prayers as if this ceaseless anguished moan came from a single throat and carried to that unregarding marble the hopeless longing of all the world (p. 138).

Such scenes clearly move Theo, but he hardly sees how an extraordinary leap of religious faith would make things any better. Like so many modern readers of the Christian creeds, he can only imagine conception and childbirth in such circumstances as highly improbable medical events. For him, celibacy or sterility are strictly biological matters; he cannot imagine them to be spiritual or emotional or theological in nature.

When Theo returns to Oxford, he finds the mood increasingly depressed, and he has a sense of impending danger. It falls upon him a few nights later, when one of The Five Fishes, a Jamaican woman with the significant name of Miriam, appears at his door. One of the group has been picked up by the police, and they are on the run. Julian has asked for Theo to come and help them. Against his better judgment, and almost against his will, he does so. On the way, Miriam tells him something unbelievable: Julian is pregnant.

The second half of the novel relates the story of this apparently miraculous pregnancy and its significance. The narrative provides a wide range of insights about the same sorts of questions that are raised by the creed: How can one birth be of such significance? How can the child be protected against those who would respond to the birth with violence or take advantage of it for personal gain? What would it be like to be the mother of this child, to bear the responsibility and the hardships of bringing such a child into the world? And the book also faithfully refuses to give any precise answer concerning the question that we, too, don't know how to answer: How did this miraculous conception happen? The book does drop a few interesting hints; the child's mother knows the identity of the father (a friend who is also a priest, and whose name is the same as the Gospel writer most associated with the virgin birth: Luke), and the parents were "missed" by the government's ongoing fertility-testing program. But the book refuses to offer a definitive answer on this point because, first of all, we don't really know, and more important, because *that's not the point*. The point of the new birth is *that* it happened, not *how* it happened. Its significance is not in the scientific medical details, but in its meaning for the future of the world.

The author adds a number of nice touches to complicate and deepen the mystery. Julian has not struck us, thus far, as a very likely mother for the repopulation of the earth. She is middle-aged, withdrawn, and is physically imperfect (she has a badly deformed hand). But there are hints; when Theo sees her in Magdalen Chapel, "her face gleamed with a gentle, almost transparent light" (p. 36). Just before his trip abroad, he sees her in the Oxford covered market "in a glow of effulgent colour, skin and hair seeming to absorb radiance from the fruit, as if she were lit not by the hard glaring lights of the store, but by a warm southern sun" (p. 131). The signs of fertility are all there, but they couldn't be recognized by powers that be; Julian's deformity made her exempt from the government's regular program of testing. The father of the child, Luke, was also exempt from testing due to childhood epilepsy. The author's underlying suggestion is that we have put so much faith in scientific approaches to life—indeed, that we have become so mechanically adept at *engineering* life—that we have neglected its most essential ingredients: life in community, regard for the other, a contemplative spirit, and of course, love.

Very early in the novel, Theo writes in his journal about this new religion of humankind:

> Western science has been our god. In the variety of its power it has preserved, comforted, healed, warmed, fed, and entertained us and we have felt free to criticize and occasionally reject it as men have always rejected

their gods, but in the knowledge that, despite our apostasy, this deity, our creature and our slave, would still provide for us. . . . It has been my god too, even if its achievements are incomprehensible to me, and I share the universal disillusionment of the those whose god has died (p. 5).

The remains of Western science were searching for new birth among the most likely candidates: the young, the beautiful, the strong. But when fertility finally breaks back into the world, it arrives among the weak, the lowly, the unlovely. "The stone that the builders rejected has become the chief cornerstone" (Ps. 118:22).

I have already noted that the book gives no definitive medical or scientific explanation as to how this pregnancy occurred. Nor does the author explain why and how the curse of sterility is broken at this particular *moment* and among these particular *people*. Again, though, there are some tantalizing hints: both the mother and the father are part of a community that has found a reason to feel and to care, and both are Christians—not the official ones, not the newly rationalistic or gushing ones, but Christians of the old school, complete with the *Book of Common Prayer* and the Eucharist. We are privy to very little of the practice of their faith, but they seem to be able to maintain Christlike virtues of patience and gentleness, even as the world around them is falling apart. Eventually, the father dies to save the life of the mother, and we later learn that the profundity of his feeling was part of the reason that Julian was attracted to him: "I envied him because he could love so much, could feel so much. No one has wanted me with that intensity of emotion. So I gave him what he wanted" (p. 189).

Perhaps *love* turns out to be the essential ingredient—not the sentimental love of the American televangelist (who revives the Beatles song "All You Need is Love" as her theme song!), but the profound, other-directed, community-building love that is the very heart and soul of the Christian faith. In the beginning, Theo cannot imagine such love without a bad taste in his mouth; he refers to its "appalling subservience" (p. 47) and believes himself incapable of it: "I am fifty years old and I have never known what it is to love. I can write those words, know them to be true, but feel only the regret that a tone-deaf man must feel because he can't appreciate music, a regret less keen because it is for something never known, not for something lost" (p. 133).

But by the end of the book, some of Julian's focus on community, love, and the other has begun to rub off, however lightly, on the cold and skeptical Theo. Once he looked upon The Five Fishes with disdain, and could only wish "for a second, no more, that he could share the passion and the folly which bound together that pitiably unarmoured fellowship" (p. 113); now he has, in essence, become a key member of a community that, as he himself realizes, has nurtured this new life. He rediscovers prayer; lost bits of verse from his childhood reappear in his mind as he quotes Scripture and the liturgy (in some cases perhaps without realizing it) from long-forgotten memories. He gives up on his "god of science," finally coming to understand and to accept Julian's desire to give birth in secret, away from the gleaming machinery that we have developed to engineer life (p. 225). And most significant of all, he is learning to love (p. 226):

> He contemplated the gulf fixed between Julian and himself by her belief, but without dismay. He could not diminish it but he could stretch his hands across it. And perhaps in the end the bridge would be love. . . . The emotion he felt toward her was as mysterious as it was irrational. He needed to understand it, to define its nature, to analyse what he knew was beyond analysis. But some things now he did know, and perhaps they were all he needed to know. He wished only her good. He would put her good before his own. He could no longer separate himself from her. He would die for her life.

He is, in fact, a very different person than the emotionally numb figure whom we encounter in the book's opening pages. And he is only one example of how a life can be so thoroughly transfigured by the event of new birth.

The story of the birth of the child seems deliberately to parallel the traditional accounts (perhaps, some critics have suggested, too much so): a three-sided room, like a stable, in the midst of "the holly and the ivy," is the location; there is a complete cast of characters, including the mother and child, the older man in the background (not the child's father), and a wicked despot who claims to want to see the child but really plans to use the new birth for his own self-promotion. There are "no simple shepherds at this cradle" (p. 198), but there are some Magi— the powerful but somewhat chastened members of the Council, who arrive to pay homage to the newborn babe. And at the end, Theo is brought back into the faith of his childhood, at least deep enough to do what needs to be done (p. 241):

> There was very little water left in the bottle, but he hardly needed it. His tears were falling now over the child's forehead. From some far childhood memory he recalled the rite. The water had to flow, there were words which had to be said. It was with a thumb wet with his own tears and stained with her blood that he made on the child's forehead the sign of the cross.

## Questions For Discussion

1. How have you traditionally understood the language about Jesus being "born of the Virgin Mary"? Has your own faith emphasized this claim, and if so, in what ways?

2. How do you think that this aspect of traditional Christian belief is heard and understood by people in your culture who are not well acquainted with Christianity?

3. This phrase of the creed emphasizes the work of the Holy Spirit in the conception of Jesus. In what ways would you describe the Holy Spirit at work in the narrative of this novel?

4. Why do you think that stories and images of childbirth continue to have such a powerful effect on our lives? Have the technologies and the privacy surrounding childbirth in contemporary culture had any effect on this?

5. What are some of the factors, operative in our culture, that make it so hard for us to accept that something extraordinary and monumental might be accomplished without the initiative of human beings in general, and of men in particular?

## For Further Reading

Boff, Leonardo. *The Maternal Face of God: The Feminine and Its Religious Expressions.* Trans. Robert R. Barr and John W. Diercksmeier. San Francisco: Harper and Row, 1987. (Advanced/Specialized)

Macquarrie, John. *Mary for All Christians.* Grand Rapids: Eerdmans, 1990. (Introductory)

Tavard, George. *The Thousand Faces of the Virgin Mary.* Collegeville, Minn.: Liturgical Press, 1996. (Advanced)

Williams, Rowan. "Waiting on God" and "Born of the Virgin Mary" in *A Ray of Darkness: Sermons and Reflections.* Cambridge, Mass.: Cowley Publications, 1995. (Introductory)

Wood, Ralph C. "Rapidly Rises the Morning Tide: An Essay on P. D. James's *The Children of Men.*" *Theology Today* 51, no. 2 (July 1994): 277–88. (Introductory)

## Other Books and Films Related to "Born of the Virgin Mary"

Margaret Atwood, *The Handmaid's Tale*
William Faulkner, *Intruder in the Dust*
Jean-Luc Godard, *Hail Mary* (film)
Ron Hansen, *Mariette in Ecstasy*
Flannery O'Connor, "A Temple of the Holy Ghost"
Anne-Marie Miéville, *The Book of Mary* (film)
Daniel Stern, *Rookie of the Year* (film)

# four

# "Suffered under Pontius Pilate, Was Crucified, Died, and Buried"

After having just examined one of the most controversial and disputed phrases in the Apostles' Creed, we now turn to a statement that is, in some ways, its most straightforward claim. In fact, it may appear at first glance not to be a *theological* claim at all, but rather a simple historical statement referring to an event in the past. Some theologians have suggested that this is the point at which the creed is most clearly connected to the rest of human history. Pontius Pilate was, in fact, a Roman official. He was the Procurator of Judea, a region that had been habitually troublesome to the Roman Empire and was not expected to remain stable under a puppet king or some other form of self-rule; it needed a direct Roman presence. According to Roman historians, Pilate had experienced the wrath of the local population well before Jesus came along to trouble him; having set up graven images in the temple, he was met by a group of angry Jews who were prepared to commit mass suicide rather than leave the desolation in place. That was already enough of a sign to him that things would not go well in his new assignment, but he didn't have much choice. As an unpleasant flash point at the outer reaches of the Empire, Judea was not exactly a place for officers deemed to be on their way up the corporate ladder of the Roman bureaucracy.

Thus, Pontius Pilate serves as the officially designated, externally corroborated link between the broader theological claims of the creed and the specific point of human history into which Jesus entered. All the other claims are either timeless conceptual claims (belief in forgiveness, for example, or in the Holy Spirit), or else refer to specific events for which the biblical texts are our only witnesses (the virgin birth, for example, or Jesus' ascent into heaven). The name of Pontius Pilate becomes the historical "hook" that fastens the creed into the broader sweep of human events.

And yet, this phrase is more than just a statement that, at a particular point in history, "something happened." If this were its only purpose, we would be forced to think of this part of the creed as nothing more than a laundry list of statements to which we're being asked to offer our assent. But as I suggested in the introduction to this book, the opening words of the creed ("I believe") are supposed to remind us that we are here describing an orientation of *our whole lives* toward the beliefs that the Christian creeds describe—as exemplified by the practices that are bound up with those beliefs. Such an orientation might *include* certain claims about events that took place in the past, but these would most likely remain in the background; when we say that we "believe in" a particular person or idea, we're usually making a claim that goes far beyond the affirmation of a past event. We're declaring our allegiance to that idea, announcing that it is part of what structures our entire identity.

It would hardly seem to make much difference, for the shape of one's whole life-orientation, to affirm the simple historical claim that there once was, in fact, a man named Jesus who was executed by the Roman Empire when Pilate was the governor of Judea. A great many people have been willing to accept and affirm the historical accuracy of such a claim without committing themselves to anything vaguely Christian. Indeed, such affirmations are offered by various ancient Roman historians of the period, none of whom would have dreamed of shaping their lives according to Christian principles. Why, then, is this apparently "historical" statement in the creed?

We might begin by mentioning two reasons. First, the creed employs the word *suffered* rather than just *lived* or *dwelt on earth* or some such term. It therefore points to more than simply the claim that the lives of Pilate and of Jesus coincided or overlapped. It suggests, rather, that Jesus did indeed *suffer*—that he was capable of suffering, that he was not immune from this very fundamental aspect of the human condition. In this way, the Apostles' Creed continues its arguments against Docetism—that is, against the belief that Jesus only "seemed" to be human (discussed at length in chapter 2). Contrary to the Docetists, Christians eventually asserted their belief that Jesus was not only fully divine but also fully human. He was *so* human, in fact, that he was subject to the same slings and arrows to which we are subject; he could suffer. That means that he could be tempted, that he felt pain, that he experienced joy and sorrow, and that he could (and did) die. Above all, then, this phrase of the creed affirms the reality of human suffering and of Jesus' participation in that suffering.

Second, the mention of Pontius Pilate can be understood in a deeper and broader way through the use of a strategy of language use called *synecdoche*. This is when the part stands in for the whole, as when we use the name of a country's capital city to refer to the whole country or its government ("Beijing reacted to the news") or the name of a person to refer to a larger entity ("Lee surrendered at Appomattox"). In this sense, "Pontius Pilate" is an abbreviated reference to the Roman Empire—and thereby a reference to all empires and other organizations that seek to exercise coercive control over others. In some sense, then, Pilate stands for all the power structures under which human beings have suffered and continue to suffer. Consequently, this phrase in the creed holds up such suffering as particularly significant and relevant to our lives.

It would have also been accurate, no doubt, to have said that Jesus suffered from a variety of forces that bear upon all human beings. The Biblical texts tell us that Jesus suffered from hunger (Matt. 4:2), from loneliness (Matt. 26:40), from frustration (Mark 8:21), from anger (Mark 3:5), and from a feeling of abandonment (Mark 15:34). The writers of the creed could also have emphasized his sufferings under the religious authorities of his day, or at the hands of his compatriots. But by focusing on Pilate (and therefore on the Empire), the creed draws our attention to the temporal power structures that seek to dominate our lives. These structures may be political, economic, familial, or cultural; they may draw their strength from illegitimate appeals to difference in race, gender, and other biological realities; and they may achieve their dominance through violent coercion, subtle suggestion, or the incitement of mass panic. Of course, human suffering is not limited to these particular forms, but neither should we forget that much of our suffering results from structures that are put in place by human beings. The creed emphasizes that Jesus suffered under some of the same forms of domination that we suffer under today.

This phrase of the creed therefore provides us with a good opportunity to talk about the reality of human suffering—about its pervasive nature, its extraordinary effect on our lives, and especially about Jesus' willingness to accept and assume even this aspect of the human condition. But as we will see, talking about suffering is a tricky business. If we are to avoid some of the classic pitfalls of Christian belief and practice in this area, we will have to step carefully.

Suffering is a universal human phenomenon. Most of us have known grief in the loss of a loved one. We have experienced, or at least witnessed, excruciating mental, physical, and spiritual suffering—in our own lives, among our closest friends, or in the nameless, voiceless, agony-ridden faces of the news photos. And of course, we have experienced pain in our own bodies: accidental wounds, chronic diseases of uncertain origin, or the heart-rending agony of a tormented and tormenting mind.

There is nothing easier in all the world than to multiply examples of suffering; the list could go on and on. These happenings make us sad, they make us angry, and we cry out (to God, or to other people, or to no one in particular): WHY? Why does this happen? Why is it inflicted upon us—by other human beings, by the power structures that they create, and even by the natural world? Is it really necessary? Is it part of some great cosmic world order that I alone am unable to understand? Yet that hardly seems likely, since no one else seems to understand it either. Is it some bizarre form of justice, in which the total amount of suffering in the world has to add up to the total amount of wrongdoing? And yet, in any given individual, suffering and wrongdoing seem so poorly proportioned. Too often, it seems, the sun continues to shine on sinners, while rain falls on the good and the just. Is the apparent randomness of suffering just one more indicator that the world is simply a site of chaos, where we would be foolish to expect anything to happen for a good reason?

All of this is made yet more difficult by the fact that so much of our suffering does not seem to be traceable to any one person or cause. Many happenings that cause extraordinary suffering for one person can be seen as a great victory or a cause for rejoicing by someone else. (Think of children enjoying sunny summer weather while farmers go bankrupt for lack of rain.) Other forms of suffering are not caused by a single identifiable action, but by layers and networks of decisions and assumptions made over time and across all social and political boundaries. (An African-American may be surrounded by good friends of all races who only wish him well and would never harbor a racist thought; yet he is still oppressed by deeply embedded societal structures and by the often unrecognized phenomenon of white privilege.) In still other cases, we imagine that it might be *possible* to trace the cause of suffering to its roots, but the path is so overgrown with a thicket of conflicting opinions, statistics, cover-ups, and lies that we never expect to be able to successfully locate the source. We often do not know the causes of suffering; we only know that they have left us in a horrible muddle.

The experience of suffering has led human beings to propose and construct a wide variety of systems and structures that seek to explain, justify, rationalize, or even simply to *understand* the pain and agony that seems so pervasive in our world. At certain points in history, we have imagined arbitrary and capricious gods who manipulate us like puppets on a string. ("As flies to wanton boys are we to the gods," says Gloucester in Shakespeare's *King Lear:* "They kill us for their sport.")

Alternatively, we have made suffering into a virtue, suggesting that divine favor is bestowed more abundantly on those who are beaten down by the world. In moments of intellectual fervor, seeking some grand scheme that will explain it all, we have hypothesized elaborate systems of retribution. We imagine that every experience of suffering is an act of cosmic revenge against malicious thoughts and deeds—even if done secretly, unwillingly, or by others on our behalf. We have postulated alternative worlds, a paradise above our heads or a shadowy realm beneath our feet, where fairylike creatures will mete out happiness to the sorrowful and sorrows to the happy, thereby evening the score. We have even gone so far as to condemn our own bodies: to treat them as wretched, usurping, unworthy chunks of flesh and blood weighing down our otherwise freewheeling spirits, a temporary and rather unfortunate stage in the ascent of the beautiful soul.

Before we start imagining this list to be simply a condemnation of others, we should pause to think about how frequently the Christian faith has fallen into just exactly these habits of explaining, justifying, or rationalizing the experience of suffering. Throughout history, plenty of Christians, most of whom should have known better, have depicted God as capriciously punishing his creatures at random. Christians with worldly power have disenfranchised and marginalized those who are biologically "different" from themselves and have justified their actions by telling their victims that their suffering makes them holy or acceptable in the eyes of God. Priests and pastors, faced with inexplicable suffering, have, by hints or suggestions or even outright proclamations, attributed it to some hidden sin on the part of the victims or of those closest to them. Many Christians have profited by describing heaven as "pie in the sky when you die," hoping that it will persuade the have-nots to wait at least one more generation before fomenting some kind of revolution (more on this point in chapter 12). Christians have all too regularly participated in the condemnation of the physical body—denouncing its biological drives for food, sex, and rest as inherently evil manifestations of gluttony, lust, and sloth (more on this in chapter 11). Never mind that every one of these strategies is officially opposed in the traditional teachings of the Christian faith; never mind that they contravene Christian proclamations of divine justice, free will, prevenient grace, salvation by faith, and the essential goodness of the created order. When we Christians have found it convenient to think something, we've never let the official statements of our beliefs get in the way!

On the other hand, it has to be admitted that Christians have not always been particularly clear or persuasive about how we ought to understand the experience of suffering. We don't proclaim it as an article of faith that created beings *have* to suffer, so it seems a little odd that they do. But we *do* proclaim that Jesus suffered: Jesus Christ, the Son of God, our Lord, entered into this world and suffered at its hands. This provides us with our first clue: suffering is, apparently, so much a part of the human condition that, part of what it meant for God to become fully human was to experience suffering as well. We worship Jesus Christ,

> who, though he was in the form of God, did not regard equality with God as something to be exploited, but emptied himself, taking the form of a slave, being born in human likeness. And being found in human form, he humbled himself and became obedient to the point of death—even death on a cross. Therefore God also highly exalted him and gave him the name that is above every name, so that at the name of Jesus every knee should bend, in heaven and on earth and under the earth, and every tongue should confess that Jesus Christ is Lord, to the glory of God the Father (Phil. 2:6–11).

In Jesus, God experiences what we experience: the impermanence of mortal flesh, the impersonal forces of our environment, and the apparent obliviousness of most of the created order to our experiences and concerns. And, as a human being in the person of Jesus, God also encounters other human beings—endowed as they are with free will, and therefore fully capable of bringing suffering upon one another. If we keep in mind the extraordinary *limitations* of human beings (our incomplete knowledge, our biological needs and drives, and our incomplete control of our own will), we realize that God's willingness to become a human being was tantamount to a decision to suffer. These divine sufferings have always been connected with the carrying out of our salvation. Somehow, the redemption of the world is tied up with God's willingness to take on the reality of its suffering.

What does it mean to live with that suffering, day in and day out? What does it mean to experience the structures of domination in our own day—whether they be those of the government, the economic order, the aesthetic assertions of our culture, or the intimate structures of our own families? What does it mean that so much suffering does not even seem to be traceable to any particular source? And most important, what does it mean that God was willing to experience that suffering as well, to bear it in a human body? Even if we know from the outset that we are hardly likely to "make sense" of suffering, can we at least gain some clarity about how we might respond to the experience of suffering in an intelligent, pastoral, and theologically sound way? Might we also begin to draw some appropriate distinctions between, on the one hand, the false glorification of suffering (as a means of justifying abuse, domination, and the endless deferral of justice), and, on the other hand, the possibility that there might actually be something worth suffering *for?*

In selecting a novel that might help us through these questions, the field is wide open. The experience of human suffering has probably inspired more literary production than all other experiences combined. Much of this literature is about extreme and extraordinary suffering: slavery, rape, torture, the Holocaust, the abuse of children, and the violation of the mentally ill. Such works are powerful and important; some of them are examined elsewhere in this book, and others are listed in the various reading lists at the ends of chapters. Here, however, I have chosen a novel that draws us into a world of less extreme, more garden-variety suffering—the sort that most of us experience on a daily basis. Here the reader will find families that suffer from being broken apart, and others that suffer from being held together. Children suffer under the watchful eyes of their teachers, and workers under the watchful eye of the factory owners. People suffer from not fitting in with the crowd, or from forcing themselves to fit in *too* well. And on a very regular basis, the characters suffer from the illusions that they have built up around themselves and that they use to insulate themselves from the harder realities of the wider world. The novel in question is the one that, as I mentioned in the preface to this book, first started me thinking seriously about the integral relationship between fictional narrative and Christian belief: Charles Dickens's *Hard Times*. The novel takes us to the not-so-imaginary world of Coketown, a British mining and milling center in the midst of the Industrial Revolution. It is a place of exhaustingly long workdays, sterile education, enormous gaps between rich and poor, and a constant longing for some means of escape. Sound familiar?

\* \* \* \* \*

"Now, what I want is, Facts. Teach these children nothing but Facts." This demand expresses the most strongly held belief (we might even say "the creed") of Mr. Thomas Gradgrind, whose job is to supervise the inculcation of facts in the minds of schoolchildren. An ordinary schoolroom may seem an odd place to begin our search for the meaning and significance of human suffering: no shocking scenes of gun violence here, no race riots, no subversion of the authority of the teachers. On the contrary: a well-regulated, thoroughly organized, well-trimmed classroom, in which all the little pitchers are being filled to the brim with "imperial gallons of Facts." In just such classrooms, throughout the brief history of universal public education, have some of the most painful and poignant moments of suffering that anyone has ever experienced occurred.

Dickens could not be clearer about this: the program of education being visited upon these children is laughable and crude. But not only that: their treatment is also injurious, deformative of character, and morally inexcusable. In these opening scenes—not as much of a parody of Victorian education as some might like to believe—we see children catalogued, molded, and filled with as many Facts as their dear little heads can hold. Little wonder that they try to get away from the place as soon as they can, and seek entertainment at the circus (or worse). The humor of the scene is painful to experience, for very often—and in precisely this way—is the natural, sponge-like enthusiasm for learning knocked out of the heads of children at an early age. Dickens catches the depth of the crime in the title of an early chapter: "Murdering the Innocents."

From scenes of suffering in the classroom, we are transported to scenes of suffering in the home. Dickens peels back the layers of Mr. Gradgrind's household, showing us the utilitarian father, the cluelessly mean-spirited mother, and the stultified life of the children (who have been so painstakingly raised on a diet of Facts). The portrait is pure hyperbole, but it makes its point: suffering is a part of everyday life, and its source is never particularly clear. The whole "system" is at fault—the economic system, the educational system, the political system. The origins of all the suffering seem to lie in the power exercised by those empowered to exercise it, but it is very difficult to put one's finger on a particular perpetrator. All that we know for certain is that people are in pain.

Thomas Gradgrind believes he has hit upon the solution to every problem in the world—the education problem, the family problem, the economic problem, the political problem. His particular solution ("Facts") is certainly the most immediate target of Dickens's scorn; but we would do the author an injustice if we assumed that, simply because *we* don't harbor the same extreme Utilitarian convictions, we are therefore free from the temptation to impose our own particular program for the salvation of the world. The two eldest Gradgrind children, Louisa and Thomas, have suffered mightily under their supposed savior. All the joys of childhood have been displaced in them by Facts, and the household's Great Commandment is that the children must shut down their imaginations; their father's oft-repeated motto is: "never wonder."

As a display of his confidence that "Facts" can cure even the most reprobate of wonderers, Mr. Gradgrind takes into his household the freespirited Sissy Jupe. She has been orphaned by her father's sudden departure from a local circus troupe, and Mr. Gradgrind intends to use her as a sort of demonstration of the master's skill at sculpting perfect practicality. (One is reminded of Shaw's *Pygmalion* and the musical *My*

*Fair Lady* that was based on it. Just as Henry Higgins can make a a cockney flower girl into a social success, so does Gradgrind intend to knock the flights of imagination and wonder out of Sissy's head.) As readers, we fear at first that she might suffer the same fate as the other Gradgrind children. As it turns out, however, Sissy not only has resources of her own for fending off the bombardment of Facts; she also comes to evangelize the entire household with her Gospel of the Heart. But not, of course, until after a great deal more suffering has taken place.

At this point, into the novel enters one Josiah Bounderby, a factory owner who has found ways to rationalize every form of suffering such that the victim always gets the blame. He claims to have had no privileged upbringing, but to have made his own way in the world, having pulled himself up by his bootstraps—and he is not afraid to say so (over and over again!). He too inserts his fair share of suffering into the world. He never misses an opportunity for self-promotion; he obscures the legitimate grievances of his factory hands by accusing them of extravagance; he fabricates his own history of suffering and self-redemption; and he uses his supposed high respect for his own household as an excuse for proclaiming the inferiority of everyone else, and badgering the life out of them to boot.

If Bounderby provides the extreme example of a character able to *cause* suffering, Stephen Blackpool—one of the factory hands—is the one who seems most thoroughly on the receiving end of it. His marriage has turned horribly sour; his wife is a perpetually drunk woman who returns occasionally to pawn all his property and soil his living quarters. He can do nothing about it, because the rabidly inequitable divorce laws of the time (which Dickens was here mercilessly skewering) made the process easy for the rich and impossible for the poor. As a result, Stephen's beautiful friendship with Rachael cannot blossom into love and marriage. His conscientious refusal to do anything that might get him labeled a "troublemaker" not only puts him at odds with his fellow workers; it also provides Bounderby with an excuse, by means of a tortuously inverted logic, to fire him for subversive behavior. Stephen's trusting disposition makes him an easy mark for those in search of a scapegoat.

The plot of this novel is nothing more than the sum total of the characters. Once they are drawn in this fashion, they all do pretty much what we would expect them to do. Gradgrind suggests that his daughter marry Bounderby; he is thirty years her senior, but that hardly seems an obstacle, since mutual affection (or the lack thereof) is not reducible to Facts. He is, of course, providing for her in the only way that his system of Facts allows to him—by marrying her to a man of wealth. Louisa, having had all imaginary flights of anything romantic or beautiful rooted out of her life from the beginning, accepts the marriage proposal with a sigh of indifference: "What does it matter!" (p. 136). James Harthouse, a sort of Bounderby-in-training, employs his oily, weasel's disposition to befriend young Tom Gradgrind for the purpose of obtaining information about his sister—and then maneuvers his way into her life. His motives are not completely clear; perhaps he is hoping to receive romantic favors, to discredit her household, or simply to be able to say that he did so. Mrs. Sparsit, a sort of well-born-woman-fallen-from-grace who works as a servant of sorts in Bounderby's house, personifes mean-spirited gossip. She sees adultery on the horizon and relishes the opportunity to see others brought to shame.

Meanwhile, suffering continues to expand in every direction. Bounderby cannot abide Stephen Blackpool's soft-spoken description of the wretched lives of the workers, and so fires him; Louisa tries to help him out; her brother Tom takes advantage of him in order to cover up his own crime of theft. Tom is purposeless in life and deeply in debt; Louisa is locked in a loveless marriage and is pursued by a scoundrel; Stephen is unemployed, destitute, and marked as a troublemaker; Rachael is abandoned; and Mrs. Sparsit is jealous and lonely. Surrounded by all this suffering, the elder Thomas Gradgrind cannot quite understand why the perfect system of utilitarian calculus did not somehow manage, in the end, to put everything to right. "Mr Gradgrind was forever working, in print and out of print, at this eccentric sum, and he never could make out how it yielded this unaccountable product" (p. 90).

In short, the suffering is nearly universal, and much of it seems useless or perverse. No one is suffering for a good cause or in pursuit of a higher goal; all are suffering from the sad circumstances that fortune has laid at their doorstep, or from the sheer perversity of other people, for whom causing such suffering is found to be convenient. In fact, practically all the suffering that takes place in this novel can be traced not to a cosmic toss of the dice, but to the decisions of human beings—sometimes individuals acting in isolation; more often groups and classes, acting so as to insure the survival of economic and social structures that will continue to mete out the suffering in ever-increasing doses. Clearly, Dickens is unwilling to romanticize this suffering. It isn't virtuous, it doesn't automatically elevate its victims, it isn't "God's will," it's not a punishment visited upon the sinful. And yet, somehow, much of the suffering of this novel is transformed into something redemptive. How does that take place?

In the case of Louisa, her loveless marriage and Harthouse's pursuit eventually drive her back to her home and to a confrontation with her father. She finds herself finally able to say the things for which she could not previously find words: she tells him what he has left behind in his relentless pursuit of Facts. "How could you give me life, and take from me all the inappreciable things that raise it from the state of conscious death? Where are the graces of my soul? Where are the sentiments of my heart?" (p. 239). Pent up for years within her, the emotion comes rolling out; she accuses her father of having deformed her very soul. He listens to her, takes in all this sudden news, and he is moved. He may be a Utilitarian to the core, but he is not stupid. He can see his daughter's sufferings when they are shown in so vivid a light, and he begins to undo some of the damage that he has done. We also sense that it is precisely her sufferings that open her up so gloriously to the love that Sissy Jupe has brought into the Gradgrind household.

Sissy herself is another example of the redemptive quality of suffering—as are most of the characters associated with Sleary's Circus. They clearly lead a very hard life, and are often thought ill of by the very people who patronize their entertainments. The physical hardships and uncertain future that they constantly face are only the tip of the iceberg of their suffering. As readers, we are not privy to the day-to-day experiences of their lives. But we do know that Sissy's father, who was an acrobat, was so humiliated by the crowds who watched him falter in the ring that he felt it necessary to leave the circus, and with it, his dear daughter. The suffering that this must have caused for them both is almost unbearable, as is the fact that Mr Gradgrind attempted to cloister Sissy from all outside communication. But precisely because the circus life is such a difficult one, those who live it understand themselves as bound together as a sort of family—in fact, they comprise the most well-functioning family unit in the novel. And this communal life, in which they depend upon one another for everything from their daily bread to the care of their children, is held up as so much better a life than anything experienced by the "privileged" Gradgrinds and Bounderbys.

Another example of the redemptive power of suffering is that of Mrs. Pegler, the mysterious figure who seems to lurk just at the edges of Josiah Bounderby's life—peeking in on his activities, unnoticed, once a year. She is clearly suffering from her isolation, and would dearly like to participate in this man's life in some way, but the reader doesn't learn why until the end of the novel: she is, in fact, his mother. He has paid her off (at a pittance) to keep her quiet about his privileged upbringing so as not to jeopardize the enormous myth of "the self-made man" that he has carefully constructed about himself. In her long, revelatory speech toward the end of the novel, we learn about the sacrifices she has made and the suffering that she has endured for the sake of her son (made tolerable to us only by the fact that she doesn't know just how despicable a character he really is!). "I am well contented," she says, "and I can keep my pride in my Josiah to myself, and I can love for love's own sake!"

(p. 280). Her endurance of her sacrifice and her isolation enable her to describe all that she has done for her son and thereby to reveal, to the rest of the characters, just how thoroughly they have been duped by Bounderby. "Detected as the Bully of humility, who had built his windy reputation upon lies, and in his boastfulness had put the honest truth as far away from him as if he had advanced the mean claim (there is no meaner) to tack himself on to a pedigree, he cut a most ridiculous figure" (p. 281).

But the most profound example of redemption through suffering is that of Stephen Blackpool, who quite literally "gives his life for the ransom of many" (cf. Mark 10:45). Accused of robbing the bank and then attempting to return to town to clear his name, he is badly injured in a fall down an abandoned mine shaft. He is eventually found, very near the point of death, by Rachael and Sissy. He gives them information that leads to the revelation of young Tom Gradgrind's guilt in the robbery, helping to relieve the extraordinary anguish that the whole family has felt as their suspicions about young Tom had grown stronger and stronger. The anxiety produced by Stephen's absence (and by his failure to return to town in a timely manner) serves to unite three women of radically different dispositions and social classes: Rachael, Sissy, and Louisa. And Stephen's reconciling work is broader still, for in working together to get him out of the mine shaft, the people of the town achieve a solidarity that neither their own slave-like conditions nor the demagogic speeches of the labor organizers had managed to muster among them.

The parallels to Christ's redemptive suffering are obvious, right down to the women at the tomb, and Dickens does not hesitate to remind us of them. Like the suffering servant of Isaiah, Stephen is "neither courtly, nor handsome, nor picturesque, in any respect" (p. 190); he is brought up from the pit in a pose that reminds readers of artistic representations of the deposition of Christ from the cross ("with the two men holding on at the sides . . . and tenderly supporting between them, slung and tied within, the figure of a poor, crushed, human creature" [p. 289]). In this state he is described as a "form without form" and is "laid upon the bed of straw" (p. 289). Both Stephen and the narrator make an explicit connection between the star that shines above him and the star of Bethlehem (pp. 290–92), and his dying prayer is that "aw th' world may on'y coom toogether more, an get a better unnerstan'in o'one another" (p. 291). The words are a very close parallel to Christ's prayer in his farewell discourse "that they may all be one" (John 17:21).

Far too much is made of "Christ figures" in literature; the term is employed too often, applied to any character who suffers, teaches, plays the "holy fool," or dies for the sake of others. Rarely is any theological

nuance brought to such discussions, which accounts for the fruitlessness of the endless literary debates as to whether a particular character
is or is not a "Christ figure." For Christians, the portrait of Jesus in the
Gospels ultimately cannot be replaced by anything or anyone; there is
no "Christ figure" who can adequately portray for us the full identity of
Jesus Christ. However, characters like Stephen Blackpool, who mirror
*certain elements* of the life and death of Jesus, can be useful to us insofar as they help us to understand some aspect of our belief. In this case,
I think we are given some hints about the pervasiveness of human suffering, about some of its more obvious causes, and about the ways in
which it can lead to reconciliation and redemption.

Does all of this mean that suffering is "good"? Is it meant to imply
that we should go out and seek to bring it upon ourselves? That we should
bear it, no matter what? That we gain some kind of moral superiority
by suffering more than the next person does? The answer to all these
questions must clearly be "no"—at least in the general and universal
sense in which they are presented here. Take the case of Stephen Blackpool's sufferings, for example: his terrible living conditions and his treatment at the hands of Bounderby and his fellow-workers was neither
good nor excusable. He was right to seek ways of redressing it, and others were wrong to make it so difficult for him to do so. Stephen is not a
"better person" just because he suffers, and his status as victim cannot
be cashed in for a free ticket into heaven (though the narrator seems
quite sure that he's headed there). In no way does the novel suggest that
we would all be better people if only we suffered as much as Stephen
Blackpool. It does suggest, however, that, faced with such suffering,
Stephen provides a model of how to bear it; and he also helps us see
that, if we are willing to bear it, we need not thereby allow suffering to
have the final word.

Because suffering is a universal experience, our question is not so
much about how to avoid it, but how to understand it. As long as we
simply rail against it, question it, and seek to avoid it at all costs, we will
not really be facing it squarely. Reading a novel like *Hard Times* can help
us see suffering as something that is (at least in some cases) given meaning by the actions and attitudes that it brings about. If we can imagine
how ordinary human suffering might lead to a greater good, then we
can also begin to understand how God's willingness to take on our
human flesh might bring about the redemption of the world. This in
turn can help us understand our own experiences of suffering—not to
"make sense" of them, not to justify or rationalize them, but to recognize them as part of life. We know that free and limited human beings
will often find themselves in the midst of suffering. Knowing that God
dwells in the midst of such suffering does not eliminate it, explain it, or

justify it; but it may help us to bear it. And it certainly serves to remind us that we do not suffer alone.

## Questions For Discussion

1. Describe other forms of suffering that you have seen depicted in this novel or other fiction. Some of the details will clearly be specific to an author's own time and place; consider what some of the modern-day equivalents might be for the problems that novelists have identified.

2. What are some of the causes that human beings (or fictional characters, in this book or others) have sometimes believed to be worth suffering for? Worth dying for? Do you think that people are as willing to suffer or die for a particular cause as they once were? If not, what might have contributed to this change?

3. Think of other examples (fictional or otherwise) in which suffering seems to lead to reconciliation or redemption of others. What are some of the conditions that are present when this happens? What role is played by those on whose behalf the suffering takes place?

4. "Jesus suffered and died to save us from our sins." Discuss your reaction to this common Christian claim. How, in your view, does this come about? Have you had any exposure to particular "theories" that seek to explain this process? (Some of them are referred to by names such as "substitionary atonement," "salvation by example," "the ransom theory," and so on.) If you have heard of any of these approaches, what do you see as their advantages and disadvantages?

5. What other analogies can you imagine to explain how suffering might have redemptive (or generally positive) effects? Consider whether any of the following examples help to illuminate the relationship between suffering and redemption: athletic training; pregnancy and childbirth; working to prepare for a celebration.

## For Further Reading

Crysdale, Cynthia S. W. *Embracing Travail: Retrieving the Cross for Today.* New York: Continuum Press, 1999. (Introductory/Advanced)

Frei, Hans W. "Jesus Christ and Modern Christ Figures" in *The Identity of Jesus Christ: The Hermeneutical Bases of Dogmatic Theology.* Philadelphia: Fortress Press, 1975; reprint, Wipf and Stock, 2000. (Advanced)

Hauerwas, Stanley. *Naming the Silences: God, Medicine, and the Problem of Suffering.* Grand Rapids: Eerdmans, 1990. (Introductory/Advanced)

Lowe, Walter. *Theology and Difference: The Wound of Reason.* Bloomington: Indiana University Press, 1993. (Specialized)

Nouwen, Henri J. M. *The Wounded Healer: Ministry in Contemporary Society.* Garden City, N.Y.: Doubleday, 1972. (Introductory)

Young, Frances. *Can These Dry Bones Live? An Introduction to Christian Theology.* New York: Pilgrim Press, 1993. (Introductory/Advanced)

## Other Literary Works Illustrating Suffering and Redemption

Fyodor Dostoevsky, *The Brothers Karamazov*

David James Duncan, *The Brothers K* (discussed in chapter 5)

T. S. Eliot, *Four Quartets*

Graham Greene, *A Burnt-Out Case; The Heart of the Matter; The Power and the Glory*

Victor Hugo, *Les Misérables; Notre Dame de Paris*

Nikos Kazantzakis, *The Last Temptation of Christ* (discussed in chapter 2)

Herman Melville, *Billy Budd, Sailor*

Toni Morrison, *The Bluest Eye; Beloved* (discussed in chapter 7)

Flannery O'Connor, "The Artificial Nigger"; "The Displaced Person"

Iain Pears, *An Instance of the Fingerpost*

William Shakespeare, *King Lear*

Leo Tolstoy, *Anna Karenina*

# five

# "Descended into Hell, On the Third Day Rose Again"

The two phrases that we examine in this chapter have inspired a good deal of theological controversy, in two very different ways. In the case of the first phrase, referring to Christ's descent into hell, the controversy has been primarily among academic theologians, having mostly to do with how the effects of God's redemption are brought to those who lived before the time of Jesus, and sometimes bearing on the question of the relationship between Christianity and Judaism. In the case of the second phrase, however, the controversy has been much more public and popular; here, the arguments tend to divide out among traditionalist/modernist lines, and they tend to engender strong feelings on all sides. Most Christians, it seems, tend to regard the resurrection of Jesus as much more crucial to their faith than his descent to the realm of the dead. And yet, in the legendary creation of the Apostles' Creed by the Twelve, these two claims are welded together as the contribution of a single voice. (Significantly, these words are spoken by Thomas—who, according to John 20:25, doubted the resurrection of Jesus!)

Once again, the modern tendency has been to treat these two statements as though they were nothing more than bits of documentary history—as eyewitness accounts (whether credible or otherwise) of specific events. But for much of Christian history, the emphasis was less on their historicity (which, as we have already noted, is a uniquely modern anxiety) and more on their much deeper and more significant theological ramifications. In emphasizing this point, I am not attempting to deny the historical reality of these claims. I simply want to argue that, like most of the statements in the creed, the significance of these phrases goes far beyond that of an account that one might read in a newspa-

97

per—and might or might not accept—about some particularly significant event.

To understand this more clearly, try reversing the example. Imagine
what might happen if people living in ancient Palestine could receive a
report from the distant future about something that was as "unbelievable" to them as Christ's descent and resurrection seem to us. Imagine,
for example, that they are told that human beings will walk around on
the surface of the moon. Some people might accept this claim; others
might brush it away as a vain leap of imaginative fancy. But whether or
not one accepted the claim that "it really happened" would not necessarily say anything about whether one understood its significance. Even
to *assert* the claim that people have walked on the surface of the moon,
one must already have in place all sorts of assumptions about technol-
ogy, human creativity, the structure of the physical universe, and so on.
In the end, such assumptions would be far more important for understanding the significance of a lunar landing than would be the acceptance or denial of a particular historical event. The person who can't
accept that a moon landing could actually happen, but who can nevertheless imagine a world within which such a feat would be possible, will
be closer to the "truth" about such matters than will a person who accepts
the factuality of the event without understanding what it means.

Similarly, the significance of the creed's mention of Christ's descent
to the dead and his resurrection goes far beyond the question of their
historical factuality. They make claims about the relationships among
God, the world, and human beings (living and dead). When we express
our belief in these teachings, we situate ourselves in relationship to such
deep and difficult mysteries as life, death, God, time, and the physical
universe. And our relationship to these deep and difficult mysteries is
typically more important  than our assertions as to whether some particular event "happened."

Christ's "descent to the dead" is sometimes translated as "descent into
hell"; this difference is due to the difficulty of rendering the Latin word
into English. The word *hell* is somewhat misleading, since it tends to conjure up a complex and fiery place of torment that so dominated later Christian imagination. On the other hand, the Latin term clearly suggests the
idea of a *place*, so the phrase "descended to the dead" remains a little
abstract. Perhaps "descended to the realm of the dead" would be best,
which leads us to ask what that might be like. I will return to this point.

The claim that Christ "descended to the realm of the dead" has traditionally had two purposes. First, it extends the work of the previous
phrase in the creed (suffered, died, and was buried) by making it clear
that Jesus experiences the full range of human existence. He not only
suffers and experiences the "moment" of death; he also experiences death

as a moment of potential separation from the communion of others. He experiences the profound anxiety, the utter loss, and the potential God-forsakeness felt by those who die. His death is not a pretend death, not an apparent death for the purpose of "seeming" to be a human being, but a real death with all the horror and terror that we human beings associate with it.

The Eastern Orthodox theologian Alexander Schmemann remarks that Christians have sometimes tended to play down the true horror of death, glossing over it with remarks about God's will or about how everything will come out all right in the end. He suggests that, while Christians do have certain convictions about eternal life, these beliefs should not lead us to pretend *either* that death is irrelevant *or* that it is just a normal part of life. Christianity, says Schmemann, proclaims death "to be *abnormal* and, therefore, truly horrible. . . . The horror of death is not in its being the 'end' and not in physical destruction. By being separation from the world and life, it is *separation from God*" (p. 100). This separation is what makes death so terrible and terrifying, and this is one of the things that we emphasize about Christ's death when we proclaim that he descended to the realm of the dead.

At the same time, the descent to the dead makes two important claims about the relationship between God and the dead: first, that death's potential to separate us from God is, through Christ's descent to the dead, definitively overcome; and second, that God brings even the dead into participation in the divine life. As the author of the letters of Peter puts it, "This is the reason the gospel was proclaimed even to the dead, so that, though they had been judged in the flesh as everyone is judged, they might live in the spirit as God does" (1 Peter 4:6). This further implies that the salvation wrought through Christ is extended through time, forward and backward, in ways that our own linear constructions of time can barely imagine.

In sum, then, Jesus dies a real death and so experiences what other human beings experience when they die. And what do they experience? Well, of course, we don't actually *know* the answer to that question. In this matter, all is speculation; all the stories and tales, all the creative films and "near-death-experience" documentaries, all the fire-and-brimstone preaching—in the end, it's all guesswork. As human beings, with our reflective intelligence but also with our obvious limitations, we find ourselves, like Shakespeare's Hamlet, meditating on the reality of death—but with no certainty about what may follow:

> But in that sleep of death, what dreams may come
> When we have shuffled off this mortal coil
> Must give us pause.

Did similar thoughts cross Jesus' mind? The depth of feeling that he displays when praying in Gethsemane suggests that the answer is yes.

Indeed, Jesus would not be "truly human" if he had had vastly greater certainty about what lies beyond death than do we. He can believe in the future; he can have faith; he can trust in the benevolence of God—and surely he does all of these things better than we are able to do. But it is precisely with this faith and trust and hope that he must go to his death, rather than with some kind of empirically certified knowledge of what the future holds. And when he dies, he experiences what we all experience. We don't know what that will be, but we use a wide variety of images, metaphors, and other communicative strategies in an attempt to speak about our faith and trust and hope. In the ancient world, one of the most well-worn images was that of a "realm of the dead," typically located under the earth's surface or in some deep abyss, where those who have died continue to experience some form of existence—typically a rather shadowy one, and not always very pleasant. It was not usually a place of extreme torture and pain, as in the later imaginative portraits of hell, but neither was it a place of eternal bliss. Instead, it was simply a rather boring place, where people continued to "exist" (if we can call it that) as empty shells of their former selves.

For the ancient cultures within which the creeds were written, the claim that Christ "descended to the dead" was the most vivid and communicative way of saying that he really experienced what we experience when we die. They expressed that claim in the imagery of their era, employing language that suggested a specific place, a specific direction (down), and a specific length of time (forever). We may find this language "culturally specific" or even "mythological," but do *we* have any clearer sense of "what happens when you die" than they did? Probably not; and unfortunately, we're usually not even as imaginative as they were about trying to express whatever faith or hope or trust that we *do* have. But there is a certain sense in which we can translate this claim into something like, "Jesus experienced what we will experience after we suffer and die," and not be too far afield from this first meaning of the phrase "he descended to the dead."

A further aspect of the meaning and significance of this phrase, however, requires a bit more imaginative work on our parts, because it reorients our entire understanding of time. We tend to construct our experience of time in linear fashion, such that whatever happened "before" a certain point in time is unaffected by what happens "after." Not all cultures understand time in this way, and in particular, circular or cyclical reckonings of time have played a significant role throughout human history. We still have vestiges of these cyclical reckonings in the structure of our days, weeks, months, and years as regular cycles, repeating certain patterns. But our version is less like a circle and more like a spiral; we're fairly convinced that, once something is done, it's past. We can return to it, but only with a sense of distance.

But the Christian claims about salvation have not been made any easier to accept among modern people schooled in this linear logic. From early in the Christian era, theologians worked hard to develop accounts of the salvation of the world that distanced themselves from describing it as some kind of divine salvage operation. In other words, they were dissatisfied with a picture in which God suddenly noticed that the world was going awry and so decided to have a Son who could be sent to repair the damage. Rather, they claimed that God *has always been* a communion of persons, and that the incarnation of the Word—while taking place at a distinct moment in time—has a significance that is shot through time, time before and time after, and cannot be fully comprehended by just plotting it as a particular point on a linear timeline. These beliefs were expressed in credal statements about the timeless relationship among the divine persons. (Thus the Nicene Creed's phrases "eternally begotten of the Father" and "proceeds from the Father"—not the past tense, *proceeded*, but the present tense—describe an ongoing, and indeed an eternal, reality.)

These claims are closely related to the claim that the salvation brought about through Christ must also be timeless. It is offered just as much to those who lived before the time of Jesus as to those who lived during and after that time. Jesus' "descent to the dead" is a particularly picturesque way of expressing the breadth and depth of God's saving work: it transcends boundaries of time and space. Because we don't tend to use a specific physical location to specify the "place of the dead," we may find this imagery to be less than adequate in expressing our belief in the timeless and unbounded nature of salvation; but we may find other, equally useful images to be quite useful in thinking through the idea.

The resurrection of Jesus presents a different kind of problem. It does not confine itself to speculative ruminations on some otherworldly realm "where people go when they die," and therefore cannot be so easily "translated" into a different set of images. The biblical resurrection accounts claim not only that Jesus was raised from the dead, but also that his bodily presence was experienced by those who knew him. (One of the evangelists emphasizes Jesus' bodily resurrection by having him participate in a breakfast of broiled fish: Luke 24:41–43.) Few of us can claim to have actually experienced, in bodily form, a person who has died (though most of us have come closer than we think; I will take up this point again when I turn to the Christian belief in "the resurrection of the body" in chapter 11). Making sense of our belief in the resurrection will not, therefore, be simply a matter of saying, "ancient cultures imagined it in one way; we imagine it in another way." Our examination of the resurrection of Jesus will have to take a slightly different course.

Here too, however, matters may not be quite as they seem. The resurrection of Jesus clearly has a meaning and significance that transcends any play-by-play description of events. It is, above all, an *authentication* of the life of Jesus: a claim that God officially approves of his teachings and his willingness to die at the hands of the state. The particular *form* of Jesus' life and death is thereby described as a *good* form, a divinely sanctioned form. In addition, the resurrection of Jesus makes a statement about suffering and death—namely, that death does not have the final word. God's mighty act of raising Jesus from the dead is, as Paul puts it, a defeat of death by death (1 Cor. 15:54). "Death no longer has dominion over him" (Rom. 6:9); and, by extension, death no longer has dominion over us.

The resurrection of Jesus has also served as a way of emphasizing God's willingness to overcome the separation or alienation that seems to have developed over time between humanity and God. In the stories of the Garden of Eden, human beings can even "hear the sound of the LORD God walking in the garden at the time of the evening breeze" (Gen. 3:8); but Moses can only see God's back (Exod. 33:23), and before long people are beginning to think that God has abandoned them. This feeling reaches a fever pitch in the book of Isaiah, when the prophet cries out: "O that you would tear open the heavens and come down" (64:1). Precisely because this gulf has resulted from our turning away from God, it can only be overcome by God's gracious initiative toward us. In Jesus' experience of utter alienation from, and complete restoration into, communion with God, we discover our own potential for a similar process of restoration.

I consider it quite significant that Jesus' descent to the dead and his resurrection are fused into a single article of the Apostles' Creed. In some sense, these two beliefs are two sides of the same coin: Jesus' utter estrangement from God in death would be incomprehensible without the resurrection, but the resurrection would be nothing but a piece of stage magic if it were not understood as a divine response to the alienating power of death. We cannot really recognize the exhilaration of reaching the highest heights unless we are able to descend into the deepest depths. Or as Friedrich Nietzsche put it, with characteristic cleverness: "In the mountains, the shortest way is from peak to peak; but for that, one must have long legs." Most of us find that any journey from height to height takes us through some frighteningly shadowy valleys.

The "death and resurrection" motif is actually rather common in literature, and a number of novels can be used to illustrate the general principle. But it's rather more difficult to find novels in which this motif of death and resurrection is keyed quite deliberately to the death and resurrection of Jesus. More often, what some literary critics refer to as "death and resurrection" is little more than the downward slide of a particular character followed by some kind of rock-bottom experience and then a gradual rebuilding. Such novels illustrate the general point well enough, but they may do very little to help us understand how the specifically *Christian* belief in Jesus' descent into hell and resurrection into new life can become the prototype for our own experience of alienation and reconciliation. But at least one recent novel is able to show how characters descend into hell and rise again while keeping Jesus somewhere in the picture at all times: David James Duncan's brilliantly conceived, gripping, and frequently hilarious book *The Brothers K*. It is a profound meditation on the great eternal themes, including death, life, and of course, *baseball*.

\* \* \* \* \*

*The Brothers K* is a chronicle of the Chance family: Hugh and Laura (Papa and Mama) and their six children (four boys—Everett, Peter, Irwin, and Kincaid—and twin daughters Beatrice and Winifred, known always as Bet and Freddy). Kincaid narrates the story (though he interrupts himself from time to time to quote a letter from Everett or a long high-school essay by Irwin). Kincaid tells a little about himself and provides some fascinating details about Bet and Freddy, but the bulk of the story is about, first, the relationships between all six children and their parents, and then, in the second half, about the three eldest brothers.

Papa Chance is a baseball player—a phenomenally good pitcher— and a true devotee of the game. He has spent most of his life in the minor leagues, but he's just about to get a break into the big leagues when an accident at the paper mill (where he works to supplement his meager bush-league earnings) destroys the thumb of his pitching hand. Deprived of (what seemed to be) everything important to him in life, he more or less gives up. He takes to moderately heavy drinking, chain smoking, and sitting inertly in his chair, watching and commenting on the baseball games that appear on the television screen—games in which, it once seemed, he was destined to *be* watched and *be* commented upon. Given what has happened to him, he is not terribly bitter—at least on the outside. But his children, and especially Kincaid, recognize that his quiet resignation is killing him.

One day, Kincaid is sitting in the pickup with his father, who is chain smoking Lucky Strikes and drinking one can of beer after another. The boy cannot get an image out of his mind: the image of Vera, a girl in his sabbath-school class, who has a harelip and who is constantly teased in that particularly merciless way that only grade-school children can manage. But she is always the only one to volunteer to say the prayer at the end of the class, and so she always says it. And she goes on, and on, and on. Children begin by snickering; a few of the braver souls let out a guffaw from time to time; and even the teachers, Brother Beal and Sister Harg, cannot abide the ludicrousness of it all (p. 86):

> *"Nyearest Nyeesus!"* she calls out, her voice, her whole body quivering. *"Nank nyou! Nank nyou!, for yall nyour nyimmy nyimmy nmlessings, nand for nthis nay of Nhristian Nyellowshipt!"* . . .
> Noses blow violently; half-stifled giggles circle the room like pigeons trapped in a barn. Beal keeps his head bowed, but clears his throat and steps threateningly around his podium.

Vera goes on, and on, even after Sister Harg interrupts with "Amen!" and "Thank you, Vera!" Kincaid's first reaction is one of compassion; "if she was my sister I would take off my coat, and I'd wrap her up and hold her, and I would beg her never, ever to do this naked, passionate, impossible thing again" (p. 86). Her parents say only that "it's the cross that she bears"; but Kincaid's brothers think it's cruel to put a child on a cross.

Sitting with his father in the pickup, Kincaid relates the story of Vera to his father, hoping that he'll recognize the beauty of her willingness to push onward through her horrible disfiguration and say what she feels, despite it all. He wants his father to listen, to see the connection. But he doesn't; perhaps he can't. "I don't know what all goes on at your church," he says. "That's your mother's department" (p. 98). But Kincaid has worked himself up into a frenzy in telling the story of Vera, so that he almost feels as she feels—namely, that he just *has* to say what has to be said:

> I want to control myself, I want to calm down, but I also want to slug Papa so hard I knock the smoke right out of his head. Because it's a *lie*. It's a bald-faced, idiotic lie for him to sit there with his wrecked thumb and dead eyes telling me that Vera and her lip and his own sons and crosses are all "Mama's department." . . . "Get those muddy boots down off that glove box!" he snaps. And out it comes. "Then *you* quit smoking!" I shout. "And quit lying! And quit sitting there like a god----ed *corpse* out of some damned—"

> I see the fury come into his eyes, but I don't see the fist that smashes
> the left side of my face (p. 98).

Kincaid's father is normally a pretty peaceful man; this violent action stuns his son and turns the father into a regretful, apologizing, sobbing wreck. His descent to the dead is utterly complete: he has attacked his own flesh and blood. At this point, there is nowhere for him to go but up.

He begs his son: "Tell me *please*, right now if you possibly can, what it is you want from me. Tell me what you and your brothers think I should be doing different, and if it's in my power, if it's possible at all, I swear I'll try to do it." Kincaid responds that he wants his father to be like Vera: to live, despite what life has dealt her. "All I want is for *you* to fight, Papa. To fight to stay alive inside! No matter what" (p. 99).

And so he does. He goes to the high school track and does sixteen quarter-mile laps ("as fast as he could run, walk, or stagger them"). He then comes home, takes his cigarettes down from the top of the refrigerator, and instead of lighting one, "grabbed the carton in a stranglehold, hissed 'You did this to me!,' ripped open every pack, shredded and pulped every last cigarette, then swept up the whole mess and flushed it down the toilet. From that day forward he ran four miles every day after work, and didn't smoke another cigarette" (pp. 103–104). Papa then built an odd-shaped shed in the backyard and hung a mattress on the side of the garage wall, so that he could throw pitches year-round. His four sons, all of whom are baseball fans (and some of whom are rising high-school stars), watch from a hedge, dreaming of a comeback. Papa reminds them that he has no such hopes. Nevertheless, they (and we) can tell that he now looks at his own life, and life in general, very differently.

Then an old friend, a surgeon, offers to undertake an experimental operation on old Papa Chance: to remove a toe, replace it with a prosthesis, and graft the toe on in place of his wrecked left thumb. The boys pitch in to landscape the doctor's new office as payment for the operation, and it seems to be a success. Papa throws better and better pitches in his makeshift bullpen, but refuses to entertain thoughts of returning to the bush leagues.

Enter one Gale Q. Durham, who had made a career of working with baseball's equivalent of junk—aging major-leaguers, injured stars, men with whom most big-league teams would never take a chance (but who might be taught a few new tricks). His goal was to help them reverse the ugly win-loss record and solve the attendance problem (thereby saving the manager's job) at some unknown Double-A backwater in Oklahoma or Oregon. The Junk Genius had already brought Papa Chance back from a devastating shoulder injury earlier in his career and had put him on the road to success before the mill rollers changed all that. Now he has come to Camas, Washington—through the secret intervention of one of the sons—to persuade this one-toed, one-thumbed piece of "junk" to go for one last tryout. Many pitches (and many beers) later, he has not found one argument to which Papa Chance does not have a ready reply. So he unleashes his secret weapon as the boys listen in (p. 257):

> "What I'm gonna do, my onetime ballplayin' friend," Durham said softly, "is die lovin' the game of baseball. An' what you're gonna do, if you betray that same love, is die confused."
>
> That did it. The old man had finally loosed an arrow that flew straight to Papa's heart; we felt it hit; we saw Papa start to bleed. . . . Durham said, "Just tell your kids and me the truth here, is all I'm askin' o' St. Hubert the Confused. Don't, number one, throw fifty pitches better'n the best fifty o' my big league life, then tell us you ain't got the stuff. An' don't, . . . Hubert, try tellin' me it's good for these kids to see their old man stay a factory hand, an' hate it, for a buck. Don't tell me that not bein' true to the work you've always loved most an' did best is a help to your kids. Just repeat after me, if it's the truth: 'I give up on baseball, Gale. I just don't love the game no more.'"
>
> Somehow the silence that followed, in my ears, had a stadium roar. And Papa found nothing to say to quiet it.

Soon, Papa is hearing that stadium roar himself, after landing a job as pitching coach and "stupid-situation reliever" for the local minor-league team. And shortly afterward, he's turning some of those stupid, hopeless situations into wins because the players play better when this inspiration of a man is on the mound. G. Q. Durham, with typical literary license, describes Papa's toe as having died on the cross and been resurrected as a thumb. It wasn't, of course; but whatever it was, as far as this baseball-baptized family was concerned, it would do. "Starting in 1965, at the preposterous age of thirty-five, Papa proceeded to enjoy five and a third seasons as a coach and left-handed pitcher of 'stupid relief' for the Triple A Portland Tugs. Which was resurrection enough for us" (p. 266).

Papa Chance has learned that in life, as in baseball, there are two entirely different ways to strike out. One is to stand there and watch as the fastballs whiz by, to allow the power of the pitcher to overwhelm you. As a result, you end up assuming that—whether on account of your own faults, the faults of others, or sheer fate—things were just meant to be this way, and that the way to respond is through stoic resignation. For the girl in Kincaid's sabbath-school class (whose name, after all, means "truth"), that certainly would have been the easier path. Indeed, it's that path that the world rather expects her to take: to sit quietly and to endure her deformity in silence. But the other way to strike out is to "go down swinging": to give it all you've got, to dig yourself clear into the ground, so that your failure at least bears some of the marks of success. In Papa Chance's case, it was a matter of recognizing that if you're going to strike out, it's better to go down swinging than to sit in a half-drunken stupor and watch life slip away. Only in this way could he realize that the blow that had been dealt to him at the paper mill did not need to be the end of his baseball-playing, baseball-loving life.

Thus ends the first half (roughly) of the book—which, to this point, has been primarily about Papa, and has set the scene for the second half, which is primarily about the three eldest brothers and the very different directions that their lives will take. Before returning to them, however, I need to say a bit more about how the book fuses together the ideas of utter alienation (descent to the dead) and complete reconciliation (resurrection and new life).

The book is full of theological details—epigrams that quote the Bible or some mystical Hindu text, Dostoyevsky or Thoreau, or less well known commentators like Antonio Porchia, who offers this deeply theological gem (p. 411):

> Suffering is above, not below.
> And everyone thinks that suffering is below.
> And everyone wants to rise.

There is also a constant undercurrent involving Mama's devotion to the Seventh-Day Adventists, whose fire-and-brimstone theology leads most of the children to prevaricate, bluff, or barter their way out of the church. (Only Irwin, and later Bet, seem captured by Mama's passion for her denomination—Irwin, because of his childlike simplicity, and Bet, because she has stumbled onto some secret knowledge about her mother's past.)

Because of these elements, the book's overall theme of descent and resurrection never loses its essentially theological focus. It never becomes just another rags-to-riches story. The theological focus is written into the book's very title. I'm not thinking of its important reference to Dostoyevsky's inimitable *The Brothers Karamazov*, which (thankfully) this book makes no systematic attempt to imitate (though there are some lovely cross-references: one character falls in love with a Russian lit major and decides to read every great work of Russian fiction in order to win her heart; when she leaves him, she places on the kitchen table a speech from Dostoyevsky's novel). However, the three main brothers in the novel are vaguely based on the Karamazovs—Irwin, like Dmitri, is a big, stubborn optimist who eventually goes to war; Everett, like Ivan, is a reckless intellectual with atheistic leanings (but without the passions and instincts to match); and Peter, like Alyosha, is a religiously minded introvert (though his tastes run toward Indian religions, rather than Russian Orthodoxy). The book even includes an unannounced reference to a Russian dance troupe that appeared on the Ed Sullivan show in the 1950s under the name The Flying Karamazov Brothers.

These references are all clever, and they help to move the book along—which is good, because it's about seven hundred pages long (another imitation of Dostoyevsky?), but none of them really explain the secret of the title. The secret, of course, is *baseball*. The letter "K" is not an initial, name, or abbreviation. It's a *verb*. And as all baseball fans know (at least if they've ever kept a box score), to "K" is *to strike out*.

By analogy, to "K" is also to mess up, make a mistake, take a wrong turn of one sort or another. It is "to descend to the dead," "to lose your life, utterly and completely"—and not always just metaphorically. Through this connection, the book helps us to understand that striking out—the baseball equivalent of "descending to the dead"—is part of what makes the resurrections in baseball, and in life, so very glorious.

One of the brothers in the novel, Everett, offers a definition of the verb "to K." It's long, but it's clever, and it is central to the book. So here it is:

> **K** (Kā) *verb,* K'ed, K'ing. **1.** *baseball:* to strike out. **2.** to fail, to flunk, . . . to fizzle, or **3.** to fall short, fall apart, fall flat, fall by the wayside, or on deaf ears, or hard times, or into disrepute or disrepair, or **4.** to come unglued, come to grief, come to blows, come to nothing, or **5.** to go to the dogs, go through the roof, go home in a casket, go to hell in a hand basket, or **6.** to blow your cover, blow your chances, blow your cool, blow your stack, . . . buy the farm, bite the dust, only **7.** to recollect an oddball notion you first heard as a crimeless and un-K'ed child but found so nonsensically paradoxical that you had to ignore it or defy it or betray it for decades before you could begin to believe that it might possibly be true, which is that **8.** to lose your money, your virginity, your teeth, health, or hair, **9.** to lose your home, your innocence, your balance, your friends, **10.** to lose your happiness, your hopes, your leisure, your looks, and yea, even your memories, your vision, your mind, your way,
>
> **11.** in short (and as Jesus K. Rist once so uncompromisingly put it) to lose your very self,
>
> **12.** for the sake of another, is
>
> **13.** sweet irony, the only way you're ever going to save it (p. 380).

Or, somewhat more accurately, what The Master of the K "so uncompromisingly" said was, "those who want to save their life will lose it; and those who lose their life for my sake will save it" (Matt. 16:25; Luke 9:24; cf. Mark 8:35).

Of course, we have all heard those words before. But we may not have witnessed a wide enough range of examples of "losing one's life" to really make sense of these hard words. As far as I can tell, the words are most often spoken at military funerals and memorial services, in which we offer up our hope of eternal life for those who have quite literally lost their lives. I don't want to suggest that we have no business doing so (though I might want to quarrel with the particulars). And yet, this is not only a statement by Jesus about how we all should live our lives; it also describes Jesus' own life. When we say that he "suffered under Pontius Pilate, was crucified, died, and was buried," we are pointing out that we believe in a Savior who, quite literally, lost his life. When we claim that he descended to the dead, we emphasize he suffered death as completely and thoroughly as do we. We also claim that God raised him up from death, so there is a sense in which, by losing his life, he "saved" it. But I think very few of us could offer a clear description of exactly how that process worked; nor do we have the faintest idea of how we, as Christ's disciples, might follow in his footsteps. Perhaps it might mean that only by experiencing death—utterly, completely, with all its horror and terror and sorrow fully intact—will we know what it really means to rise again.

Living as we do in a culture of tolerance, individualism, and a very privatized understanding of religious belief, we are very unlikely to be called upon to lay down our lives, at least in a literal sense, for our faith. Indeed, one of the great hallmarks (some would say "achievements") of Western culture is that we have made it very unlikely that you will ever need to die for your faith—so unlikely that, if you actually do so, you will surely be called a zealot or a fanatic. Hence we don't really know much about what it means, from a theological perspective at least, to lose our lives and thereby save them. This lack of knowledge does very little to help us understand Jesus' descent to the dead and his resurrection—that is, to help us understand how one might lose one's life and thereby save it (and save others in the process). And so I think we need a greater store of examples and illustrations about what it means to lose our lives—to be utterly abandoned, to descend to the dead—and what it means to be raised up into newness of life.

This novel offers at least four such illustrations. One is that of Papa Chance, who loses his thumb and finds a whole new life (for himself, and for his family). But his is not the best illustration of the paradigm, because Papa had been doing just fine, thank you, before the accident at the mill. His is certainly a story of death and rebirth, but not of *necessary* death and rebirth. More interesting, I think, are the lives of the three oldest brothers—each of whom *thinks* he is pursuing salvation of a sort, and each of whom meets with defeat and discovers, in that moment of abandonment, who he really is.

Everett, the eldest, sets out on his personal path to glory by finally getting shut of the small town of Camas and becoming the chief rebel, heckler, and all-around wit on the campus of the University of Washington during the height of the Vietnam War protests. He engages his professors in heated arguments in front of packed lecture halls, he writes for the student newspaper, and he pursues Natasha (the Russian lit major mentioned above, who is perhaps the only student on campus who can see him for the relatively amorphous, listless character he really is). Eventually he burns his draft card and has to lay low; but without his usual crowd of groupies, he really isn't worth much, and he spends his time reliving his glory days and pursuing mindless, loveless sex. After a quasirevelatory moment (he looks in the mirror and sees the face of a pig), he packs up and goes to Canada, where he reestablishes a life of sorts as an off-season caretaker for several vacation homes.

It is, indeed, only a "sort" of life, and soon his tendency toward drift and shapelessness begins, once again, to dominate. Finally, though, he hurls himself into the one thing for which he still has a passion—his pursuit of Natasha. He reads every Russian novel he can find, from the sublime to the ridiculous, and he starts a long-term correspondence with his beloved that is not only about, but also in the style of, the Russian greats. She is (finally!) increasingly interested in him, and one day she shows up, completely unannounced, on his front doorstep. They enjoy forty-four days of bliss until she leaves, again without announcement, leaving only the aforementioned clipping from *The Brothers Karamazov* on the kitchen table.

To say that Everett was devastated would be a rather dramatic understatement. He has now officially "K'ed." He has failed, fallen apart, come unglued, gone to the dogs, bought the farm, bit the dust. Any previous tendencies toward listlessness were as nothing compared to his present state. It is all he can do to get up and fix himself three eggs each morning for breakfast. As readers, we wonder how long Everett can continue to live, and whether this is all going to lead to suicide, or worse. But in the middle of all this, he learns that his brother Irwin has been sent home from Vietnam and committed to a mental institution. And Everett does something that might, at one time, have seemed out of character: he comes back to the United States (knowing that he's likely to get arrested for draft-dodging), stands before the members of the First Adventist Church of Washougal (an institution and a group of people whom he despises), and pleads with them to go to Los Angeles and rescue Irwin. The people at the church mostly despise him back in turn, and when he goes home to change clothes, he does get arrested. But his speech before the church members plants a seed, and several of those in attendance, including a visiting Elder from Korea and the indomitable Sister Harg (of sabbath-school fame), show up at the Chance home to plan strategy. Both of these characters are eventually instrumental in securing Irwin's release from the institution.

To understand the relationship between Everett's "strike out" and his ability to help bring about his brother's eventual freedom, one need only imagine what might have happened if Everett had been enjoying Natasha's company and living in a state of bliss when the message about Irwin had arrived. Would he have packed everything up and headed to Washougal? Or would he have been too eager to save the life that he had made for himself, even at the cost of his brother's salvation? The question cannot, of course, be answered definitively. But it seems at least worth asking whether Everett's "strikeout" didn't make it possible, or at least easier and therefore more likely, for him to do what he did. Perhaps he discovered that unless you really die, you never really live.

Similar accounts could be offered of the other two brothers who feature prominently in the second half of the book. In the case of Irwin, his simplistic faith and his air-headed optimism make him a rather more difficult character to break. He experiences one trial after another—an injury that ends his athletic scholarship (and draft exemption), his girlfriend's pregnancy, and the traitorous actions of the pastor to whom he was so dedicated—yet he remains unshaken. Only in the face of the most extreme horror in the book, the war in Vietnam, does he finally descend into hell. Just when we think he has reached his lowest point in watching the execution of a Vietnamese child, he suffers yet more greviously in psychiatric incarceration. But he too is raised up, and he ends up providing care for his dying father, making woodstoves, and adopting children from abroad.

Peter provides a different model. In comparison to his brothers and his father, his rise to fame and glory seems easy and pure and undiluted, but his descent into hell is just as meteoric and really is his own fault. He goes to India to live the authentic life of the native population, but there discovers that he really is a white Westerner after all. He falls for an elaborate con, which takes him very close to complete and utter depravation (he loses absolutely everything, right down to the shirt off his back), and he learns that he still holds many of the same Western prejudices and assumptions that he had regarded in others with such disdain. This experience provides him with the perspective and the inspiration that he needed to go home and design Irwin's release.

All three brothers, as well as their father, help us to understand something important about death, resurrection, and the dynamic interrelationship between the two. They remind us that Christ's descent to the realm of the dead is not just a story about how pre-Christian believers come to be saved, but also a prototype for the utter rejection, degradation, and alienation from God and from other people that most all of us experience at one time or another. They remind us that only in the midst of such experiences of abandonment and loss can we really come to know the meaning of new life. They remind us that these two experiences are interrelated: those who do not know the utter depths of despair that are manifested by death will never really taste the extraordinary joy that is known to those raised up into newness of life.

## Questions For Discussion

1. What images and language have you used to describe what happens to Jesus between the time of his death on the cross and his resurrection?

2. What kinds of human experiences do you most closely associate with the very strong language of "descending to the dead" and "rising again"?

3. Read 1 Corinthians 15. How does Paul understand the relationship between Jesus' death and resurrection and our own? What other images and symbols have Christians used to explicate this relationship?

4. What other examples of "descent unto death and rising again" do you find in *The Brothers K?* Do these examples provide you with any further explanation of what we might mean by proclaiming that Jesus "descended to the dead and rose again"?

## For Further Reading

Balthasar, Hans Urs von. "Going to the Dead: Holy Saturday" in *Mysterium Paschale: The Mystery of Easter.* Trans. with an Introduction by Aidan Nichols, O.P. Grand Rapids: Eerdmans, 1993. (Advanced)

Lewis, Alan E. *Between Cross and Resurrection: A Theology of Holy Saturday.* Foreword by John Alsup. Grand Rapids: Eerdmans, 2001. (Advanced)

Lash, Nicholas, "Friday, Saturday, Sunday," *New Blackfriars* 71 (March 1990): 109–119. (Introductory/Advanced)

McIntosh, Mark A. "The Eastering of Jesus: Resurrection and the Witness of Christian Spirituality." *Downside Review* (January 1994): 44–61. (Advanced)

Moltmann, Jürgen. *The Crucified God: The Cross of Christ as the Foundation and Criticism of Christian Theology.* Translated by R. A. Wilson and John Bowden. New York: Harper and Row, 1974. (Advanced/Specialized)

Moore, Sebastian. *The Fire and the Rose Are One.* New York: Seabury Press, 1980. (Introductory)

Schmemann, Alexander. *For the Life of the World: Sacraments and Orthodoxy.* 2d edition. Crestwood, N.Y.: St. Vladimir's Seminary Press, 1973. (Introductory/Advanced)

Williams, Rowan. *Resurrection: Interpreting the Easter Gospel.* London: Darton, Longman, and Todd, 1982; reprint, New York: Pilgrim Press, 1984. (Advanced)

## Also Cited in This Chapter

Nietzsche, Friedrich. *Thus Spoke Zarathustra*, in *The Portable Nietzsche*. Edited and translated by Walter Kaufmann. New York: The Viking Press, 1954, 103–439; quotation from 152.

## Other Works Illustrating Christ's Descent and Resurrection

Denys Arcand, *Jesus of Montreal* (film)

Fyodor Dostoyevsky, *The Brothers Karamazov; Crime and Punishment*

T. S. Eliot, *Four Quartets*

Anne Lamott, *Traveling Mercies*

Richard Matheson, *What Dreams May Come* (book and film)

Iris Murdoch, *The Red and the Green*

Flannery O'Connor, *The Violent Bear It Away*

Barbara Pym, *A Few Green Leaves*

William Shakespeare, *The Tempest* (many film versions, including *Prospero's Books*)

Muriel Spark, *Memento Mori*

# six

# "Ascended into Heaven, Sits at the Right Hand of God"

Of all the elements of Christian belief, the two that are signified by these two phrases must surely rank as among the most remote from our ordinary experience of the contemporary world. In comparison, even the phrase concerning Jesus' resurrection seems somewhat easier to imagine. We are familiar enough with the cycles of completion and renewal that come with every change of the season, and we can imagine a great variety of literary descriptions of "death and rebirth"; but in our experience, the only things that "ascend into heaven" are airplanes, weather balloons, and space satellites. So it is all the more difficult to imagine how people in another era must have understood this phrase, when the notion of the physical ascension of *anything* was even more foreign to their ordinary experience.

Moreover, the notion that "Jesus ascended and sits at God's right hand" seems to suggest that God inhabits a particular space (a space to which one might "ascend"), and that God has a "right hand" at which one may "sit." All of this language seems to be based very firmly on an imaginary three-tiered universe, in which we inhabit the middle ground, with the realm of the dead below and paradise above our heads. This description of the universe, while taken for granted by the ancient writers, is precisely what certain fashionable theologians tend to pronounce, with relish, to be wholly unacceptable to "modern people" like ourselves.

What, then, are we to do with this article of the creed? Should we simply discard it? Should we leap over it, consigning it to a place among the vestiges of a bygone era, assuming that it has no real relevance for Christians today? None of these options seems particularly attentive to the depth and breadth of the Christian tradition, which has, from the very beginning, asserted this particular claim as the concluding chapter of the story of Christ's presence among us. I have already discussed the importance of understanding our own faith to be in continuity with those who have gone before us in their Christian journeys. However strange the claim of Jesus' ascension may ring in our ears, we owe it to our predecessors to think seriously about what it might mean for us today.

But something even more significant may be at work here—something not well acknowledged by those who imagine that we "modern people" no longer live in a three-tiered universe. Think of how many elements of that supposedly "imaginary" universe lurk in our habits and our speech patterns. We use language that would certainly suggest to an outsider that we are convinced that higher places are better than lower places: "upwardly mobile," "upper classes," "the moral high ground," "reaching the summit," "flying high," "climbing the corporate ladder," "high art," "it's lonely at the top"—as opposed to "lower classes," "down in the dumps," "lowbrow culture," "dropping out," "falling by the wayside," and "hitting bottom."

Thus, to treat this phrase of the creed as irrelevant would be inattentive to the ways in which, even in an age of space travel and advanced geology, the language of "up" and "down" still has extraordinarily strong symbolic power in our understanding of God, morality, art, economics, psychology, and our entire network of social relations. This symbolic power is at the heart of the biblical narrative, and particularly in the accounts offered by Luke, at the end of his first book (the Gospel of Luke) and again at the beginning of his second book (the Acts of the Apostles). In these writings, we are told that while Jesus "was blessing them, he withdrew from them and was carried up into heaven" (Luke 24:51), and that "as they were watching, he was lifted up, and a cloud took him out of their sight" (Acts 1:9).

On the one hand, Luke is simply addressing a problem faced by every writer who has ever created a character who must eventually make an exit. Specifically, Luke has emphasized the fleshly reality of Jesus, particularly the fleshly reality of the body of Jesus even after his resurrection from the dead (Luke 24:39–43). And yet, the writer has no immediately available method of getting his main character "offstage." If Jesus rose from the dead and walked about in this fleshly form, one may legitimately ask: *Where is he now?* By describing him as having "ascended into heaven," Luke solves this problem and, in the process, provides a dramatic finish to his narrative.

But on the other hand, the story of Jesus' ascension came to take on much greater significance than would typically be allotted to a mere stage direction. The presence of this story in the work of one New Testament writer hardly accounts for the fact that this phrase became one of the very few details of the earthly life of Christ to find a place in the Christian creeds. Nor can its significance be explained as an attempt to emphasize Jesus' full humanity (as can the references to his birth, suffering, and death—all of which are universal human experiences and therefore help to demonstrate the fullness of Jesus' humanity). The ascension is at the opposite end of the spectrum: it is almost a universal human *non*experience.

Admittedly, the ascension is a particularly *dramatic* element of Jesus' life; and yet, many other dramatic events of his life are absent from the creeds. For example, so great a miracle as the feeding of a multitude of thousands—which appears in every Gospel (and in two of them twice)—was never even a *candidate* for inclusion in the creed. We cannot fully explain the significance of Jesus' ascension for Christian belief by merely noting that its absence would render our story incomplete or insufficiently dramatic. Something else must be at work.

In order to plumb the deeper meaning of the stories of Jesus' ascension into heaven, and of his being seated at the right hand of God, let us consider what they might imply. First, these beliefs suggest that the question of "Where is Jesus now?" is a real and legitimate question—which, in turn, implies that Jesus' resurrection was real and permanent. It further implies, first, that the resurrection of Jesus had been a fully bodily, fully fleshly one; if Christians had wanted to assert that the resurrected Jesus had been a spirit-like figure or a mere figment of the disciples' imaginations, they would not have had to have made any claims about what happened to his resurrected body. Second, these statements make it clear that Christians believe that, at least in the ordinary physical sense of the phrase, Jesus' fleshly body is no longer here.

Both of these elements seem worthy of our attention. On the matter of "the flesh of Jesus," we might begin by noting that, although this question is closely related to the full *humanity* of Jesus (discussed in previous chapters with attention to the problem of Docetism), the matter of Jesus' *fleshly* reality marks a slight shift of emphasis. In the ancient world, the word *flesh* was most often associated with those elements of human existence that were indistinguishable from those of other animals: our physical needs (for food, drink, shelter, and propagation of the species), our fragility, and ultimately, the fact that we will eventually die. Thus, even when Jesus' humanity is fully affirmed, the neediness and fragility of Jesus' physical body is rarely emphasized. Even if we are able to admit that Jesus experienced physical needs and that he understood the real fragility of his earthly life, these aspects are typically forgotten when we turn our attention to the nature of Jesus' *resurrected* body. In stark contrast with the immense images of suffering in at least some depictions of Jesus' passion, the resurrected Jesus always seems to be fully at peace, fully in control, and lacking for nothing.

On issues relating to "the flesh of Jesus" (and to the flesh in general), the church has not had such a stellar record. Perhaps inspired by some phrases of St. Paul and St. John that sounded, at least in some historical contexts, to drive a sharp wedge between flesh and spirit, Christians have sometimes posited theologies that have glorified the disembodied soul or the freely blowing spirit, without offering nearly so positive an evaluation of the earth-bound body or the troublesome flesh. At the very least, a good deal of Christian ethical thought has shown itself to be quite uncomfortable with the embodied, enfleshed state in which we all find ourselves.

But it cannot be too strongly emphasized that this tendency—to ignore or to minimize the significance of the flesh—is wholly at odds with the Christian doctrine of creation, which affirms that God made all things "good." Certainly, human beings fall away from this original goodness; but this fall does not make their flesh into a prison, nor a burden, nor (least of all) an inevitable locus of evil. Such negative claims about the flesh would make it difficult to understand how Jesus can live such a thoroughly fleshly existence. (According to the biblical narratives, he becomes hungry, thirsty, and tired; his flesh can be bound, can bleed, and can die.) A properly Christian theology of the flesh must therefore affirm our fleshly existence as good, redeemed, and ultimately destined for glory.

God's redemption of our flesh is made known and made clear to us in a variety of ways. Through the conception and birth of Jesus, God became Mary's flesh in her womb, reminding us of the wonder of newly enfleshed life. Through the earthly life of Jesus, God became flesh in a way that could feel, suffer, and be pleased by all the same things that all human beings feel, suffer, and are pleased by. But the redemption of the flesh does not stop here. Through the resurrection, God raised up this earthly, fleshly life—and thereby reminded us of its ongoing worth and dignity and goodness.

It is probably therefore no accident that Luke—who gives us the story of Jesus' ascension into heaven—is also so concerned to describe the resurrected Jesus as possessing a fully human, fleshly body. Admittedly, it is another of the Gospel writers who tells the story of Thomas, who needed to "see the mark of the nails in his hands" (John 20:25), yet that evangelist also narrates instances of Jesus walking through walls (thereby making him seem less "bound" by his flesh). In contrast, Luke tends to describe the resurrected Jesus as relatively indistinguishable from any other human being—so much so that the travelers to Emmaus do not recognize him (Luke 24:13–35). To his disciples, Jesus says: "'Look at my hands and my feet; see that it is I myself. Touch me and see; for a ghost does not have flesh and bones as you see that I have.' And when he had said this, he showed them his hands and his feet" (Luke 24:39–40). Afterwards, they gave him a piece of broiled fish, which he took "and ate in their presence" (Luke 24:43)—leaving no doubt in the mind of the readers that this is a fully human being, a flesh-and-blood creature like themselves.

Luke then offers us the next logical step in this stage of "the redemption of the flesh": the flesh is welcomed into heaven, taken up into the presence of God. God's willingness to "become flesh and dwell among us" is therefore not a temporary condition, not merely a short-term moment of unpleasantness that God must endure in order to set things right. On the contrary, by *permanently* taking on not only our intellectual and spiritual characteristics but also our fleshly existence, God redeems it and draws it up into the trinitarian communion of the divine life.

Consequently, the phrase "ascended into heaven" has a fairly significant impact on two other essential elements of Christian belief. One of these is the resurrection of Jesus: the physical, fully enfleshed character of Jesus does not end with his death and burial, but continues into his resurrected life. The creeds, in affirming Luke's account of the ascension, are thereby making a statement about the fleshly nature of Jesus' resurrected body. The other belief that is affected by Jesus' ascension is one that we will consider later in this book: "I believe in the resurrection of the body" (or, in some translations, "the flesh"—more on this question in chapter 11). In the welcoming of the flesh of Jesus into the presence of God, we are offered the sign and seal that our fleshly existence has a significance beyond death—and that its ultimate destiny is to be in perfect communion with the divine Trinity.

Turning now to the second of the two affirmations implied by our belief in Jesus' ascension: that Jesus' fleshly body is no longer here. Why is it important to affirm this? Its importance is related to the scene in John's Gospel, mentioned above, in which Thomas is invited to put his fingers in the marks of the nails in Jesus' hands and to place his hand in Jesus' side. Thomas had claimed that this empirical evidence was important to him; in fact, he said that he would not believe unless he were able to carry out these actions. Interestingly, however, when Jesus arrives on the scene (apparently having walked through a wall, since John emphasizes that "the doors were shut"—20:26) and invites Thomas to carry out these actions, the Gospel writer does not actually state that Thomas did so. The mere *presence* of Jesus, perhaps combined with the simple *invitation* to touch his wounds, seemed to be enough to provoke Thomas's confession of faith: "My Lord and my God!" (20:28).

But whether or not Thomas actually took Jesus up on his offer to touch his wounds, we know that this option is one that, at least in any ordinary sense, *is simply not available to us.* Our belief in the ascension of Jesus is testimony to the claim that, in our earthly lives at any rate, we do not have the opportunity to touch the wounds of Christ, for there is a very real sense that, as with the empty tomb, "he is not here." This, I want to suggest, puts a whole new light on things.

The biblical narratives set up the contrast for us. From the time of Jesus' resurrection until his ascension, he is at least occasionally present to his disciples in a physical, fully enfleshed form. After his ascension, he may still be "present" in a real and very personal way (perhaps most intensely in the blinding of Saul in Acts 9), but he is not physically present in the way he had been before his ascension. This contrast continues into the present: we may speak of the presence of Jesus, and we can describe him as being in a personal relationship with us, but he is not physically present.

If Jesus were "here" in a physically embodied way, we could expect certain questions to be answered definitively. When we had a question about an ethical dilemma or a complex liturgical revision, we could go to the resurrected Jesus and ask him for a final ruling. But the doctrine of the ascension tells us that we do not "have" Jesus in the way that his disciples "had" him. (It might also be worth reflecting on the question of whether the disciples "had" him in any more definitive a sense; we are sometimes fooled by our senses, and being physically in the presence of someone does nothing to insure that we understand that person completely. Indeed, in some cases, that physical proximity may actually obscure our capacity for discernment.) In any case, our present-day knowledge of Jesus is of a completely different order.

It may be worth pausing at this point to note the other ways in which Jesus continues to be present to us, in spite of the physical absence of his fleshly body in the ordinary sense in which we think of such language. First, the Holy Spirit is the continuing presence of God in the world, taking up much of the ministry of Jesus in his life and enacting his ongoing presence in the world (more on this point in chapter 8). Second, the church is called "the Body of Christ" because there is a very real sense in which all Christians are called to embody the person and work of Jesus in their own lives and to be the face of Christ for one another. (I will also address this point in greater detail in chapter 9.) Finally, in many Christian communities, the Eucharist is considered a site of Christ's presence in the world: it is an outward and visible sign of God's grace—made known to us in Jesus, and made known to all the world by the Holy Spirit. I mention these three aspects of Christ's ongoing presence in order to avoid suggesting that, after his ascension, Christ somehow abandons the world. And yet, while we insist on the reality of Christ's presence, we must also acknowledge the *differences* between the presence that we experience today and the fully human embodiment of Jesus during his sojourn on the earth.

Since Jesus is not here as a single, fully human, fully enfleshed being, this implies that our Christian faith is not *compelled* by God. God does not force us to believe by means of a physical presence that would, as it were, quiet all doubts. Our freely given faith is, in some sense, superior to the faith of those who, like Thomas, seemed to have little choice in the matter. (In John 20:29, Jesus says, "Have you believed because you have seen me? Blessed are those who have not seen and yet have come to believe.")

The physical presence of another person is an overwhelming experience; no longer does our relationship to that person require much action or initiative on our parts. We are almost *compelled* to acknowledge the existence of the other by that person's sheer physical presence. In that person's absence, our faith and love are put to the test; now it will require an act of our own will, a determined decision, to bring the other person to mind, and to place our trust and devotion there. Our belief in the ascension of Jesus is therefore a sign and seal of the depth and breadth of our faith.

We also confess our belief that Jesus "is seated at the right hand of the Father." In one sense, of course, this is a metaphorical claim; God does not have a physical body in the ordinary sense, possesses no hands (right or left), sits in no throne. The language arises from the ancient vocabulary of monarchy, in which the power and authority of the single ruler was mediated to others by the monarch's closest advisor and most trusted subject. (Long after he stopped sitting at anyone's right hand, we retained the phrase "right-hand man"—that is, the one through whom a leader's will is most diligently enacted.)

On the other hand, the claim that Jesus "sits at God's right hand" provides us with another way of emphasizing the more general claim that "he is not here." He is not directly within our grasp; we can't call him up for a brief conversation, can't join him in an Internet chat room. This implies, first of all, that a few things about him are likely to remain unknown; and second, that we bear a greater responsibility for the ongoing promulgation of the faith than would be the case if its "founder" were still around to do all the work. Our relationship with Jesus, though certainly a matter of our response to God's initiative, must still be an active *response* rather than the passive acceptance of an obvious fact.

In sum, then, the two claims that seem most strongly bound up with this part of the creed are, first, that God redeems the whole of humanity—including our physicality, our flesh (and not just our disembodied spirits or minds); and second, that the physical absence of Jesus implies a different sort of relationship than would otherwise be the case—a relationship that requires of us greater initiative and greater faith. In order to explore both of these claims, I turn to one of the less frequently performed plays of William Shakespeare. The play is a vast canvas of human emotion, kingdoms in conflict, and obstacles to love overcome; it contains many wonderful theological elements, as do all of Shakespeare's plays. Although all these elements are certainly worthy of attention, most of them will not be taken up here. My focus is primarily on the play's final act—though of course, you'll need to gain some sense of the whole play in order to make sense of its ending. I want to suggest that, in the final act of *The Winter's Tale*, we are offered some interesting observations about "believing" in someone who has "gone away"—and about the positive significance of the *flesh* as part of what makes us truly human. If you don't have time read the play yourself, listen to an audio recording of it; most people find Shakespeare more comprehensible in this form anyway, since it was written to be read aloud. Another rewarding option is to get together with a group of friends and divide up the parts to read it aloud. You can also see a film version (several are available), or best of all, watch a performance on stage.

*  *  *  *  *

Before turning to the specifics of this play, I want to say a few words about its dramatic form. Most of the other works of literature that we are examining in this book are novels or short stories—extended narratives that combine dialogue and description to form a continuous whole. Drama is different; it typically has no narrator to explain what the characters are feeling or thinking, no lengthy discursive accounts to set the scene or provide an account of "the story so far." Everything must be expressed through the characters' dialogue—aided, of course, by scenery, props, movement, and stage magic (which is why it's always more meaningful to hear or see a work of drama performed rather than to read it silently). But when it is performed, drama can exert a kind of power that is truly remarkable.

What is it about drama that makes it so compelling? Is it the realism, the lifelike nature of what transpires on the stage? Is it the complexity of drama, allowing the reader or viewer to step into the shoes of various characters, seeing things from that person's point of view, at least for a moment? Is it, perhaps, the way that the characters interact, weaving themselves into one another's lives such that their interrelationships become more important than their individuality? Whatever factors may combine to make the dramatic arts so gripping, anyone who's spent much time in the theater knows this much: it works. It grabs us, draws us in, involves us in the lives of the characters in ways that few other forms of narrative can accomplish.

The German philosopher G. W. F. Hegel believed that drama was the highest form of literature. He described it as a synthesis of epic and lyric, of parable and poetry. Like the former, it tells a continuous story; but like the latter, it brings us into intimate contact with the inner world of the characters. Personally, I love drama above every other art form, so I am inclined to agree with Hegel on this point. But I think it might be better to say that the various genres of literature do not stand in a hierarchy to one another, but that each has certain advantages and disadvantages with respect to the other two. I would not wish for a world of nothing but drama any more than the poetry lover would want to wish away stories and plays, or the avid reader of novels would seek to banish poetry and drama.

All the same, there are reasons why I have chosen a drama to help us think through this particular element of the creed. It has something to do with drama's ability to help us understand transformation and change. Drama can demonstrate, as few other art forms can, how changing circumstances and relationships can bring about a transformation of the mind or a change of heart. Understanding such change is key to a better understanding of the relationship between God and us, particularly with respect to the extraordinary transformation signified by Jesus' ascension.

*The Winter's Tale* is a play about the entangled relationship of two kingdoms: Sicily and Bohemia. As the play opens, the former kingdom is in the foreground. King Leontes is anxious about his wife Hermione, whom he believes to be in love with Polixenes, the visiting king of Bohemia. His jealousy grows so fierce that he asks one of his courtiers to murder the visiting king (in spite of the fact that the two men have been friends since childhood). Fortunately, the courtier decides that he cannot possibly undertake his assigned task. He informs Polixenes of his host's plot upon his life and flees with the visiting king back to Bohemia. Leontes sees this act of flight as further evidence of his wife's adultery; he imprisons her and plans to sentence her to death. She bears a baby girl while in prison; the child is presented to him by his wife's maid, Paulina, who remarks on the baby's close resemblance to the king. But Leontes' jealousy is too strong; he insists that the child must be the issue of Polixenes. He therefore exposes the child to the elements, expecting her to die abandoned. All these actions so terrorize everyone around him that the king's own son dies of grief, leaving him without an heir. Just as Leontes is beginning to recognize the error of his ways, he receives news from Paulina that Hermione, his wife, is dead.

At this point, the action of the play switches to Bohemia, where the exposed daughter, Perdita (whose name means "lost"), is found by an old shepherd and his clownish son. Perdita grows up and falls in love with Florizel, the son of the Bohemian king (Polixenes, whom we met in Act I). It appears that the children of the two estranged kings are destined to marry and live happily ever after, but Polixenes learns that his son is going to attempt to conceal this marriage from his father, and in his anger, he forbids it.

Now the action returns to Sicily, and we discover what King Leontes has been doing these many years (while his daughter—unbeknownst to him—has been growing up). Encouraged by Paulina, Leontes has gone to the gravesite of his wife and his son every day, mourning their loss and repenting of his own rash action that brought about their deaths. But today his visit is interrupted by the news that Florizel and Perdita have suddenly arrived in Sicily—supposedly to deliver an official greeting from the King of Bohemia, but in reality, attempting to flee his prohibition of their marriage. We also learn that they are pursued by the King of Bohemia himself, who intends to make short work of their intended elopement.

Despite these ominous events, the play's resolution comes in the comic, rather than the tragic, mode—on several fronts. In a grand scene of discovery (which actually occurs offstage and is reported to the audience by several "gentlemen"), Perdita is discovered to be Leontes's daughter, and the two kings consent to the marriage of their two children. Leontes and Polixenes—who last parted amidst hatred, jealousy, and fear—are now reconciled. Indeed, children and parents and adoptive parents and entire kingdoms are reunited in a grand scene of revelation and recognition: "I never heard of such another encounter," says one of the narrators, "which lames report to follow it, and undoes description to do it" (V.2.55–57).

In the play's final scene (V.3), Paulina claims to have had a lifelike statue of Hermione sculpted. She reveals it to Leontes and Perdita, and they marvel at it so greatly that Paulina worries about them and threatens to cover it up again. But there is more amazement to come: after Paulina indicates that part that her audience must play—"It is required/ You do awake your faith" (V.3.94–95)—she calls the statue to life, and it descends and speaks. So perhaps Hermione has not been dead after all? At any rate, she—or someone who very much resembles her—is certainly alive.

This itself is something of a "resurrection" story, and the play might profitably be used as an illustration of the part of the creed that we discussed in the previous chapter. Nevertheless, this is not the use to which I want to put it here; I am more interested in how it can help us understand Jesus' *ascension*. Of course, there is no literal ascension in *The Winter's Tale*. But the play does allow us to focus on the two issues that, as I have suggested, are implied by our belief in Jesus' ascension: the significance of the flesh, and the importance of continuing to believe in someone who is not physically present. Leontes begins the play by assuming that the flesh is a negative thing, a site of lust and anxiety; but he ends the play convinced of its positive significance. In addition, Leontes continues to "believe" in his wife for the sixteen years during which she is dead (as he assumes), and during which time she is certainly absent (as he does not merely assume, but experiences).

Very early in the play, as Leontes' jealousy erupts, he has little good to say about the passions of the flesh. Seeing his wife spending time with his friend, he draws aside and worries:

> Too hot, too hot!
> To mingle friendship far is mingling bloods.
> I have tremor cordis on me: my heart dances,
> But not for joy, not joy. . . .
> But to be paddling palms and pinching fingers,
> As now they are, and making practised smiles
> As in a looking-glass, and then to sign, as 'twere
> The mort o'th'deer—O, that is entertainment
> My bosom likes not, nor my brows (I.2.108–11, 115–19).

He goes on to enumerate the pangs of jealousy that he feels as having attacked his very body: he speaks of "the infection of my brains / And hard'ning of my brows" (145–46); the possibility that his wife has been untrue is like an illness of the body: "Physic for't there's none" (200); "Many thousand on's / Have the disease and feel't not" (206–7). The flesh is the place where we are most severely tempted to unfaithfulness; and so Leontes can see only its worst elements. "Were my wife's liver / Infected as her life, she would not live / The running of one glass" (304–306).

After Leontes imprisons Hermione, he finds himself unable to rest, and blames this on his own body's weakness; and he wishes that his wife's body were no more:

> Nor night nor day no rest. It is but weakness
> To bear the matter thus, mere weakness . . .
>     say she were gone,
> Given to the fire, a moiety of my rest
> Might come to me again (II.3.1–2, 7–9).

At the same time, Leontes's son has fallen ill, and he laments the weakness of his child's body as much as his own (14–17). When Paulina brings in Hermione's newborn daughter to present her to the king, it is the baby's physical appearance that marks her as Leontes's own and gives the lie to his accusations of adultery against his wife (97–107).

How different all this looks to Leontes, in the face of the loss of his wife and his children! We may choose to look upon our frail human flesh as a burden, a temptation, or a curse; and yet, our experience of others in this world in necessarily mediated by that very flesh. The flesh provides the only real channel of communication between human beings, and when it is not present to us, we long for it. We may be willing to accept the fact that, for many people, the transition from life to death is a release of some kind, a journey out of this vale of tears. And yet we still mourn those who die; however assured we may be that they now dwell in paradise, we can no longer see them, hear them, touch them in the flesh. And that is a grievous loss.

So Leontes pines after his wife and son (and, he now realizes, his daughter as well). He holds fast to his memories, but that is simply not enough: "I might have looked upon my queen's full eyes, / Have taken treasure from her lips" (V.1.52–54). Nor can some other fleshly body replace that which has been lost; our bodies are an important part of what differentiates us from one another, and we cannot pretend to substitute one for another. Leontes is therefore resigned (V.1.56–60):

> No more such wives, therefore no wife. One worse,
> And better used, would make her sainted spirit
> Again possess her corpse, and on this stage,
> Where we offenders now appear, soul-vexed,
> And begin, "Why to me?"

Paulina confirms his anguish: "Had she such power, / She had just cause."

The importance of the flesh is drawn out again in Leontes's encounter with Florizel and Perdita. As Leontes gazes upon the young couple, he takes a bit too much interest in the girl; she is beautiful, captivating. Her physical presence is enough to draw him away from attention to his mourning, however dedicated he had been to it up until then. Paulina hastily checks him (V.1.223–26):

> Sir, my liege,
> Your eye hath too much youth in it. Not a month
> Fore your Queen died, she was more worth such gazes
> Than what you look on now.

He claims, however, that he is only looking lovingly at her because he reminds him so much of his own wife. (As well she might! She is their daughter, of course—though Leontes does not yet know this.)

And finally, in the final scene, Leontes's encounter with the "statue" becomes more and more passionate as he recognizes its fleshly reality. As the scene begins, Leontes expresses little more than the aesthetic interest of an art lover. But when he has seen the statue and considered how closely it resembles her, his speech becomes much more animated; he is more enthralled to be in the presence of what at least appears to be flesh, even if it is more "wrinkled" and "aged" than he remembers her (V.3.28–29). But he is still distraught over the memory of the difference between the reality of the flesh and (what he takes to be) the mere appearance of the stone: "O thus she stood, / Even with such life of majesty— warm life, / As now it coldly stands" (34–36). Perdita wants to kiss the statue's hand, and Leontes senses that it might breathe; his passion is stirred to the breaking point: "What fine chisel / Could ever yet cut breath? Let no man mock me, / For I will kiss her" (78–80). And then Paulina allows the scene's intensity to build to a climax by announcing that she can even make the statue move.

Over the course of the play, Leontes has been brought from an attitude of despising the flesh as a temptation and a burden to affirming it as that which he seeks after most intensely. His journey serves as a poignant reminder to us—in a culture that maintains something of a love-hate relationship with our frail fleshly existence—that our flesh is a creation of God, and like all of creation, God has pronounced it good, indeed "very good" (Gen. 1:31). It is to be loved and cherished and treated with respect, for it is the medium through which we encounter other creatures, and in fact, it is "a temple of the Holy Spirit" (1 Cor. 6:19). This positive evaluation of the flesh is emphasized even more by the fact that, in Jesus, God takes on human flesh and dwells among us, in all our fragility and vulnerability. God's fleshly existence somehow transcends death and is taken back up into the divine life—thereby sanctifying human flesh and restoring it to goodness in which it was created by God.

*The Winter's Tale* also speaks to the other significant element of our belief in the ascension of Jesus: namely, the importance of continuing to believe in someone who is physically absent. Clearly, Leontes has done so—even though he has, in a sense, brought this requirement upon himself. For sixteen years, we are told, he has "performed / a saint-like sorrow" and has "paid down / More penitence than done trespass" (V.1.1–4). At the beginning of Act V—in spite the presence of the king's attendants, who are urging him to forget the past and to remarry—he is resolute (V.1.6–12):

> Whilst I remember
> Her and her virtues, I cannot forget
> My blemishes in them, and so still think of
> The wrong I did, myself, which was so much
> That heirless it hath made my kingdom, and
> Destroyed the sweet'st companion that e'er man
> Bred his hopes out of. True?

Paulina answers: "Too true, my lord."

In fact, Paulina seems to work very hard to reinforce Leontes's penitence. She sometimes appears to the audience as harsh, even unkind, in refusing to show him mercy. She seems almost to rub salt in the wounds, emphasizing that the king himself killed his wife, and that the death of his children, too, was his own doing. Depending on how the opening lines of this act are played, they can be painful to watch; we know that Leontes has done terrible things, and in fact we witnessed many of them in Act I. Nevertheless, sixteen years of penitent mourning seems like quite a lot.

One of the King's advisors is worried about the implications of his behavior for the future of the country. As long as Leontes remains fixated on the dead Hermione, he will not produce an heir to the kingdom. The advisor chastises Paulina accordingly (V.1.25–29):

> You pity not the state, nor the remembrance
> Of his most sovereign name; consider little
> What dangers by his highness' fail of issue
> May drop upon his kingdom and devour
> Incertain lookers-on.

But Paulina responds that the king's advisors have too little faith; they have allowed the physical absence of a queen and an heir to weigh more heavily than the prophecy of the oracle (V.1. 44–49):

> 'Tis your counsel
> My lord should to the heavens be contrary,
> Oppose against their wills. Care not for issue;
> The crown will find an heir. Great Alexander
> Left his to th'worthiest; so his successor
> Was like to be the best.

And so, encouraged by Paulina and by her faithful devotion to Hermione even in her absence, Leontes resolves never again to marry.

*The Winter's Tale* thus gives us ample opportunity to reflect on what keeps us going, what keeps us "believing" in someone who is physically absent for an extended time. I will mention three such elements: memory, community, and resolve.

First, we need memory. In describing his ongoing process of mourning to those who would like him to forget the past, Leontes emphasizes that he has kept a clear picture of his wife in his mind, and that this has sustained him. He describes her physical features in detail, once again bringing home the point that our bodies, our flesh, are an essential part of who we are; it differentiates us from others. Leontes has had to learn, the hard way, just how important the flesh is: once he regretted having to encounter it, but now, his memory of its features is a significant part of what sustains his faith. In reminding himself of what she was like, what she did and how she lived, he brings her back into his presence, even in her absence. So too do we tell stories of the physical presence of Jesus on the earth; in doing so, we help to maintain our faith in him even in his physical absence.

Second, we need community. Specifically, we need other people who are invested enough in our lives to help us through the difficult work of believing in that which we cannot see, hear, or touch. In our culture, we have become accustomed to the idea that the only people who can help us are the professionals whom we pay to do so: therapists, lawyers, financial advisors, and the like. Even pastors and priests can sometimes fall into the trap of allowing "professional duty" to become the primary rationale for their care for others. But at a deeper level, what we really need are not people whom we *pay* to be our advocates and advisors; we need a loving community of friends who care about us for our own sake. In this sense, a friend is someone who will not only provide nurture and support, but who is also willing to criticize us when we head down the wrong path.

In this sense, Paulina is a genuine friend to Leontes—perhaps the only friend that stays with him through the entire play. When he leaps into fits of jealous rage in Acts I and II, his advisors come to fear him and, one by one, they stop trying to counsel him to better behavior. But Paulina never relents: even under extraordinary threats from the king, she continues to upbraid him for his bad behavior, including his injustice toward his wife and his appalling neglect of his own children. Perhaps Leontes would have been able to develop greater faith with much less suffering had he been surrounded by an entire group of friends as resolute as Paulina—friends who were willing to risk the king's ferocious displeasure in order to heal him of his misguided jealousy.

Finally, in order to maintain faith in those who are absent, we need something like "resoluteness of will." How easy it can be to drift away from people who, however much they meant to us when they were present, do not bear a similar weight in our lives in their absence. As I have suggested throughout this chapter (and indeed throughout this book), the flesh is a powerful thing: it is the medium through which we most intimately come to know other people. In order to overcome its absence, we need to direct our hearts and minds to the absent person in very intentional ways. Leontes was very single-minded in his jealousy in the opening acts; but after the death of his wife, he is able to put that resoluteness of will to good use. He stays committed to the course of action that he has chosen, in spite of those who are tempting him to forget the past. His wife is not present, and her physical absence becomes a good reason, at least in the eyes of most, to dispense with any ongoing attention to her. But Leontes is decided: "No more such wives, and therefore no wife." In our Christian journeys, developing this kind of resolve requires us to cultivate habits of commitment and constancy, such that we can remain faithful to the One whom we cannot see and touch in any ordinary sense. This is part of the rationale for regular devotional practices such as common worship, Bible reading, and works of mercy. Only through such habits can we develop the firmness of will to say that, even though we cannot see, yet we believe.

To maintain such resolve in the face of physical absence, we need to recognize how thoroughly steeped we are in the assumption that knowledge and certainty are based on empirical observation. If we want to know something for certain, we go and "take a look." To have real proof, we need to "see the evidence." We tend not to trust the testimony of others, however much expertise and reassurance they may offer. The Christian faith is truly countercultural in this respect, claiming that, although we cannot see and touch Jesus, although we have no empirical evidence to offer, we still believe. Yet to say this is to walk a fine line, for it would be easy to allow the Christian faith to dissolve into a dualistic mysticism in which physicality is irrelevant. Our belief in the ascension of Jesus is our constant reminder to choose the path between these two false alternatives. We proclaim, at one and the same time, the real significance of our physical bodies—as well as the possibility of a faith that does not depend on physical presence alone.

## Questions For Discussion

1. Think of additional examples to show how the language of "up" and "down" continues to have symbolic value in our culture, in spite of modern astronomy and geology. Consider also what it means for someone to "sit at the right hand" of someone else.

2. Examine some of our cultural assumptions about "the flesh," that is, our physical bodies. Be sure to think of both positive and nega-

tive assumptions—ways that we are encouraged to *overvalue* the flesh and ways that we are taught to ignore or minimize its significance. After reading this chapter, what do you understand the Christian belief about the flesh to be?

3. Consider your own experiences of believing in someone who was not physically present. In what ways does this physical absence change the nature of the relationship?

4. In what ways does our culture encourage us to rely only on empirical evidence for our knowledge and for certainty? Think about the impact of the natural sciences, the media, and even how we judge sporting events (the instant replay!).

5. What are some of the specific habits and practices that Christians might develop in order to improve their ability to maintain faith in Jesus despite his physical absence, and in spite of our empirically minded culture?

## For Further Reading

Farrow, Douglas. *Ascension and Ecclesia: On the Significance of the Doctrine of the Ascension for Ecclesiology and Christian Cosmology*. Grand Rapids: Eerdmans, 1999. (Advanced/Specialized)

Robinson, John A. T. *The Human Face of God*. Philadelphia: Westminster Press, 1973. (Introductory)

Vogel, Arthur A. *Radical Christianity and the Flesh of Jesus*. Grand Rapids: Eerdmans, 1995. (Introductory/Advanced)

## Other Literary Works Exploring Jesus' Ascension

Graham Greene, *The Human Factor*
Toni Morrison, *Beloved* (discussed in chapter 7)
Iris Murdoch, *The Flight from the Enchanter*
Iain Pears, *An Instance of the Fingerpost*

# seven

# "He Will Come to Judge the Living and the Dead"

This is the first of several phrases in the Apostles' Creed that state a belief in something that will take place in the future. Such claims can sound a bit odd in our culture; to "believe" in some future event sounds as though it might involve the work of a fortune-teller or an astrologer. Perhaps it reminds us of those books that appear with great fanfare at the bookstore (and then disappear quickly) predicting some major change in our economic or political system, books that claim to provide secret knowledge about "the next big thing," and even books that predict the precise day and time that the world will end. Such books are easy enough to write (and to sell); since no one has yet *experienced* the future, it doesn't cost anything to make claims about it. No one can prove that a prediction is wrong until well after it was supposed to take place— and by then, all the books are already sold!

But claims about what will happen in the future can't always be dismissed as mere "fortune-telling." A good deal of our day-to-day conversation includes comments about the future and our expectations of it; we make plans, undertake various kinds of preparatory work, and sometimes organize our entire day's activities around some event that we expect to take place in the future. Some of our most significant life commitments—going to college, getting married, having children, planning for retirement—are based on what we think the future will be like as a result of an action in the present. We embark upon a particular career path because we expect it to be fulfilling (in one way or another), even though it may take many years of preparation and a number of sacrifices in order to get there. We have children because we "believe in them," in their growth in love and their future happiness, even before they are born.

Two very important genres of Christian literature—prophecy and apocalyptic—speak boldly about what will take place in the future, but it would be a mistake to lump them together with astrology and weather forecasting. These writings are really quite different from those briefly popular books that claim to tell us about the next big consumer trend or the upcoming stock-market crash. The prophetic and apocalyptic writings in the Bible and other Christian literature are not mere fortune-telling; they are attempts to provide us with whole new ways of seeing ourselves and understanding our context. They are meant to direct us toward the future, but also to help us orient our lives rightly in the present.

Prophetic and apocalyptic texts do make claims about what will take place, but they typically place these events in an *indefinite* future. In other words, these texts rarely make claims about the particular time or place that something will happen. Such specific information about, for example, the end of the world would distract readers away from the text's significance for the present; it would begin to sound more like a weather forecast. In fact, Jesus seems to discourage speculations about the specific moment of the end of the world, even suggesting that he himself is not privy to such knowledge: "About that day and hour no one knows, neither the angels of heaven, nor the Son, but only the Father" (Matt. 24:36; Mark 13:32).

In most cases, the prophet's goal is not so much to demonstrate skill at predicting a future event by announcing that it will happen on a given date. In fact, prophets often don't expect to live long enough to see their own prophecies fulfilled. When we read the Old Testament prophets, for example, we don't get the sense that they were looking forward to a moment when people would look at them with awe and say, "Wow, you said it would happen just like that, and it did! Your ability to predict the future is simply amazing!" The prophets seemed to have a more ambitious goal in mind: they were looking to change the whole orientation of their hearers' lives by urging them to rethink their relationship with God and the rest of creation. No matter how many of their future predictions came true, most of the prophets would have considered themselves failures if no one's life was changed as a result of their proclamation.

Take, for example, a classic piece of Hebrew prophecy that has been interpreted by Christians as having predicted the coming of Jesus Christ: "Look, the young woman is with child and shall bear a son, and shall name him Immanuel" (Isa. 7:14). This verse is quoted in the Gospel of Matthew (1:23), and Christians have certainly interpreted it as predicting a future event. (So have Jews—though they believe that, since the messiah has not yet come, the prophecy has not yet been fulfilled.) But

Isaiah's goal was surely not just to impress his listeners with his predictive power; in fact, given that he wrote many centuries before the coming of the messiah, none of his contemporaries would be around to congratulate him on his foresight. The prophetic message of the book of Isaiah was meant to draw Israel into a closer relationship with God and with one another, and to prepare them for an event that was to come in the future. Even though Jews and Christians differ in their interpretation of whether Isaiah's prophecy has yet been fulfilled, they share a common belief that his words were meant to strengthen the relationship between God and human beings. The ultimate meaning of the prophecy is that God continues to love and care for the people, and will send the Anointed One to earth to save them.

So although prophetic literature may actually predict the future, it also seeks to *interpret* the current context and to *orient* and *prepare* people for the future. One particularly vivid and dramatic form of such literature is that which describes the end of the world and its final consummation. This is often referred to as "apocalyptic" literature, from a Greek word meaning "to reveal." Apocalyptic writing seeks to reveal to its readers truths that have remained hidden and to unveil the future; it is often dramatic in structure and cosmic in scope. Again, it would be easy to mistake such writing as a simple prediction of the future; but precisely because of its grand drama and its cosmic scope, it has profound implications for how we should live *today*. It encourages us to develop a certain kind of *attitude* about the future—whether or not we're around to see all the details of its predictions come true. Prophetic and apocalyptic texts encourage us to develop a faith in God's ability to bring about the salvation and the judgment of humankind, and to bring human history to a close and to a final consummation.

So, for example, when reading the New Testament book of Revelation, we would miss something very important if we thought that its only point was to let us know just how many people are going to die in what kinds of spectacular ways (so that, when the time comes, we'll be able to look on in wonder, saying, "Wow, that St. John the Divine, he really got all the details exactly right!"). The deeper significance of the book of Revelation is that, because human history will eventually come to a close and because God will vindicate the righteous, we ought to live our lives with a certain amount of *distance* from this world, which is passing away. We ought to live in such a way that God becomes the true focus of our allegiance; for in the end, God will be all that really matters. When we read the book of Revelation, we should feel called to orient our lives toward God—not just at some time in the indefinite future, but right now.

We should not be surprised about the close relationship that these texts seek to establish between the present and the future. As I suggested above, our beliefs about the future have a significant impact on the shape of our lives in the present and on how we will interpret the events that are taking place all around us. We know this intuitively—even in our ordinary, everyday encounters. If we believe that a major snowstorm is on its way, we stock up on groceries and make sure we know where the snow shovels are hidden. If we believe that interest rates will drop in the future, we might put off a major purchase until we can take advantage of that change. If we think we're likely to be moving again in less than a year, we don't bother to unpack all the boxes.

Now, it's perfectly possible that our assumptions about the future will turn out to be false; after making about a hundred trips to those still-packed moving boxes over the course of four or five years, we realize that it would probably have been better to unpack them. But our *belief* about the likelihood of an upcoming move is what made us leave those boxes packed. Beliefs about the future influence action in the present, whether or not we think of them as accurate predictions of the future. So when the prophets speak about the future, they expect that, if their claims are persuasive, this will make some difference for how their audiences will live in the present.

I have offered these detailed comments about the role of prophetic and apocalyptic literature because their future orientation is related to the future-oriented claims of certain Christian beliefs. In the last two chapters of this book, we will discuss the Christian beliefs in the resurrection of the flesh and in life everlasting; in the present chapter, we are focusing on our belief that Christ "will come again, to judge the living and the dead." When we make this claim, we declare that we understand ourselves to be living in a "time between the times"—between Christ's first advent in lowliness and his second coming in power and great glory. This in turn emphasizes our belief that, although God has acted decisively to redeem the world, this work is not yet completed—not yet fully consummated. There is still work to be done; there are still accounts to be settled. Our savior will come again, "to judge the living and the dead," and to establish the reign of God. God's supreme reign will dislodge and overshadow all the various claims that human beings make, on a daily basis, to rule over one another and to proclaim themselves the true source of power. The Nicene Creed accents this belief by adding to the aforementioned phrase the line "and his Kingdom will have no end."

So our belief in Christ's return *does* have a future-oriented element; it is a belief about something that will happen. But it also has profound significance for our lives in the present. For if we truly believe that God will come again, this means that we do not believe that everything on earth has already achieved perfection—nor that it will ever do so through our efforts alone. It will take another decisive act of divine intervention to set everything right. This does not mean, of course, that there is no value to our own efforts to do God's work in the world; we are certainly called to a life of gratitude for God's grace, and to allow the fruits of the Spirit to be produced in our lives (Gal. 5:22–26; see also chapter 8 of this book). We should proclaim our thankfulness for God's love and care toward us by reflecting that love and care toward others. But if our efforts are successful, it can become all too easy to see this as *our own* accomplishment, *our* solving of all the world's problems, rather than God working in and through us. By stating our conviction that *God* will eventually bring human history to a close, we are making a claim of personal humility. We will not ourselves bring about the reign of God; God will do so.

The language of "judgment" in this part of the creed can sound slightly menacing, as though the main purpose of God's return to earth were to rain down a great many lightning bolts on people who haven't been paying good attention. In later chapters, I will return to the Christian beliefs in the forgiveness of sins and in life everlasting; I hope my comments on those elements of the Christian faith will provide a further context for interpreting our belief in divine judgment. In the meantime, it is important to note once again that our convictions about a future judgment have implications for the present. We choose to live a certain kind of life because we believe that, in the end, "what goes around comes around": sorrow turns into joy, and joy turns into sorrow. We believe in a certain sense of justice that does not allow for some people to receive all good things all the time while others receive nothing. This seems to be the upshot of Jesus' message that those who lack many earthly comforts are blessed because of their future life of abundance, while those who are happy now are destined to a less fortunate future (Luke 6:20–26).

Our belief in the future coming of God is an attempt to expand the time frame within which we usually view such matters. We are accustomed to relying on a snapshot of the present, the moment in which we currently live, as a framework or context within which to understand the events that we see taking place in our own lives and all around us. By broadening that context to include events that took place thousands of years ago (such as Jesus' life, death, and resurrection) and events that will take place in the indefinite future (Jesus' second coming), we begin to see the good and bad things that happen to people as part of a much wider frame of reference. We become a little less eager to seek temporary forms of pleasure in the present if we believe that they will be balanced by a radical absence of such pleasures in the future. The sacrifices that we make today bring us into a closer relationship with our fellow human beings and with God—both now and in the future.

The beginning of the musical version of Victor Hugo's *Les Misérables* includes several songs in which various classes of people reflect on the relationship between their present lives and their expectations for the future. Quite consistently, they remind each other that what one thinks about the future will impinge quite significantly on how one lives in the present. As the play opens, a group of prisoners express their own sorrow and pain that grows out of their inability to see anything positive on the horizon; all they can imagine is a seemingly endless prison sentence. When some of their number attempt to express hope, others respond by reminding them of their bleak future: "You'll always be a slave. . . . You're standing in your grave."

Similarly, in a later scene, the Paris factory workers and the destitute of the streets express their expectation for the future and its effect on their present lives: "At the end of the day it's another day over / And that's all you can say for the life of the poor." The workers feel fortunate to have a job, but they observe that, by the time they have purchased the bare necessities of life, there is no money left over. The two groups unite to express a larger vision of the future—an expectation that provides them with greater inner resolve than has anything they have experienced in the present. They believe that "At the end of the day there's another day dawning"—and that, in the future, those who have made their way to the top by walking over the backs of the poor and the destitute will be brought up short: "There's a hunger in the land, there's a reckoning still to be reckoned / And there's gonna be hell to pay, at the end of the day." Because the workers and the poor are convinced that something will happen to bring about justice, they are able to face each day of their difficult lives with at least a modicum of energy and hope. If these words had been spoken by the rich and the powerful, they would sound like an attempt to defer justice into the indefinite future. But when spoken with conviction by the poor themselves, these words can provide inspiration for hope and a spur to action.

We can see, then, how closely our beliefs about the future are tied to how we live in the present, but such beliefs are also related to a certain kind of attitude toward the past. In the Christian context, our belief that "Christ will come again" is a way of reminding ourselves that Christ's first coming was of urgent importance—and thus, that we are called to *remember* and to *live into* the life, death, and resurrection of Jesus until he comes again. We spur ourselves to remember the past by thinking about the future, and we spur ourselves to think about the future by remembering the past.

To see how closely our beliefs about the past, the present, and the future are interwoven, we need only pause to consider how we treat our loved ones who have died. Even though their lives are now an event of the past, we do not simply forget them; they continue to have an effect on how we live today. We tell stories about them, look at pictures, and treasure certain keepsakes—not out of mere nostalgia, but because we think it matters for our lives in the present. It also matters for the future: we tell our children about their forebears because we believe that the joys and sorrows of those who have gone before us can teach us something about how we might reshape our own lives in the present and in the future.

In sum, then, our belief that Christ "will come again to judge the living and the dead" is a belief about the future, but it orients our lives in the present. It calls us to remember Jesus' life, death, and resurrection; it draws us together as a community governed by a common hope; it emphasizes our ongoing accountability to God with the explicit mention of *judgment;* and it gives our lives direction for the future and identity in the present.

All of these issues and images spin around throughout the text of Toni Morrison's brilliant novel *Beloved.* Winner of countless prizes, including a Pulitzer Prize and the Nobel Prize in literature, this book has met with almost universal critical acclaim. It is deep, rich, and filled with a thousand insights and implications for the Christian life, only a few of which can be explored in this chapter. (I've placed the novel on the reading lists of several of the chapters of this book; it could be used to explicate a wide range of Christian beliefs.) We also have a very fine film treatment of the novel, directed by Jonathan Demme and starring Oprah Winfrey and Danny Glover. (The film is an excellent adaptation, in my opinion, and this is not an easy book to adapt. The film can, however, be hard to follow unless the viewer has also read the book.)

*Beloved* is a book about our memories of the past, about the shape of our lives in the present, and about our expectations for the future. Its title character is someone who "comes again," in judgment and in love—and the book explores what it means for others to live into that second coming in a faithful way. Of course, the novel does not provide an exact parallel (no book ever does); it is less about the *expectation* of this return and more about how one can live *in the midst* of it. I am not suggesting that the one who returns is a Christ-figure, nor that the various crimes and misdemeanors represented in the novel are in any way descriptive of God. But I do believe that the book helps us better understand the implications of our belief that Christ will come again. Living into this belief requires that we remember our connection to the past, that we allow ourselves to be reshaped in the present, and that we establish a direction in our lives that leads us into the future.

\* \* \* \* \*

From the very beginning of the novel (and also quite early in the film version), we learn that the house at 124 Bluestone Road is haunted—possessed by the ghost of a baby girl who died many years ago. This is not mere wisp of memory, but a very palpable presence. The ghost does what the girl would have done, and spitefully: breaking a mirror, putting her hands in the cake, throwing food, kicking the dog. We learn early on that the child died violently (the novel comments on "the baby's fury at having its throat cut," p. 6), but the narrator does not divulge the horrific details until the halfway point of the novel. We as readers are asked to go through the process of remembering, just as the child's mother, Sethe, must do. For in spite of the presence of the ghost, the dead child has not yet "come again"; that second advent will be a fully incarnate one. So as the book opens, we are aware of the real and spiritual presence of one who has died long ago, but we are about to be stirred into vivid remembering by her fully enfleshed "second coming."

The first visual presence of the visitor is witnessed by Sethe's only living daughter, Denver, who looked into a bedroom window and saw that "a white dress knelt down next to her mother and had its sleeve around her mother's waist" (p. 29). Sometime later, the significance of this presence is accented by the visit of Paul D—a old friend from Sethe's days as a slave on a plantation with the highly ironic name of "Sweet Home." The combined appearances of these two figures from the family's past has the effect of orienting the household toward the future (p. 38):

> Sethe had given little thought to the white dress until Paul D came, and then she remembered Denver's interpretation: *plans*. . . . It was a luxury she had not had in eighteen years and only that once. . . . [Yet] the word that her daughter had used a few years ago did cross her mind and she thought about what Denver had seen kneeling next to her, and thought also of the temptation to trust and remember that gripped her . . . Would it be all right? Would it be all right to go ahead and feel? Go ahead and *count on something?*

Because they are beginning to make space that will allow the past to come back into their lives, Denver and Sethe can actually think about the future, and can begin to think about their present-day lives in the context of that future.

The film version does not depict Denver's vision of the kneeling white dress; however, the director does make it clear that she is very aware of the ghostly presence. In fact, Denver welcomes it as a sort of companion in an otherwise lonely house. (Her older brothers couldn't abide its spiteful presence and took off as soon as they were old enough to do so; friends and neighbors seem to be avoiding the house and the family, for reasons that become clear later in the novel.) Denver's awareness of the ghost is very intense; Paul D recognizes her feelings, remarking that "She's got a waiting way about her. Something she's expecting and it ain't me" (p. 41). But Sethe cannot quite acknowledge the past to Denver, cannot allow it into her house in full form. "To Sethe, the future was a matter of keeping the past at bay. The 'better life' she believed she and Denver were living was simply not that other one. . . . As for Denver, the job Sethe had of keeping her from the past that was still waiting for her was all that mattered" (p. 42). Notice the author's careful reconfiguration of the imagery of time in the last sentence of this quotation: the "past" is described as though it were in the future, "waiting" for Denver.

Paul D has no idea what might be haunting this house; he remembers Sethe as a wonderful woman and is taken aback by the degree to which her life is oppressed by this presence. He recognizes it immediately, in a lovely moment early in the novel that is nicely echoed in the film:

> Paul D tied his shoes together, hung them over his shoulder and followed [Sethe] through the door straight into a pool of red and undulating light that locked him where he stood.
> "You got company?" he whispered, frowning.
> "Off an on," said Sethe.
> "Good God." He backed out the door onto the porch. "What kind of evil you got in here?"
> "It's not evil. Just sad. Come on. Just step through" (p. 8).

But when Sethe and Paul D embrace in the kitchen, the ghost flies into a temper, and the whole house threatens to shake apart. In a fit of anger, Paul D drives it out of the house; Sethe seems relieved, but Denver senses that he has robbed her of her one companion and friend.

But the past is not so easily pushed out of the present. A new character arrives on the scene, no longer an invisible spiteful child, but a mature, bodily presence: "A fully dressed woman walked out of the water" (p. 50). After a night and a day this mysterious figure makes her way to a stump in front of the house where Paul D, Sethe, and Denver see her upon their return from a local carnival. We are immediately alerted to Sethe's maternal relationship to this newcomer: "The moment she got close enough to see the face, Sethe's bladder filled to capacity. She said , 'Oh, excuse me,' and ran around to the back of 124. . . . There was no stopping water breaking from a breaking womb and there was no stopping now" (p. 51). The newly arrived visitor says her name is Beloved, which we have already learned is chiseled on the tombstone of Sethe's dead child. (She seems to have been unnamed at the time of her death. In life, she is referred to only as the "crawling already? baby"; "Beloved" comes from the first words of the baby's funeral service, the only ones Sethe remembered: "Dearly Beloved.") Although the visitor appears to be about nineteen or twenty years old (thus making her the age she would have been, had she not died), her manners and skills are those of a small child. The newcomer is able to recall a memory of Sethe's crystal earrings, which she has not seen on this visit but which she would have seen as a baby, and she wears white cotton lace around her neck to cover her scar (in the film version, the scar is visible from the outset; it's unclear whether Sethe is aware of it at first).

Thus, as readers, we have plenty of evidence that Beloved is Sethe's "crawling already? baby" who has come again. But in spite of it all, Sethe cannot bring herself to admit that her dead daughter has returned. As the novel moves along, we begin to see why Sethe might well want to avoid calling too many memories to mind. The horrors of her life of slavery are really beyond description and almost beyond imagination, but Morrison brings them to life vividly and with persuasive force. The physical, psychological, and sexual abuse visited on the African women and men who were forcibly brought to this country is something that we must never forget. Like the Nazi genocide of the past century, it must be kept in mind lest it be repeated; and yet, for inhabitants of the United States, it is much harder to keep in mind, because it was our own doing. It was our own Holocaust—a point about which Morrison reminds us in her dedication of the book to "Sixty Million and more"—this being the estimated number of deaths caused by the slave trade (and ten times the number of deaths usually associated with the Nazi Holocaust).

But the point of the novel's explicit depiction of the horrors of slavery is not to make us feel guilty about our past, but to help us empathize with those who suffered it. As readers, we need to understand that, for a former slave, being returned to slavery would be the worst thing imaginable: hell on earth. Only if we understand this can we make sense of the truth about Sethe and about Beloved—the truth which Sethe herself is trying so hard not to remember. For what we discover is that, in order to prevent her baby from being taken back into this place of torment and utter despair, Sethe *killed* the baby. In fact, she tried to kill all four of her children, but succeeded in only one case. For the past eighteen years, Sethe has had to live with this reality: the only way she could save her daughter was to kill her.

Now Beloved has come again, in order to draw out Sethe's memory of this horrible event—not to force her to relive it in some gruesome way, but to accept it as part of her own life story. The entire community—much of it composed of people who are themselves escaped slaves—has shunned Sethe ever since that day. She has had no one to whom she can pour out her soul, to whom she can explain that nothing, not even death, could be worse than the fate that awaited her and her children if they had been returned to their former master under the Fugitive Slave Law. Beloved's presence forces her to remember the past, to accept it as part of who she is, and to draw her and her daughter back into the community from which they had become estranged.

Eventually the book moves in a different direction. It explores the intense relationships among mother, daughter, and sister, and how this knot of family ties both attracts and repels those who are outside it. I will not go into these details here, as it is less germane to our present topic; the latter part of the book does, however, have implications for our understanding of divine and human relationships, and I have commented on its significance in my book on the Trinity, *These Three Are One*. It is a tribute to Morrison's extraordinarily rich and deeply theological writing that the novel explores so many themes related to the Christian faith. The book is filled with biblical allusions—from the party at Sethe's house that turns into a scene of the feeding of the multitudes, to the "tree" on Sethe's back (imprinted by the slavemaster's lash) that recalls the crucifixion, to the book's deeply meaningful epigram, from Paul's letter to the Romans: "I will call them my people, which were not my people, and her beloved, which was not beloved." The characters obviously have deep lives of prayer, and live into their relationship to God with seriousness and with joy.

A book so rich in theological meaning cannot be easily summarized, so I will not try to tie up all the loose ends that remain. Instead, I will close this chapter with a brief discussion of three ways in which the novel helps us better understand our belief that Christ "will come again to judge the living and the dead." First, the accent on judgment is an attempt to call us to accountability: we are asked to own up to our own thoughts, words, and deeds. Second, the Christian belief in this future event has the effect of binding the community together in solidarity and hope. And finally, the belief is key to our own personal identity: it gives us purpose and direction in life, reminding us that we are children of God and that God will never abandon us.

Turning first to the question of judgment and accountability: as readers, we get the impression that one of the reasons that Sethe is nervous about accepting the identity of the new visitor is that she is anxious about being judged or hated for having done this deed. She does not seem to have flagged in her conviction that it was the right thing to do; after the moment of the killing she walked out of the woodshed with her head high and her back straight (p. 152), and even now she can explain it all to Paul D with conviction: "I took and put my babies where they'd be safe" (p. 164). But she still knows that she hurt her own child, even if she felt forced to do so. And so it is with genuine gratitude and a bit of surprise that she realizes that "She ain't even mad with me. Not a bit" (p. 182). But this does not absolve her from a felt need to explain her act to the victim so that she can be released from having to repress the horrible memory of it all. "Be nice to think first, before I talk to her, let her know I know. Think about all I ain't got to remember no more" (p. 182). In the last part of the book, Sethe and Beloved engage in a number of poetic dialogues that speak of confession, acceptance, judgment, mercy, and release.

The idea of a future judgment is meant to remind us of our ultimate accountability, to God and to one another, for our actions. As I noted earlier in this chapter, any talk of judgment often sounds rather threatening, as though we are about to punished for every fault we ever committed. But judgment is also about the clearing of accounts—being required to set the record straight, to admit to the realities that one has covered up or refused to acknowledge. The "judgment" that Beloved exercises over Sethe is not, in the end, a harsh condemnation of the woman who killed her; it is, rather, a way of making sure that Sethe can herself remember and acknowledge what she did. It is not so much the act being judged as the conscience: to what extent can the wrongdoer actually accept the act as part of who she is? We see a similar dynamic at work in the biblical depiction of the last judgment in Matthew 25. The story does speak of reward and punishment, but what stands out for most readers is the process of recognition that takes place among both the rewarded and the punished. They realize that the words and deeds of their lives, directed toward other human beings, are ultimately directed toward God: "Just as you did it to one of the least of these who are members of my family, you did it to me" (Matt. 25:40). To be judged is to be reminded of true meaning and significance of our actions, and to be required to be accountable for them. We do this not just because we are under the compulsion of the judge, but because living an authentic human life requires that we be honest with ourselves about who we are—the parts that we don't like as well as those that we do. I will return to these matters again in chapter 10 when we examine the question of forgiveness.

Second, the Christian belief that Christ will come again provides a way of binding the community of believers together in solidarity and hope. In the novel, we learn that Sethe's harsh actions against her own children were really a result of a breakdown in community. There had been a lavish party at her house the day before, and the guests, who had enjoyed themselves at the time, were feeling guilty, jealous, and disapproving of the sheer abundance of it all. This was why no black person did what they always did when slavecatchers arrived in town—get the fugitives out of harm's way. "That explained why nobody ran on ahead; why nobody sent a fleet-footed son to cut 'cross a field soon as they saw the four horses in town hitched for watering while the riders asked questions. . . . Not anybody ran down to Bluestone Road, to say some new whitefolks with the Look just rode in" (p. 193). The community had been successful at protecting its own, but the dissension and hurt feelings that followed the party were enough to break it apart. This led to eighteen years of disapproval and isolation for Sethe. But when the community discovers that the dead child has come again and is wreaking a new kind of havoc at Sethe's house, they are galvanized to do something about it. They finally come to the house to pray and to sing—eighteen years later than they should have, perhaps, but they come all the same.

Part of what defines a community is its direction and orientation—where it understands itself to be headed. A group needs to know not just what beliefs it holds dear and what common practices its members participate in; it also needs to have a sense of its own future. For all the reasons I have discussed in this chapter, we need a sense of the future in order to be bound together into a common life in the present. Our belief that Christ will come again provides this direction and orientation; it is the goal toward which we are all headed. Even if we each have our own gifts and purposes within the larger community, we know that we share that common goal and hope.

Finally, the novel has something to say about how an orientation to the future can give meaning and identity to our lives, helping us see that we have something to live for. After her experience of the return of Beloved and the reconciliation that she accomplishes, Sethe falls into a painful experience of uncertainty and self-doubt. When Beloved leaves again, Sethe goes to the bed in which her mother laid down to die, and seems to be planning to die as well. She is certainly threatening to give up on the plans that she was able to imagine when Beloved began to appear. But Paul D comes to her and reminds her that she has done much good in the world, that she has a future and something to live for. This is, in fact, how the novel (and the film) ends (p. 273):

"Sethe," he says, "me and you, we got more yesterday than anybody. We need some kind of tomorrow."

He leans over and takes her hand. With the other he touches her face.

"You your best thing, Sethe. You are." His fingers are holding hers.

"Me? Me?"

Sethe is not yet convinced that an orientation toward the future will be enough to allow her to accept that she is "her own best thing," but one suspects that Paul D may be able to help her see far enough into the future to believe it.

In the hectic world of our day-to-day lives, it is easy to forget about the importance of an orientation toward the future. We sometimes speak nonchalantly about the need to have "something to live for," but we have become so accustomed to just skipping down to the next item on our planning calendars that we sometimes lose sight of the final goal. Our belief in Christ's return to earth is our way of reminding ourselves that we always have something to live for, that we always have a future direction, and that it will always involve God. We believe that God put the wheels of human history in motion, and God will eventually bring that history to a close. God is in complete control of the world—all appearances to the contrary notwithstanding. God reminds us that we are loved and treasured by God as God's very own children; we are God's own, and we will never be abandoned.

The injustices that Sethe faced and the desperate measures to which she was driven are poignant reminders of the sinful state of humanity—and of our deep need for salvation. However much we may have been created in the image of God, we must surely have fallen far from that image if we can so dehumanize other human beings on account of their race. And of course, the injustice continues in so many ways. I would never want our belief in God's future reign to allow us to forget the sins of the past, nor to blind us to our continued participation in them in the present. Nevertheless, I believe that the Christian orientation toward the future—our conviction that Christ will come again—can become the basis for both a gathering up of the past and a reorientation in the present. We are called to live lives directed toward the reign of God, even if we know that it will not be fully established until the end of time.

In their struggles against South African apartheid, Christian leaders often called upon their Christian convictions to ensure that justice, reconciliation, and love remained the primary motivation and goal. They called upon the Christian hope for the coming of the reign of God to remind us that God is ultimately in charge. In that way, a conviction about the future led to a real victory in the present. One African pastor put it this way:

It may appear as though the powerful, the rulers of this world, are in full control. Their arrogance seems to know no bounds. But the Church knows: Jesus Christ is the Lord of history. Christ is the Lord of life. And Christ's word shall have the final say.

## Questions For Discussion

1. How have you generally understood the prophetic and apocalyptic language of the Bible? Do you see it mostly as a prediction of the future, or does it have other significance as well?

2. Think of some additional examples from everyday life that show how our actions and attitudes in the present can sometimes depend on what we think is going to happen in the future.

3. Given that we do not know the day or the hour when Christ will return to earth, we have to be content (in the meantime) with an expectation or foretaste of that future. List some of the experiences that you believe give you something of a taste of what that future might be like.

4. How have you understood the idea of God's *judgment* of the world? Do you think of it as something to be welcomed? Feared? Does it create anxiety in you, or a feeling of acceptance? Read Matthew 25:32–46 and discuss how it shapes your attitudes about God's final judgment.

## For Further Reading

Douglass, James W. *The Nonviolent Coming of God*. Maryknoll, N.Y.: Orbis Books, 1991. (Introductory/Advanced)

Grey, Mary C. *Prophecy and Mysticism: The Heart of the Postmodern Church*. Edinburgh: T & T Clark, 1997. (Introductory/Advanced)

Groh, Dennis E. *In Between Advents: Biblical and Spiritual Arrivals*. Philadelphia: Fortress Press, 1986. (Advanced)

Peters, Ted. *God—The World's Future: Systematic Theology for a Postmodern Era*. Minneapolis: Fortress Press, 1992. (Advanced/Specialized)

Robinson, John A. T. *Jesus and His Coming: The Emergence of a Doctrine*. New York: Abingdon Press, 1957. (Introductory/Advanced)

## Other Literary Works Related to Christ's Second Coming

Natalie Zemon Davis, *The Return of Martin Guerre;* also the film of the
    same name directed by Daniel Vigne; adapted as the film *Sommersby*
    by Jon Amiel, and as the musical *Martin Guerre* by Alain Boublil and
    Claude-Michel Schonberg

Victor Hugo, *Les Misérables;* also the musical, also by Boublil and
    Schonberg

W. W. Jacobs, "The Monkey's Paw"

Henry James, *The Turn of the Screw*

Flannery O'Connor, "Judgment Day"

Walker Percy, *The Second Coming*

# eight

# "I Believe in the Holy Spirit"

In chapters 1 and 2, I discussed the importance of the Christian belief in a very specific God: the triune God, the Trinity. At that point, I offered some initial explorations into that complex question by discussing the two persons of the Trinity that have been traditionally referred to as "the Father" and "the Son." I suggested that what is most important about these terms is not so much their analogy to *human* fathers and sons, and especially not the masculine metaphors that they draw upon. Rather, their importance is to be found in their *relatedness* to each other: *father* and *son* are *relational* terms that depend upon one another for their meaning. No children without parents, of course; but no parents without children, either! One does not become a parent until the child is born; and, with respect to the *relations* being described here, parenthood is as much "caused" by the child as the child is caused by the parents. The incarnation of God in the world was not the sending of a subordinate being or a mere divine messenger; rather, one of the divine Trinity took on human flesh.

The early Christians began to use this language to make sense of their experience of Jesus, whom they understood as Emmanuel, "God with us" (Matt. 1:23). It was the only way they could understand God as, on the one hand, continuing to dwell beyond their immediate grasp, and yet, on the other hand, simultaneously walking along the shore of the Sea of Galilee. After Jesus' death and resurrection, they had another experience that eventually broadened their understanding of God further. This was an experience of God who was present in their day-to-day world, just as Jesus had been; yet unlike Jesus, this presence of God was not incarnate in a single human being with whom they could converse and interact in ordinary ways. This experience of God was not bodily—or perhaps we should say that it was bodily in an entirely different sense than had been their experience of Jesus. God was entering the world, not in the person of a single human being, but through the work of a community of human beings. God was inspiring the souls of faithful Christians to go out into the world and do the work they had been given to do.

In order to give voice to this experience of God, the early Christians drew upon ancient Hebrew sources, which spoke of the Spirit of God at work in the world. In the book of Acts, the experience is described as follows (Acts 2:1–6):

> When the day of Pentecost had come, they were all together in one place. And suddenly from heaven there came a sound like the rush of a violent wind, and it filled the entire house where they were sitting. Divided tongues, as of fire, appeared among them, and a tongue rested on each of them. All of them were filled with the Holy Spirit and began to speak in other languages, as the Spirit gave them ability. Now there were devout Jews from every nation under heaven living in Jerusalem. And at this sound the crowd gathered and was bewildered, because each one heard them speaking in the native language of each.

Peter interprets this miraculous event as the fulfillment of an Old Testament prophecy (Joel 2:28), which he quotes to them in Acts 2:16–18:

> This is what was spoken through the prophet Joel: "In the last days it will be, God declares, that I will pour out my Spirit upon all flesh, and your sons and your daughters shall prophesy, and your young men shall see visions, and your old men shall dream dreams. Even upon my slaves, both men and women, in those days I will pour out my Spirit; and they shall prophesy."

Peter then goes on to tell the story of the life, death, and resurrection of Jesus, who provides the concrete reference point for the outpouring of God's spirit to which these people have been witnesses.

The Holy Spirit is sometimes called the "neglected" or even the "forgotten" member of the Trinity. It is certainly the case that throughout Christian history, we haven't been quite sure how to understand this Spirit, which "blows where it chooses" (John 3:8). From early on, Christians were not quite sure they wanted to describe the Spirit as divine, as *God;* they were much more willing to describe Jesus as God. Was the Spirit worthy of worship? Should we pray to the Spirit? Questions like this were not actually sorted out until the fourth century, when the Council of Constantinople finally agreed upon the language that appears in the Nicene Creed:

> We believe in the Holy Spirit, the Lord, the Giver of Life,
> Who proceeds from the Father,

Who with the Father and the Son is worshiped and glorified,
And has spoken through the prophets.

But even these strong claims about the Holy Spirit have not rescued it (him? her?) from relative obscurity in most strands of the Christian tradition. Compared with the grandeur and mystery of God, the Source of all things, and compared with the personal, almost immediate relationship that Christians often feel with Jesus as the incarnation of the Word of God, the Holy Spirit seems a bit too ordinary, too everyday—and at the same time too elusive and indefinite.

In fact, the Spirit has always been associated with some of the more indefinite, uncertain, and free-form elements of Christianity, and in some quarters this has made the Holy Spirit a bit suspect. The stories that we tell about Jesus tend to be very concrete: his birth, his ministry, his words to his disciples and the crowds, his death and resurrection. The narrative detail in these stories makes it relatively more difficult to remake him into whatever we might want him to be (though admittedly, Christians have proven themselves quite resourceful in this regard!). But with the Holy Spirit, there seem to be virtually no constraints; anyone can say "the Holy Spirit told me that I should . . ." and thereby justify almost any behavior whatsoever. So from the earliest period of Christian history, the Holy Spirit proved to be incredibly powerful, working the most amazing works among the people of God—and yet at the same time extraordinarily subject to abuse, allowing people to justify reprehensible actions by claiming to be inspired by the Spirit.

Paul was evidently facing this problem within the Christian community at Corinth. Apparently, Christians there were interpreting various events within the community as having been inspired by the Holy Spirit—including not only preaching and teaching but also speaking in tongues. Some may have been relying on the Spirit to propose more radical claims within the community, including (perhaps) greater authority for women. Others may have been appealing to the Spirit as a way of absolving themselves from all constraint, including widely held taboos against gluttony and incest. Paul responds to this situation by insisting that the Spirit is not a "different God" from the God who became incarnate in Jesus. If we cannot discern at least a "family resemblance" between the ministry of Jesus Christ and the present-day actions of Christians who claim that their work is inspired by the Holy Spirit, then this would tend to cast doubt on the validity of that inspiration. Paul puts the matter as follows (1 Cor. 12:1–7):

Now concerning spiritual gifts, brothers and sisters, I do not want you to be uninformed. You know that when you were pagans, you were enticed and led astray to idols that could not speak. Therefore I want you to understand that no one speaking by the Spirit of God ever says "Let Jesus be cursed!" and no one can say "Jesus is Lord" except by the Holy Spirit. Now there are varieties of gifts, but the same Spirit; and there are varieties of services, but the same Lord; and there are varieties of activities, but it is the same God who activates all of them in everyone. To each is given the manifestation of the Spirit for the common good.

Here Paul is, quite legitimately I think, trying to prevent appeals to "the Spirit" from justifying every form of nonsense that anyone can dream up.

But of course, in the process of elaborating such restrictions, one may very well end up placing obstacles in the way of God's attempt to do a new thing. Elsewhere in his letters, Paul refers to the process of setting up such obstacles as "quenching the Spirit" (1 Thess. 5:19), and many people now think that a great many Christian leaders through the ages, including perhaps Paul himself, occasionally engaged in work that tended to quench the Spirit. Many scholars, for example, believe that some of the early Christian communities were engaged in lively debates over the possibility that women might have considerably more freedom and authority within the church than they had in other spheres at that time. Undoubtedly, some of the arguments in favor of a larger role for women were based on claims about the work of the Spirit. But Paul (and many others) seem to have worked to shut down this particular movement, perhaps worrying that this was just self-interest parading as divine inspiration. Other early Christian groups—the Montanists, for example—were much more willing to discern the Holy Spirit's reordering of the cultural assumptions of the day; they also gave much greater authority to women. On the other hand, the Montanists developed their own highly authoritarian structures, as have most other Christian communities that have claimed to be especially devoted to the work of the Holy Spirit. So we need to be careful about assuming that all the problems of the faith would be solved if only people paid more attention to the Holy Spirit.

All in all, Christianity has often found it very difficult to draw the line between authority and freedom, between its core identity and acceptable novelty. While the concrete narratives of Jesus stress the value of a central point of reference, the free-wheeling power of the Holy Spirit encourages change and innovation. Different branches of Christendom have seen this differently. The Roman Catholic Church, faced with the upheavals in almost every field of knowledge and the literal rearrangement of the known world in the nineteenth century, tended to place its focus on the life of Jesus as authoritatively interpreted by bishops and, especially, by the bishop of Rome. Eastern Orthodox Christians saw this as an attempt to impose authoritative control on the work of the Holy Spirit. Many Protestant Christians, however, thought the Eastern Orthodox were also unwilling to let the Spirit blow where it chooses, particularly in their continuing commitments to national alliances and their willingness to side with Rome in their devotion to an all-male priesthood. Still others argued that the Spirit was calling us away from the very idea of priesthood, or away from traditional liturgical forms, or away from creeds and from the biblical texts. At the far extreme, some forms of Protestant Christianity seem willing to adopt any testimony that is claimed to be "of the Spirit" as the genuine article. It is no surprise that many people have come to think of the Holy Spirit as God's wax nose—something that can be reshaped into any form at a moment's notice.

However guilty Paul may have been of "quenching the Spirit" in some respects, he was surely on the right track when he insisted that there should be some kind of correspondence between the work of the Spirit and the life, death, and resurrection of Jesus. We ought to be dubious about any action, person, or idea that seems to contradict the teachings of Jesus, no matter how loudly it is proclaimed to be a manifestation of the Holy Spirit. If someone claims the Spirit's authority for something that we cannot even imagine Jesus asking or requiring of us, or that forces us to rewrite the basic narratives of his life among us, we should remind ourselves of Paul's words that "no one speaking by the Spirit of God ever says 'Let Jesus be cursed!'"

On the other hand, we need to avoid interpreting this too narrowly; Jesus was necessarily a part of his own time and place, and what he did in conformity with that cultural setting cannot necessarily be taken to be a universal mandate. For example, the fact that Jesus appears to have chosen male disciples for his "inner circle" does not, in itself, speak against the ministry of women. Women were certainly among those who followed Jesus, and he says nothing to suggest that they are any less able to be his disciples than are men. (The fact that the twelve are all men probably has more to do with the historical allusion to the twelve tribes of Israel than it does to any suggestion that the Christian ministry is an exclusively male club.) Therefore, I see no reason to doubt the claim that the Holy Spirit is presently inspiring the church to make more use of the extraordinary gifts that women bring to ministry, and I would make similar arguments for the greater incorporation of other marginalized groups into the Christian family. These efforts seem very much to be the work of the Spirit, identifiably in continuity with Jesus' own ministry to the marginalized and the outcast of his own day.

On the other hand, claims that the Holy Spirit has inspired a person or a group to work for the installation of a certain form of government (or for its overthrow), or that the Spirit has directed us not to be compassionate to one another or to injure one another—such claims are not to be trusted. This is because they do not sit well with the narrative of Jesus. He never suggested that the salvation of our souls or the coming of the reign of God was dependent upon a certain form of government being present or absent. (Living as he did in a land where the oppressive hand of a colonial power was so much in evidence, he undoubtedly encountered many people who thought precisely this, which is why the absence of any revolutionary or reactionary rhetoric in his teachings is so remarkable.) Because Jesus' own life and works are so broadly shaped by his compassion for others and his refusal to strike out in revenge against those who wronged him, any claim that the Spirit has inspired such revenge or such lack of compassion is nothing but a self-interested attempt to justify one's evil deeds by coating them with a veneer of divine sanction.

In short, we should be able to recognize lines of continuity between the life of Jesus, the transcendent God who is beyond our grasp, and the Spirit who dwells within us. This is part of what it means to think about the work of God in trinitarian terms: that we not become so focused on one aspect of God's character that we allow the other aspects to be neglected. God is transcendent, infinitely beyond our grasp; but God is also nearer to us that we can imagine. God has no body, yet God became incarnate in a human body and inspires many such bodies to become the body of Christ in the world. We will not set these elements against one another as long as we are thinking in terms of the mutuality and internal relationality of the triune God.

All the same, even bearing in mind that all of God's work is the work of the entire Trinity, we can speak of certain works of God as particularly associated with the Holy Spirit. Traditionally, we have spoken of three such works as having a special "appropriateness" to the Spirit. First, the Holy Spirit is engaged in the ongoing transformation of sinful human beings into greater resemblance to the image of God in which we were created. Second, the Spirit is our advocate and guide, offering direction to our lives and "taking our side" when we are confronted with obstacles. And finally, the Holy Spirit is God acting in us, enabling us to respond to God's own initiative in new and creative ways—ways that we would be unable to pursue if left unassisted. It should be emphasized that all three of these "works of the Spirit" focus not on individuals, but on the whole community of the church, the body of Christ. The Spirit is the transformative power of God, the advocate, and the responsive voice—not just for a few particularly needy (or particularly gifted) individuals, but for the entire Christian community. I now want to say a few words about each of these works of the Holy Spirit.

First, we particularly associate the Holy Spirit with the ongoing transformation of humanity and our restoration to the divine image in which we were created. I have observed previously that all the works of God originate in the Source, are carried out through the Word, and are perfected in the Spirit. So it is this "perfecting" of our human capacities that is most appropriately understood as the work of the Holy Spirit. Of course, this perfection is never fully achieved; we are human beings, after all, and not God. But if we open ourselves to the work of the Holy Spirit, we can allow ourselves to be transformed into something more closely approximating the divine image. As Paul puts it, "All of us, with unveiled faces, seeing the glory of the Lord as though reflected in a mirror, are being transformed into the same image from one degree of glory to another; for this comes from the Lord, the Spirit" (2 Cor. 3:18).

Second, the Holy Spirit is described as the Advocate and Comforter, someone who takes our side in all the difficulties that we face. In this sense, the Spirit continues the work of Jesus on earth. In his farewell discourses in the Gospel of John, Jesus says, "And I will ask the Father, and he will give you another Advocate, to be with you forever. This is the Spirit of truth, whom the world cannot receive, because it neither sees him nor knows him. You know him, because he abides with you, and he will be in you" (John 14:16–17). Notice in particular the use of the phrase "another Advocate." This seems to imply that Jesus was the first advocate, our advocate on earth; after his ascension into heaven, God comes to us again, to perfect the work that was begun in the Source and carried out through the Word incarnate. Jesus describes the Spirit as God's continuing presence, to be with us whenever we ask, and a constant reminder that God will never abandon us.

Finally, the Holy Spirit is God's action through us and in us, helping us to accomplish that which we could never accomplish on our own. This takes place in many areas of our lives. The Spirit is the cause of our love for God and for one another: "Since God loved us so much, we also ought to love one another. . . . if we love one another, God lives in us, and God's love is perfected in us. By this we know that we abide in God, and God in us: because God has given us the Spirit" (1 John 4:11–13). The Holy Spirit is therefore the basis of whatever capacity we have for doing good work. In Galatians 5, Paul elaborates a list of virtues that he describes as "fruits of the Spirit" (Gal. 5:22): "love, joy, peace, patience, kindness, generosity, faithfulness, gentleness, and self-control." These are the elements of God's character that can also become habituated in us if we allow the Spirit to animate our lives. Even our ability to pray to God is ultimately the work of the Holy Spirit: "the Spirit helps us in our weakness; for we do not know how to pray as we ought, but that very Spirit intercedes with sighs too deep for words" (Rom. 8:26).

In short, then, the Holy Spirit is God's presence among us today, actively inspiring Christians to do God's work in the world. But I have always found that discussions of the Holy Spirit tend to veer toward the "warm and fuzzy" end of the spectrum—so much so that we can't imagine why anyone wouldn't welcome the Spirit with open arms. What we forget, of course, is that being on such intimate terms with God can be an overpowering, overwhelming experience. It means giving up control of our lives and placing them in the hands of God. This is something that has always been difficult for human beings to do—but never more so than today, when having complete control over one's life is so highly valued.

Therefore, in choosing a work of literature to illustrate the work of the Spirit, I turned to one in which the presence of the Spirit was seen as something of a threat—an unwanted presence and a call to give up control. Of course, sometimes we feel that our lives are in complete chaos. In such moments, we are thankful for the gift of God's Holy Spirit to take our side and to put our lives in order. But I suspect that, most of the time, we are quite happy with the order that we ourselves have imposed on our lives—and the last thing we want is to have God jump in and start rearranging things! That is exactly how the main character feels at the beginning of Flannery O'Connor's brilliant short story, "The Enduring Chill."

*  *  *  *  *

"The Enduring Chill" begins as a sort of retelling of the parable of the Prodigal Son (see Luke 15: 11–32). Asbury Fox has been living in New York City, having jumped at the chance to flee his overprotective mother and her dairy farm. He had planned to become a writer, but things didn't work out that way; he destroyed most everything he wrote. After living in squalid conditions and beset with some chronic illness that he cannot define, he decides to give up and go home, where he knows his mother will welcome him with open arms.

But this prodigal son is not enthusiastic about his return. He regards himself as a failure, and his purpose in coming home is only to allow the disease to run its course so that he can die. Just as he sought to take matters into his own hands by leaving home, he now means to be in control of the final days of his life. But his best-laid plans go astray: at home, he finds a number of people who seem intent on reminding him that his fate is not in his hands alone. This cast of characters includes his doting mother, who will go to any length to make him comfortable in spite of himself; a clownish country doctor, who ignores Asbury's resignation to the embrace of death and persistently visits him until he is able to diagnose his ailment; a couple of black dairy workers, once the object of Asbury's condescension, who turn out to be much smarter than he is; a hilarious country priest, who doesn't show the slightest interest in Asbury's overly intellectual disdain for religion; and, just like in the parable, a jealous older sibling (a sister, though, rather than a brother), who is loudly annoyed at the attention lavished on the wayward son.

Of particular interest to us, however, are the story's persistent references to the Holy Spirit. They begin very early, with a flashback to Asbury's time in New York and his encounter with a Jesuit priest named Ignatius Vogle. (*Vogel* is the German word for *bird*—the first of many references in the story to the most common pictorial representation of the Holy Spirit as a dove or similar bird.) Asbury meets the Jesuit when a group of people who have just heard a lecture on Buddhism are discussing the question of salvation. After several of them have put forward their own thoughts on the possibility of human salvation (or lack thereof), Asbury asks the priest for his opinion. He replies in language sufficiently technical that Asbury seems unlikely to have understood it: "'There is,' the priest said, 'a real probability of the New Man, assisted, of course,' he added brittlely, 'by the Third Person of the Trinity'" (p. 330). (The first part of his reply refers to the then-current translation of a passage in Ephesians in which Paul refers to sinful humanity as "the old man" and redeemed humanity as "the new man.") The priest is emphasizing the first aspect of the Spirit's work as I described it above: the ongoing transformation of sinful human beings into their original divine image.

Neither Asbury nor the others in the discussion group are much moved by this comment, but something about the man's self-assurance sticks with Asbury, such that he becomes almost obsessed with having an intellectual conversation with a Jesuit priest before he dies. Unfortunately for him, the only priest that his mother is able to scour up is a man who introduces himself as "Fahther Finn, from Purrgatory," who has decidedly not arrived for worldly conversation about, as Asbury puts it, "the myth of the dying god." Instead, the priest drills him on the Roman Catholic catechism until Asbury relents, or tries to relent, by divulging his secret—revealing that the request for a priestly visit was just a ruse: "'Listen,' he said, 'I'm not a Roman.'" The priest is manifestly undeterred: "'A poor excuse for not saying your prayers!' the old man snorted" (p. 344).

The exchange brings forth another truth about the Holy Spirit, offering an important nuance to the second of the three "roles" mentioned above. There, I noted that the Spirit is understood as an advocate and guide, orienting our lives and taking our side. But this work of the Spirit is not merely an act of divine intervention or an attempt by God to overtake and overturn our free will. We must still make the choice; we must be willing to invite God into our lives if we want the Spirit to be an advocate on our behalf. This is the upshot of Asbury's final exchange with Father Finn:

> "God does not send the Holy Ghost to those who don't ask for Him. Ask Him to send the Holy Ghost."
> "The Holy Ghost?"
> "Are you so ignorant you've never heard of the Holy Ghost?"
> "Certainly I've heard of the Holy Ghost," Asbury said furiously, "and the Holy Ghost is the last thing I'm looking for!"
> "And He may be the last thing you get," the priest said (p. 344).

We are certainly capable of blocking the Spirit's work; we can "say no" to God, because even though God is certainly powerful enough to overcome our resistance, this could only happen through a denial of our freedom. The whole story of the Jewish and Christian faiths is that God is more heavily invested in our freedom than in anything else. We are allowed to make mistakes, allowed to go wildly astray, even allowed to turn away from God.

But that doesn't mean that God will give up on us. God "keeps at us," keeps prompting us to respond to the divine initiative, even when we have attempted to turn our backs on God. This is related to the third point made above: whatever capacity we have for a right response to God's loving care is ultimately given to us by God. This is a hard truth for human beings to learn, particularly in a cultural context that encourages us to "fend for ourselves" and to "shape our own destiny." Asbury has taken these cultural proddings to their logical conclusion: he has arranged all the elements of his own life, and now plans to arrange his death. He consistently rejects the idea that anyone else can help him. He even plans to control his mother's emotional reaction to his death by leaving her a lengthy letter of complaint to be read after he is beyond her reach.

But every now and again, Asbury seems to understand that he may not always be able to be in control. He realizes, however vaguely and confusedly, that there is a greater power at work in the world. It is symbolized for him, once again, by the image of a bird:

> He lay for some time staring at the water stains on the gray walls. Descending from the top molding, long icicle shapes had been etched by leaks and, directly over his bed on the ceiling, another leak had made a fierce bird

with spread wings. It had an icicle crosswise in its beak and there were smaller icicles descending from its wings and tail. It had been there since his childhood and had always irritated him and sometimes had frightened him. He had often had the illusion that it was in motion and about to descend mysteriously and set the icicle on his head (pp. 334–35).

There are other hints that Asbury can't quite get God out of his mind: a "presence" that manifests itself in his dreams and in his room, particularly when he anticipates that a significant event is about to transpire; a brooding sense of a future for himself that he cannot understand; and an ongoing concern about the water stain on his ceiling: "He even looked at the fierce bird with the icicle in its beak and felt that it was there for some purpose that he could not divine" (p. 345).

All of these hints come into resolutely sharpened focus in the final scene of the story, in which the water stain bird on his ceiling is explicitly linked with the Holy Spirit. Asbury has just learned that his illness, while chronic, is not fatal, and that he will have to live out his life in the care of his much-maligned mother and her troublesome coterie of friends and relations. Perhaps he has also begun to realize that he brought this disease upon himself, having drunk unpasteurized milk in a rather haughty effort to "liberate" the black dairy workers from their bondage to his mother's commands. The presence of Another in the room is almost overwhelming: when he looks in the mirror, he sees his own eyes "shocked clean as if they had been prepared for some awful vision about to come down on him" (p. 349). The author takes us back to the earlier reference of the Holy Spirit's necessary assistance in bringing about the "New Man": "The old life in him was exhausted. He awaited the coming of the new" (p. 349). He now realizes the fruitlessness of his effort to resist the divine power that seeks him and pursues him. At the very least, resisting that power will not just be a matter of saying "no," for God will never cease to pursue him:

> The fierce bird which through the years of his childhood and the days of his illness had been poised over his head, waiting mysteriously, appeared all at once to be in motion. Asbury blanched and the last film of illusion was torn as if by a whirlwind from his eyes. He saw that for the rest of his days, frail, racked, but enduring, he would live in the face of a purifying terror. A feeble cry, a last impossible protest escaped him. But the Holy Ghost, emblazoned in ice instead of fire, continued, implacable, to descend (pp. 349–50).

The Christian belief in the Holy Spirit might be well summed up in that single word, *implacable*. God is implacable. God cannot be placated, accommodated, or turned aside from the divine pursuit of our souls—

and certainly not by a mere word of rejection or opposition. We can turn our backs on God, we can run as fast as we like in the opposite direction, but God will run after us, undeterred.

All his life, Asbury has been running away from God. Like all of us, he wants to be in full control of his life and his death; meaningful experiences must be something that he makes for himself, "out of his own intelligence. He had always relied on himself and had never been a sniveler after the ineffable" (p. 346). This thought leads him to recall an incident when he was five years old, when his sister had lured him, on the vague promise of a present, to a preacher at a tent revival.

> "Here," she said in a loud voice. "I'm already saved but you can save him. He's a real stinker and too big for his britches." He had broken her grip and shot out of there like a small cur and later when he had asked for his present, she had said, "You would have got Salvation if you had waited for it but since you acted the way you did, you get nothing!" (p. 346).

So Asbury began running at a young age, and did not stop; he ran from home to New York, ran from New York to home, and did not stop running until his own efforts to torment and reject his mother pinioned him to his bed with an enduring chill. And when he finally was forced to stop running, he discovered that God was not one inch farther from him than when he had started running, twenty years before.

To acknowledge a belief in the Holy Spirit is something very much like claiming that no matter how far and how fast we run away, God will not abandon us. When we turn away, when we try to place ourselves outside the reach of the divine, God lets us turn—but pursues us relentlessly. The same story is told over and over again, from the beginning: when human beings rebel against God and become ashamed of their own nakedness, God provides clothing for them (Gen. 3:21). When a man rises up against his brother and kills him, God protects him from revenge with a mark on his forehead (Gen. 4:15). When the whole human race fills the world with violence and corruption, God saves a righteous family to begin again (Gen. 6). And when the people attempt to "make a name for themselves" by building a tower to the heavens, God confuses their language and scatters them throughout the land (Gen. 11:1–9)—but elects Israel to be the chosen people, so that all nations and races might be blessed and ultimately gathered again into one (Gen. 12:1–3).

The story continues through the history of Israel and the prophets: each time the people turn away, God pursues them. The biblical texts employ a wide range of metaphors to describe this incessant, pursuing love: God is like a jealous husband, like a jilted lover, like a nursing mother, like a mother hen: however far or fast we might run away, God will follow. The story continues in the coming of Jesus; God does not hesitate to come to us directly, in human form, in order to win us back into our rightful place as children of God. And finally, after Jesus' death, resurrection, and ascension, God pours out the Holy Spirit upon all flesh, to dwell among us until the end of the age. Our belief in the Holy Spirit is therefore a summary of the many ways in which God persists in reminding us of the power of divine love—and persists in drawing us back into relation with the One in whom we live, and move, and have our being.

## Questions For Discussion

1. What factors do you think have been involved in the Holy Spirit being the "neglected" or "forgotten" member of the Trinity?

2. Have you had the experience of hearing someone attempt to use an appeal to the Holy Spirit to justify a behavior or attitude that seemed to you out of keeping with the message of Jesus?

3. What do you think is the significance of the claim in Acts 2 that, through the inspiration of the Holy Spirit, each person heard the Christian message in her or his own native language? How is this related to the story of the Tower of Babel (Genesis 11)?

4. What other works do you particularly associate with the Holy Spirit, in addition to those listed in this chapter?

5. Describe an experience in which you suspected that the Holy Spirit might be attempting to "do a new thing." How did people react? How did they go about discerning whether the new idea or action was truly the work of the Holy Spirit?

## For Further Reading

Badcock, Gary D. *Light of Truth and Fire of Love: A Theology of the Holy Spirit*. Grand Rapids: Eerdmans, 1997. (Advanced)

Barrett, C. K. *The Holy Spirit and the Gospel Tradition*. London: S.P.C.K., 1966. (Introduction/Advanced)

Basil the Great, St. *On the Holy Spirit*. Crestwood, N.Y.: St. Vladimir's Seminary Press, 1980. (Introductory/Advanced)

Congar, Yves. *I Believe in the Holy Spirit*. New York: Crossroad, 1997. (Advanced)

Jenson, Robert W. "You Wonder Where the Spirit Went." *Pro Ecclesia: A Journal of Catholic and Evangelical Theology* 2, no. 3 (Summer 1993): 296–304. (Advanced/Specialized)

Wainwright, Geoffrey. "The Holy Spirit" in *The Cambridge Companion to Christian Doctrine,* ed. Colin E. Gunton. Cambridge: Cambridge University Press, 1997. (Introductory/Advanced)

## Other Fictional Works Related to the Holy Spirit

Richard Adams, *Watership Down*
Charles Dickens, *A Christmas Carol in Prose*
Gabriel García Márquez, *One Hundred Years of Solitude*
David Hare, *Racing Demon*
Bernard Malamud, *God's Grace*
J. D. Salinger, *Catcher in the Rye*
William Shakespeare, *The Tempest*

# nine

# "The Holy Catholic Church, the Communion of Saints"

Ask someone to define the word *church*, and you'll probably get a description of a building. If you refine your request by explaining that you're not interested in the architectural sense of the word, most people will respond by talking about the official structures of the church—its officers, organization, and bureaucracy. Occasionally, you might hear some mention of worship services (as in the phrase "going to church"). But unless your conversation partner has been encouraged (or trained!) to think otherwise, it will be some time before the focus shifts to the subject of *the people* who constitute the church. And yet, throughout Christian history—from biblical times until the present—this has been the most important meaning of the word *church*.

Before we can speak of buildings and services and institutional structures, we have to be able to think of the church as *the community of Christians*. Sometimes the church has been defined by using the phrase "the whole community of faithful people"; this reminds us that the people are more important than the building, the worship, and the bureaucracy. We also describe the church using metaphors that point to both its unity and its multiplicity—metaphors such as "the Body of Christ" (because a body is a complex, interdependent whole) or "the household of God" (because a single household is made up of many people working together). In this sense, the word *church* is not limited to any particular denomination or historical manifestation.

In fact, some theologians have argued that no one really knows *who* constitutes the church. Only God has the "inside information" that would be necessary to know whether any particular individual had really been made a part of the whole body. We certainly can't make judgments on the basis of who happens to have assembled for a particular worship service or who is listed in a membership directory. These snapshot portraits will undoubtedly include some who would give anything not to be there—as well as excluding very many people who, in spite of their absence, are members indeed. And so theologians have often spoken of "the invisible church"—those who are the church's true members, known as such to God, whether we realize it or not.

Here, however, we need to step carefully. It would be wrong to imagine that the church is only to be understood as a purely theoretical or abstract concept, divorced from the concrete practices of the people who constitute it. This abstract conception of "the invisible church" can certainly serve a useful purpose, taking the wind out of the sails of anyone who attempts to make definitive claims about "who's in" and "who's out." We really can't make any final determinations about this question, whether by choosing *particular* communities of Christians (such as denominations) or by simply looking around the pews on a Sunday morning. The concept of "the invisible church" is a reminder that, ultimately, the church is called into being by God—and therefore transcends all our efforts to designate its contours or to draw lines in the sand. In the final analysis, we are not in charge of our life in community; *God* is in charge of it.

And yet, in our highly individualistic society, too much focus on the "invisible church" can be a hazard. We tend to assume that faith is something to be negotiated between individual human beings and their God—whatever they conceive that Being to be. Thus, as I suggested in chapter 1, we are fond of highly generic portraits of God, allowing us to carry on these individualistic relationships with the divine without having to explain, understand, or justify them. In a similar fashion, we tend to be suspicious of concrete and visible manifestations of faith, particularly when they demand that we be in close relationship to others. We may show up at church from time to time, or even quite regularly, but most of us would hesitate to allow the group of people there assembled to exert much of a claim on our lives. A commonly heard refrain in our culture is: "I don't have to go to church to be a Christian." Another is: "I go to church on Sundays, but other than that, I don't get too involved." Sometimes, these claims are merely polite ways of saying something like: "I'll be darned if I'm going to let *those* people tell me how to run my life!"

So, on the one hand, we certainly need to restrain ourselves from drawing final conclusions about the inclusion or exclusion of particular members in "the whole community of faithful people"; but on the other hand, we also need to recognize the importance of the *visible* church. We need to come into contact with other Christians on a regular basis. We need to step back from our culture's strong individualistic assumptions and accept the fact that, from its origins, the Christian faith has been a communal affair. To be a Christian is not just to hold certain beliefs, not just to enter a church building from time to time, not just to have one's name on the organization's membership list. It is, rather, to be a member of the household of God, involving oneself on a daily basis with other Christians, whose lives will be woven into one's own in thorough, and sometimes uncomfortable, ways. It may be worth reviewing some of the reasons why Christianity has always insisted on this communal aspect of faith.

First, Jesus himself did not develop a set of mutually exclusive one-on-one relationships with other people. He gathered a community around him and encouraged them to pay attention to one another—indeed, to love and to serve one another. Particularly toward the end of his earthly life, Jesus insisted that his followers take over this work. He called them to go into all the world to teach, to baptize, and to make disciples (Matt. 28:19–20); to call one another to account (Matt. 18:15); to be at peace with one another (Mark 9:50); and to love one another (John 15:12 and elsewhere). Although many members of this community were scattered at the moment of Christ's passion and death, they regrouped in the wake of the resurrection, and they continued to meet and pray together. When they were sent forth at the day of Pentecost, it seemed obvious to them that their ministry would be a communal affair based on fellowship, common prayer, and the sharing of resources (Acts 2:42–47). Paul continued to emphasize this ministry of mutual care and mutual responsibility throughout his letters (see especially Romans 12, 1 Cor. 11:17–34, and 2 Cor. 13:11). Paul's lengthy analogy, comparing the community of Christians to the human body, emphasizes that the different parts of the body need to recognize the significance of all the other parts as well, and to work together for the good of the whole (1 Cor. 12:12–27).

Second, as the Christian community reflected on the nature of the God whom they worshiped, they began to realize that their own communal life could and should reflect the communal life of God. They believed in only one God, but this God had a threefold quality which later came to be understood in trinitarian categories. Christians recognized that their own community, in which many members were held together in one body, reflected the inner life of the Triune God—whose internal relatedness did not compromise the unity of the whole. Earlier in this book, I emphasized the importance of this trinitarian understanding of God and indicated that it had a number of practical ramifications. This is clearly one of them: because of our belief that we are created in the image of the triune God, and that we are destined to fuller participation in that image, God's communal identity provides an arche-type of, and model for, our human community.

Finally, and on a more practical level, the communal nature of the Christian faith was necessitated by the realization that we are all shaped, whether we like it or not, by those with whom we spend our time. These others "form" us—morally, spiritually, and even physically. The form-ative power of community is not unique to the church; in fact, in the contemporary setting, the influence of the church pales in comparison to the formative power of those institutions and communities within which we spend most of our time: schools, shopping centers, workplaces, and the places we go for entertainment purposes (whether the sports arena, the movie theater, or just sitting in front of a television or com-municating over the Internet). Even those of us who feel that we are going through life alone are actually subject to the influence of a wide range of other people, institutions, and belief systems.

From the beginning, Christian communities had to compete with the influence of other institutions of the day—for example, the Empire, the trades, and the pagan cults. If they were to be formed in specifically Christian practices, rather than the practices of these other institutions, they would need to meet together for mutual support. Consequently, "they devoted themselves to the apostles' teaching and fellowship, to the breaking of bread and the prayers" (Acts 2:42). Individuals may of course claim the label "Christian" without such communal support and mutual upbuilding, but most will find it difficult to allow their lives to be shaped in authentically Christian ways if they never spend time around other Christians. Their lives are much more likely to be shaped by the people and the circumstances that they encounter on a day-to-day basis—most of which (in our cultural setting, at least) have no discernibly Christian character and some of which are openly hostile to Christian claims.

This concern becomes more significant as the Church seeks to pro-mote a system of beliefs and a way of life that is fundamentally differ-ent from the prevalent norms of the wider culture. The Greek word for church, *ekklesia*, is derived from the verb *kaleō* (to call), prefixed by the preposition *ek-* or *ex-* (which, like its English equivalent, means some-thing like "out" or "out of"). To be a member of the church, the *ekkle-sia*, is to be "called out" of the wider society and led into a special voca-tion that may operate with radically different assumptions from those of the wider society. The Christian will be formed in habits, practices, and beliefs that are different from those who do not follow the same vocation.

This last point is especially noteworthy in our present cultural cir-cumstances. In its earliest days, Christianity was a minority movement; within the Roman Empire, most religious practices were oriented toward the traditional pantheon of gods, and pagan religious practices were indistinguishable from the ordinary duties of a good citizen. To be a Jew or a Christian in such circumstances was to mark oneself as different: different forms of worship, different moral assumptions, and different practices of everyday life. But when Christianity became the religion of the Empire (under the emperor Constantine, in the fourth century), these "differences" began to evaporate; being a Christian was pretty much like being an ordinary citizen. Most people now believe that this had a weakening effect on Christianity, diluting it into a series of social conventions and polite practices rather than a radically different way of life. Of course, today, Christianity is no longer the religion of the empire; we live in a multifaith, multicultural world. Some people call it a post-Christian, or at least a post-Christendom culture ("Christendom" designating that period of time when the church was closely aligned with the Empire). Today, as in the earliest period of Christian history, our faith ought to set us apart from the wider culture. We should once again be able to recognize the profound significance of Paul's command: "Do not be conformed to this world, but be transformed by the renewing of your minds, so that you may discern what is the will of God—what is good and acceptable and perfect" (Rom. 12:2).

Christianity has always proclaimed the significance of visible and active participation in a wider community of Christians as a way of pursuing our calling to come *out* of the wider society and *into* a special relationship with God. Over time, many different manifestations of the church have appeared; but the purpose of this book is not to argue for or against any of these manifestations in particular. Instead, our focus is on why the church is not just a convenient tool for Christians, not just a particularly useful social structure, but something in which we "believe." Why do we say in the creed that we "believe" in the church? And what are we to make of the descriptive words that surround the word *church* as it appears in the creed—words like *holy* and *catholic* and *the communion of saints?*

First, on the question of our "belief" in the church, it will be useful to recall our discussion (in the introductory chapter of this book) about the meaning of the phrase "I believe." There, I suggested that *believing in* something meant orienting one's life toward it. To believe in God is to put our trust in God, to indicate that we understand our highest allegiance as belonging to God (rather than to some other person or institution or idea). To say "I believe in the church" is to make a similar sort of claim with regard to human communities: this is the community in which I put my trust, the community to which I owe the strongest allegiance. A claim like this can make us uncomfortable; it suggests that if the church were to make a demand on our lives that was in conflict with that offered by another community (for example, a family, clan, tribe, nation-state, or economic alliance), we should side with the church rather than the other group. This probably explains why churches so rarely make demands that pose such a conflict—they aren't that confident in the allegiance of their members! But Jesus did warn us about such possible conflicts, and made it clear where our loyalties should be. He suggested that being a Christian might put one in conflict with one's family (Matt. 10:35–38), one's race (John 8:33–59), the government (Matt. 22:17–21), and/or the prevailing economic order (John 2:13–22 and parallels). To proclaim that "I believe in the church" does not mean that we must agree with and submit to everything that the visible church claims about itself, but it does mean that we are expected to give the church a place of priority among all our commitments to various communities and groups.

We now turn to the descriptive words that surround the word *church* in the Apostles' Creed. First, the church is called "holy." This does not mean that it is perfect, nor even necessarily morally sound. Certainly, such meanings of the word "holy" have crept into our language (as in the ever-popular phrase "holier than thou"). But the word's original meaning is to be "set apart," "designated for a special purpose." Think about other things that are classified as "holy": holy water, for example. What makes it holy? Certainly not its chemistry, its physical qualities, or its ability to quench thirst and put out fires; in these aspects, it is no different from other water. It is called "holy" because it has been *set aside* for a particular purpose. Similarly, the church is called holy because it consists of a group of people who have been called to a particular vocation, a calling that sets them apart from those who have not responded to this call.

The church is "catholic," not in the sense of "Protestant vs. Catholic," but in a much broader sense of the word. It derives from the Greek word *katholikos,* which in turn comes from the prefix *kata-* (meaning, in this case, "throughout") and the word *holos,* "the whole." The church is *katholikos* because it is *universal*—spread throughout the whole world. This means that the church is not a club, not a little enclave of people sheltering themselves from the nasty, cruel world. Nor is it limited by geography, culture, or historical era; people do not have to go to a particular city or live in a particular time period to be part of the church. It includes, at least potentially, the entire created order.

In fact, many theologians have argued that the church is a more fundamental reality, more basic even than what we usually call "the world." In other words, the church is not a small space within the world where people can shelter themselves, either to escape from the world or to lord it over others. Quite the contrary: the secular world is a space within the created order that has attempted to wall itself off from God. The church's mission, over time, is to move into this space and call people into relationship with God and into unity with one another through Christ. The church, therefore, is the world's destiny. In the end, at the final consummation, the church will have expanded to encompass the whole world. In the meantime, the church is often something that the secular world tries to avoid; nevertheless, the church continues, persistently, to encourage the world to pay attention to its relationship to God. (This element of persistence may remind us of the work of the Holy Spirit, who continues to pursue us even when we turn away. It is therefore not surprising that the Holy Spirit is often closely associated with the church—the body through which the Spirit acts to perfect the relationship between God and God's creation.) The universal nature of the church's mission—its potentially universal relevance to the entire creation—is part of what we mean when we speak of the church as *catholic*.

One of my favorite metaphors for the catholicity of the church is that of *yeast*. There isn't very much of it (when compared to the other ingredients in the recipe), and when you mix it into the whole lump of dough, you can't point to a particular location and say, "it's right here." It is spread throughout the whole. And by being spread throughout the whole, it enlivens and energizes the whole; without it, the loaf (and the world) would be dull and flat and boring. The followers of Christ are spread throughout the whole world, and their "little yeast" leavens the whole batch of dough (1 Cor. 5:6).

Finally, the church cuts across all barriers that we think of as dividing people: national borders, differences of race and gender, and even the line that divides the living from the dead. This is emphasized by the creed's placement of the term "the communion of saints" immediately after the word *church*. According to the legendary account of the creation of the Apostles' Creed, one apostle (Matthew) speaks both these lines, thus emphasizing that they refer to the same reality. The word *saints*, here as in the Bible, does not refer (as it has come to refer, in modern English) to an exclusive group within the church—a "designated few" whose devotion to God and passion for following the way of Jesus Christ has made them the brightest and best of the faith. Rather, the word was historically employed simply as a synonym for "Christians," "the faithful," "the people of God." We see this use in the Bible (for several examples in close proximity, see Romans 15, Ephesians 1, or Colossians 1), and it continued into the life of the early church. But as Christianity became the religion of the Empire and being "a saint" (that is, a Christian) didn't distinguish anyone from anyone else, the word took on a more and more exclusive connotation. Eventually, it tended to designate the elite group mentioned above.

It might be more helpful—particularly in the contemporary setting, when Christianity is no longer the religion of the empire—to return to the ancient biblical usage of the word. Saints are, quite simply, Christians; thus, as the grouping of these two phrases in the Apostles' Creed suggests, the holy catholic church *is* the communion of saints. It is the whole company of faithful people, whether living, dead, or yet to be born. It includes Christians of every race, language, and tribe. If you are a Christian, you participate in the communion of saints—which means that the dividing lines between nations, races, genders, and periods of time are not nearly so significant as we are often told. As members of the communion of saints, we understand ourselves to be very closely connected to a great many people whom we've never actually seen, met, or even heard of.

Our cultural setting creates a great many obstacles to belief in "the holy catholic church, the communion of saints." We have very short memories and can hardly remember what happened just a few years ago, let alone the stories of people who lived centuries before we were born. Nor do we have much time to think about the future; all around us we are reminded of the importance of keeping current and focusing on the here and now. Moreover, we like to think of ourselves as being in charge of our own destiny, so we are unsettled by the idea that we are formed by the communities in which we live and in ways of which we may be totally unaware. We are nervous about the idea that our membership in the church sets us apart from the rest of the world; we would really rather fit in, to be seen as "normal" and "with it." If we occasionally do things to display our independence, we feel safer if a great many other people are doing the same thing. (Think about fashion statements, popular music, or sports: we may boldly claim that "this is my music" or "I wear these clothes to express my individuality," but we are comforted by the fact that so many other people are listening to exactly the same music or wearing precisely the same clothes.)

Within a cultural setting that encourages and rewards conformity, autonomy, and currency, it's not so easy to make a firm statement of belief in "the holy catholic church, the communion of saints." What we would really like to say is "I believe in my own independence, in fitting in, and in living for the moment." This is why, when I teach courses in Christian ethics and the shape of the Christian life, I encourage students to spend a good deal of time thinking about the ways that we are shaped by our individualistic culture, and about how we might map out more community-oriented ways of life—in everything from how we spend our leisure time, to how we choose our professions, to how we read the Bible. In fact, I usually begin my introductory ethics course with a novel that raises questions about our culture's devotion to individualism in all its many forms. I want my students to recognize that the traditional teachings of Christianity can remind us that the widespread appeal of conformity, autonomy, and currency is ultimately an illusion, and that the way to become most truly *ourselves* is to live in communion with others.

As I noted above, our lives are decisively shaped by the communities in which we live. We are not as autonomous as we would like to believe. This process of formation is deep and broad, so our decision simply to "conform" to the cultural pressures that surround us can have profound, unforeseen, and often unhappy consequences. And the "others" who surround us (and thereby form us) constitute a much larger group than we sometimes realize. They include not just those who are alive at the moment, but also the dead—and those who are to come. We can never escape from this process of communal formation; we can only make choices about *which* communities will have the most formative effects on our lives.

The novel that I use to illustrate these points is Barbara Kingsolver's *Animal Dreams*. It is a beautifully written, vivid tale of a woman who has attempted to escape from some of the less attractive elements of life in community, and to indulge herself fully in our culture's enthusiasm for conformity, currency, and autonomy. But she ultimately finds those ideals to offer less than they had promised. She also discovers just how thoroughly she has been formed by the community in which she grew up—across the boundaries of race, gender, national origin, and even across the boundary between the living and the dead.

* * * * *

*Animal Dreams* is narrated by Codi Noline, the elder daughter of the only medical doctor in the small town of Grace, Arizona. She has been away from that town for more than a decade, and she had not been sorry to leave. The town is small and isolated; the population is inbred, and everyone knows everyone else's business; and her childhood memories are dominated by her stoic and disciplined father, who was determined that his girls were going to be different from everyone else. As the story opens, she is coming home to Grace—without any enthusiasm, and perhaps only because she had no alternative: her father has Alzheimer's, and she needs to see to his care. She has taken a one-year post as a biology teacher at the local high school. Her training, like her father's, was actually in medicine; but she never became a doctor because, according to her own self-description, she didn't have the requisite level of nerve.

But what *really* unnerves Codi is her return to Grace. She has lived more than half of her life here, but she has only hazy memories of the place; it seems very far away, even when she is in the midst of it. Everyone seems to know and remember her, but she doesn't remember most of them. Whether these memories have been actively repressed or simply left out to spoil is ultimately less important than the *nature* of the missing memories: they are often about happy occasions, moments of triumph, and events and causes that, as a child, she had led, fueled, or accomplished. She seems unwilling or unable to associate these positive aspects of her own past experience with her childhood in Grace.

Eventually we come to see one of the reasons that Codi cannot recall the most triumphant moments of her own childhood: she has so negatively evaluated her father's method of upbringing that she can't believe it could have led to anything good. Her mother died when she was very young, so all the bad memories of her childhood land squarely on the shoulders of her father. On the other hand, she seems to have a very good memory for his faults—his attempt to isolate their family from others in the community, his failure to provide them with even a small portion of the outward affection that other parents lavished on their children, and even his obsessive efforts to put his daughters into orthopedic shoes so that their feet would not suffer permanent damage from the fashionable footwear of the day. Thinking back on all this is especially painful for Codi, because she never really knew the reason why her father insisted on this separation and reserve and difference. But as the story unfolds, she begins to learn the reasons; and as she does, her perspective on her childhood changes. Her memory has been very selective; she has remembered the worst of it, but has forgotten the best of it. Slowly, she begins to realize just how much she was loved and cared for in this place—just how formative it was of her character, and how much more positively so than she had ever imagined.

The story is told through Codi's eyes, except for a few brief interspersed chapters in which her father, Doc Homer, becomes the narrator. Through these windows into his thoughts, we see him recalling the pain he has felt and the difficulties he encountered while raising Codi and her sister, Hallie, by himself. As he narrates the events, his own decisions seem to him (and indeed, sometimes to us) to be sound and sensible—what all parents should do, if only they could find the nerve to stand up to their own children. Eventually, that opinion is corroborated by others in the town—including Uda Dell, a women who often cared for Codi when she was small:

> "He just wanted awful bad for you kids to be good girls," she said. "It's hard for a man by himself, honey. You don't know how hard. He worried himself to death. A lot of people, you know, would just let their kids run

ever which way. . . . One year for Christmas I gave the two of you little cowboy outfits, with guns, and you just loved them, but he had to take away the guns. He didn't want you killing, even pretend. I felt awful that I'd done that, once I thought about it. He was right" (p. 281).

In a series of heart-wrenching vignettes, Homer remembers his efforts to show them his love—rational and unemotional efforts that were (it now seems) ultimately unsuccessful. His memories flash backwards and forwards, getting tangled with the images of his grown-up daughters, and with his patients who might well be his daughters. We watch Doc Homer losing his grasp on his own memory even as, in the longer chapters, we see Codi finally gaining hold of hers.

Several intertwined plotlines propel the novel forward. In addition to Codi's efforts to regain the memory of her own past, we also see her falling in love with Loyd Peregrina, a Native American whom she knew in high school and who teaches her about the land, the need for a home, and the dreams of animals. Codi's high school biology class discovers that the water in the local river is biologically dead; this leads to a complicated and ultimately successful protest against the local mining company that has been polluting the river. Codi's sister is in Nicaragua, doing relief work in a dangerous place; the two sisters are separated for the first time, forcing Codi to find her own identity. These elements of the plot are woven together into a rich, multilayered tapestry; and they provide a background for Codi's growing doubts about the faith that she has placed in our culture's devotion to conformity, autonomy, and currency. She had always assumed that these were the ingredients of a good life, but she discovers that people can live into their full humanity only within a community of mutual care.

Codi had always recognized that life without a community was deficient. After she left Grace, she had had a string of lovers, none of whom had seemed to mean much to her (though she did stay with one for ten years); she had also ventured all over the world, looking for something that would feel like home. Now, back in Grace and living alone, she finds it difficult to get to sleep at night without someone next to her in bed. Nor does she feel at home here.

> I'd spent my whole childhood as an outsider to Grace. . . . I'd led such an adventurous life, geographically speaking, that people mistook me for an adventurer. They had no idea. I'd sell my soul and all my traveling shoes to *belong* some place. . . . What I failed at was the activity people call "nesting." For me, it never seemed like nesting season had arrived yet. Or I wasn't that kind of bird (pp. 30, 77).

Until now, her need to "belong some place" had been partially satisfied by a huge part of *home* that Codi has always had with her: her sister Hallie, with whom she is incredibly close. From their early days they formed a united front against their father's punishing antiseptics and orthopedic shoes. They had almost always lived together, or at least in close proximity. "Hallie and I were so attached, like keenly mismatched Siamese twins conjoined at the back of the mind. We parted again and again, and still each time it felt like a medical risk, as if we were being liberated at some terrible cost: the price of a shared organ. We never stopped feeling that knife" (p. 8).

But now Hallie has gone very far away indeed: to Nicaragua, attempting to repair some of the damage that was being done on a daily basis by the U.S.-funded Contra mercenaries, and turning her skills as a plant specialist into bread for the masses. The letters between the two sisters form an important part of the moral nerve center of the novel; but Hallie's absence also means that, for the first time, Codi is really and truly on her own. As a result, all the tiny signs of the love and care that people give one another in this small community are almost too painful for Codi to behold. She can even see it on the shelves of the town grocery store:

> I stood looking helplessly at the cans of vegetables and soup that all carried some secret mission. The grocery shelves seemed to have been stocked for the people of Grace with the care of a family fallout shelter. I was an outsider to this nurturing. When the cashier asked, "Do you need anything else?" I almost cried. I wanted to say, "I need everything you have" (pp. 46–47).

Shortly thereafter, she feels intensely alone even in the midst of a party, where the close-knit family life only serves to remind her of what she believes she never had: "The party seemed like something underwater, a lost continent, and I felt profoundly sad though it wasn't my continent" (p. 64).

Of course, in the midst of all these warm and fuzzy feelings about life in community, Codi doesn't think about the other side of the story: the fact that identifying oneself with a particular community means separating oneself from certain other possible identities. Part of the reason that she doesn't "belong" in Grace is that she has always disliked so much of what it is: a tiny, tightly-knit community where the outside world is held at bay, where no one has any privacy, and where every deviation from the standard way of doing things is noticed and remarked upon. Her father had insisted on certain practices that separated them from the rest of the community, and this had caused a considerable amount of pain; but in her more reflective moments, she knows that many of Doc Homer's parenting practices really were good for her in the end. ("I will say this much for Doc Homer's career as a father: my arches are faultless" [p. 90].) But the conformity that Codi had longed for as a child, and embraced as soon as she left, had not managed to electrify her life. Meanwhile, the "cheerleader and clandestine smoker" who had been popular in high school "now smoked openly, had a raspy cough, and looked like a cartwheel was out of the question" (p. 60).

The close-knit community of Grace has also had to give up the cultural enthusiasm for autonomy. The town's clothing store and beauty parlor don't allow much space for personal expression, and privacy is very difficult to come by. Everyone in town has opinions about Codi's presence in the community, and most of these opinions circulate back to her in one form or another. In a phone conversation with a pregnant high school student who has had to drop out, Codi says, "I'm not used to living where everybody's into everybody else's business." The student responds,

> "It's the bottom level, isn't it? My mom found out I was pregnant from a lady that works at the bank. Mom goes, 'What is the date today?' and the lady goes 'The fourteenth. Your daughter will be due around Valentine's Day, won't she? I had a baby on Valentine's Day.'" Rita paused for my opinion.
> "Yeah," I said. "It's the bottom level" (pp. 151–52).

A community need not be mired in voyeurism and eavesdropping; but if we take its demands seriously, this can mean that we have to change our societally formed expectations about what kind of information remains private and what is expected to be shared with others. We cannot expect to be "laws unto ourselves" (the root meaning of the word *autonomous*); we have to expect to be held responsible to certain standards by others.

Nor can a community endure by forgetting its past in order to "keep current" in every possible way. In fact, one of the things that worries many of town's inhabitants is that satellite television will eventually destroy the community. By beaming in messages from the outside world, marketers are able to remind people of what they don't have—of their failure to keep up-to-date with the latest consumer products and fashion trends. This in turn leads to less time and interest in the traditions that have kept the community alive through thick and thin. Children are no longer speaking Spanish with their grandparents, and are refusing to wear hand-me-downs because they don't match the current fashion. Perhaps some children no longer know the town's founding myth about the nine blue-eyed Gracela sisters who agreed to come over from Spain to marry nine lucky goldminers, as long as they could bring their pet peacocks with them. ("Their legacy in Gracela Canyon was a population of blue-eyed, dark-haired descendants and a thousand wild peacocks" [p. 14].) Interestingly enough, Codi—despite her feelings of being a stranger in her own hometown—knew the story well enough as a child to take an imaginative leap into it: "I once insisted, to the point of tears, that I remembered being on the ship with the nine Gracela sisters and their peacocks" (p. 48). But the community's ability to engage in this kind of imaginative rapport with the past was precisely what Codi was trying to get away from when she left Grace.

Holding a community together means admitting that the goals of conformity, autonomy, and currency are not the highest of all possible goals, and that can be difficult in a culture that so admires these goals. Fortunately, however, the town of Grace, Arizona, seems to have enough resources to fight back against the encroachments of the individualism that have so besieged our culture. Here, I want to mention three such resources, noting their parallels to the resources that the church uses in its struggle against that same individualism. The community of Grace, like the church, is held together through time, first, by lifting up the significance of everyday work; second, by caring for those in need; and third, by developing community rituals that highlight the continuities from the past, into the present, and onward toward the future.

Almost as soon as she returns to Grace, Codi sees people who take the everyday work of their lives with great seriousness, lifting it up into a realm of extraordinary significance. Many of the men in the town now work on the railroad, which is, certainly, "just a job" and helps to pay the bills. But home life is different: whether it's the pruning of the pecan trees in the orchard, the butchering of chickens for Sunday dinner, or baking bread for a visiting son and his girlfriend—all of these activities take on a significance above and beyond their status as "daily work." They are part of what keeps the household alive: feeding the family, welcoming guests, and carrying on the trades and traditions of one's forebears.

Perhaps the best example of this kind of work in *Animal Dreams* is offered by the group of women who get together on a regular basis to embroider cloth and do other handicrafts—and to talk about the state of the town. They are actively concerned with the preservation of the community—even in the face of threats that have led most of the men of the town to give up. Their manual labor of embroidery gives them a particular focus and provides another way in which the life of the home is beautified and enriched. But this manual labor also provides the context for some fairly profound thought about what will be necessary to make the community grow and thrive. In the end, it takes a slightly eccentric scheme devised by these local matriarchs to attract media attention to the town's pollution problem, eventually leading toward its resolution.

Somehow, the residents of Grace are able to think of these activities of home and hearth not merely as chores to be checked off a "to-do" list, but as community-building activities that knit people to one another. As such, they provide something of a bulwark against a culture that tempts us to do whatever suits our fancy. The church has a similar role for Christians: it sanctifies particular forms of work as having far greater significance than the casual observer might expect. Altar guilds, musical ensembles, kitchen clean-up crews, people who shovel snow from the sidewalks—all are, at one level, just doing a job that needs to be done. But this work is necessary in order for the community to survive and to thrive; and the work is most meaningful when it is oriented toward a common purpose, toward the common good of the whole. This places it in a different category, giving it meaning well beyond the immediate effect of the work itself.

A second set of practices that make community possible are acts of mercy and mutual support. Soon after her return to Grace, Codi realizes that the women of the town have been caring for her father out of sheer gratitude that a doctor has been willing to stay in this remote town and serve it for so many years. They have been filling his refrigerator with baked goods and prepared meals, thereby offering their thanks through a form of payment in which they are particularly rich. In a similar vein, people host community gatherings in which hospitality and nourishment are in superabundance ("enough food to save an African nation," Codi remarks to herself at one such event [p. 62]). It's not so much that people *make an effort* to help one another; it's simply *habituated* in them, something they do without even thinking about it. They have been *formed* to care for one another. Codi has the habit as well, but it takes her a while to recognize it. When she quickly acts to save a baby who is choking at a restaurant, she tries to slough it off as "no big deal." But everyone who witnessed the event knows better; and when she thinks it over, Codi does too: "I kept turning my mind away from the one thought that kept coming back to me, persistent as an unwanted lover's hand, that I'd saved a life" (p. 117). Soon she is rallying her biology class to informing people of the condition of the river, teaching them respect for human life, and discovering that she is an excellent teacher.

But not until near the book's end does Codi discover how she developed these habits of care. For one thing, her own upbringing had helped her see that the societal ideals of conformity, currency, and autonomy were not quite as valuable as was often claimed. This was not just a result of her father's willingness to stay in this small town when he could easily have gone off to a more lucrative practice elsewhere. Her formation was strongly affected by the fact that, when her mother died, everyone in town had done their part to help parent the girls. They were not isolated and abandoned by the community, as Codi seems to have convinced herself. The nickname that they were given by the local matriarchs—*huérfanas* (orphans)—was not a term of sympathy for the abandoned, but a term of endearment for those whom they had themselves adopted. The girls had been cared for by "Fifty Mothers," as one chapter title puts it, and they were as much a part of the larger community as any other child:

> Several women had things they claimed we'd left in their houses when we played there as children. A doll . . . a largish plastic horse . . . Also a pink sweater, size 6X. Mrs. Muñez swore it was Hallie's. "It was behind the refrigerator. . . . She used to set up there on top of the refrigerator, because I told her she couldn't drink beer till she was as tall as her daddy." . . . Doña Althea clumped forward with her cane and set down a miniature, perfectly made peacock piñata. . . . She said, "I made one like this for both of you girls, for your *cumpleaños* when you were ten."
>
> To my surprise, this was also true. I remembered every toy, every birthday party, each one of these fifty mothers who'd been standing at the edges of my childhood, ready to make whatever contribution was needed at the time (pp. 327–28).

It may have become a cliché by the time Kingsolver's book was widely read, but it still needs to be held up as a truth: it takes a village to raise a child. Such practices of mutual care are what make a community thrive.

A final set of practices that strengthen the community are the rituals that help it link together its past, present, and future. Particularly important among such rituals are those that help to blur the easy line of demarcation that we often draw between the living and the dead. The town of Grace celebrates the Day of the Dead, a Latin American feast day with roots in both Christianity and Native American traditions. It is celebrated on All Soul's Day (November 2), and it involves the lavish decoration of cemeteries and the building of shrines to the dead (including offerings of food). It is not mournful or solemn, but thoroughly celebratory; children laugh and run and sing among the graves, begging the remains of the sweets set out for long-dead ancestors. And flowers everywhere—particularly marigolds, *cempazuchiles*, the flowers of the dead:

> Some graves had shrines with niches peopled by saints; others had the initials of loved ones spelled out on the mound in white stones. The uni-

fying principle was that the simplest thing was done with the greatest care. It was a comfort to see this attention lavished on the dead. In these families you would never stop being loved (p. 163).

At the Day of the Dead, Codi learns how our communities stay with us all through our lives, and even beyond our lives. In fact, even before she has begun to recover the memories of her own childhood, she realizes that this celebration had been part of her past as well—though she doesn't yet realize how thoroughly it has formed her. "I remembered playing Dutchman's tag with them at the graveyard on All Souls' Days— it was always a huge family picnic up there" (p. 59). Eventually, among the graves, she finds a very specific clue to her own past.

Codi is also reminded of the continuities between the living and the dead by her friend Loyd, the Native American man with whom she had had a brief relationship in high school. He takes her to see the kinishba, which he describes as "prehistoric condos." The 800-year-old buildings are made of carefully set stone, without mortar, and consist of more than two hundred rooms under a single roof. Codi moved from room to room:

> I tried to imagine the place populated: stepping from room to room over sleeping couples, listening through all the noises of cooking and scolding and washing up for the sound of your own kids, who would know secret short cuts to their friends' apartments.
> "The walls are thick," I observed.
> "The walls are graveyards. When a baby died, they'd mortar its bones right into the wall. Or under the floor."
> I shuddered. "Why?"
> "So it would still be near the family," he said, seeming surprised I hadn't thought of this myself (p. 128).

These practices remind us that the dead do not cease to be human persons; they just enter into a different phase of their personhood. They remain a part of our lives, transcending the boundaries of time and space, and even the boundary of death. (We will return to Christian attitudes toward the dead in chapter 11.)

This consciousness of the dead is just one of the many elements that help keep human communities together. So many aspects of our day-to-day life remind us of the sheer transience of human life, which tends to reinforce our assumption that we are all, ultimately, on our own. If the community is to stay together and maintain its identity, its members need to understand their identities as transcending time and space. This is why, for Christians, those who have gone before us are no less a part of the church than are those who are alive today. We are knit together with them in a beautiful tapestry, filled with a great variety of different colors and textures, but woven into a seamless whole. And so we are called to set aside our strong urges toward individualism, for in our heart of hearts, we know that a single isolated thread simply cannot compare to the beauty of that great tapestry. We are called to believe in the church, which is the communion of saints; and we are called to live in relationship with one another in a spirit of mutual interdependence and love.

## Questions For Discussion

1. Describe some of the features of our culture that strike you as promoting conformity, currency, and autonomy. What makes these features so influential?

2. What are some of the ways that we are formed in our moral and imaginative lives by institutions and associations other than the church? Why are these formative influences so powerful?

3. Have you ever experienced an occasion when your allegiance to the church came into conflict with a commitment that you had made to another community or group? If so, how did you go about resolving it?

4. What specific Christian practices help us to draw lines of continuity from our past, through our present, and toward our future? Think about not only rituals and other church practices but also about the practices of our everyday lives.

5. Identify some other practices, in addition to those named in this chapter, through which communities (such as the church) form the lives of their members.

## For Further Reading

Cavanaugh, William T. *Torture and Eucharist: Politics, Theology and the Body of Christ.* Challenges in Contemporary Theology. Oxford: Blackwell Publishers, 1998. (Advanced)

Clapp, Rodney. *A Peculiar People: The Church as Culture in a Post-Christian Society.* Downers Grove: InterVarsity Press, 1996. (Introductory)

Dulles, Avery. *Models of the Church.* Garden City, N.Y.: Doubleday, 1974. (Introductory/Advanced)

Harvey, Barry A. *Another City: An Ecclesiological Primer for a Post-Christian World.* Harrisburg, Pa.: Trinity Press International, 1999. (Advanced)

Hauerwas, Stanley. *After Christendom? How the Church Is to Behave If Freedom, Justice, and a Christian Nation Are Bad Ideas.* Nashville: Abingdon Press, 1991. (Introductory)

Hinson, E. Glenn, ed. *Understandings of the Church.* Sources of Early Christian Thought, ed. William G. Rusch. Philadelphia: Fortress Press, 1986. (Advanced)

Kenneson, Philip D. *Beyond Sectarianism: Re-imagining Church and World.* Philadelphia: Trinity Press International, 1999. (Introductory/Advanced)

Russell, Letty M. *Church in the Round: Feminist Interpretation of the Church.* Louisville: Westminster/John Knox Press, 1993. (Introductory/Advanced)

## Other Works on "The Church, The Communion of Saints"

Richard Adams, *Watership Down*
Robert Bolt, *A Man for All Seasons*
Charles Dickens, *A Tale of Two Cities*
Umberto Eco, *The Name of the Rose*
T. S. Eliot, *Murder in the Cathedral*
Louise Erdrich, *Love Medicine*
Garrison Keillor, *Lake Wobegon Days*
Arthur Miller, *All My Sons; The Crucible*
Harriet Beecher Stowe, *Uncle Tom's Cabin*

# ten

# "The Forgiveness of Sins"

In the previous chapter, concerning our belief in the church, we began to draw out some very practical consequences of Christian belief for how we live our day-to-day lives. Specifically, we are called to live lives in communion rather than in isolation, and we are called to participate in practices that can help form us as a communal people, supporting one another and holding each other accountable for our actions. This turn toward specific ethical claims continues in the present chapter; in fact, we now examine the one phrase in the Apostles' Creed that implies a specific ethical claim, in the form "we believe that, in their day-to-day lives, Christians should _____." One could also claim, of course, that our belief in Jesus as the Christ implies an acceptance of his ethical teachings such as loving one's neighbor. Yet even this simple claim would raise a great many theological questions and spark some disagreements. To what degree are we called to imitate Jesus? What counts as an act of love toward one's neighbor? These would be matters for debate and discussion.

In only one phrase of the Apostles' Creed is a specific human behavior raised to the same level as the other elements of our faith (in God, in Christ, in the Spirit, in the church)—and it's not the one that most people would expect. Try asking a few fellow Christians this question: What's the *one* action of human beings, toward one another, that has historically been considered *just as central* to the faith as is our belief in God? That we should love one another? That we should obey the Ten Commandments? That we should proclaim the gospel to those who have not heard it? No, none of these. The creed's one explicit statement about human behavior is that we should *forgive* one another. Christians believe in the forgiveness of sins.

Not that forgiveness is only about *human* behavior. Its root, its ultimate source, is in God's forgiveness of us; we forgive others as we ask for and receive forgiveness from God. In the Bible, story after story

183

reminds us of the pervasive nature of this forgiveness: God's forgiveness and protection of those who are chosen but who stray from the path (Adam and Eve, Cain, David); the divine counsel that we be forgiving, and the divine approval of those who are (Joseph and his brothers, Job, Jonah); Jesus urging others to forgive, and forgiving his own enemies, even at his death; and his many parables of forgiveness, offering examples both positive (the prodigal son, Luke 15:11–32) and negative (the unforgiving servant, Matt. 18:23–35). So frequent and consistent is the theme that the earliest Christians recognized "the forgiveness of sins" to be one of the fundamental aspects of their faith.

Deeply embedded in our claim about the centrality of forgiveness is another, somewhat more complicated belief: the belief that human beings are sinful, that they are capable of doing wrong, and that they therefore stand *in need of* forgiveness. This is not to say that human beings are inherently wicked or that we should expect that they will do evil deeds. It means that they are free but limited creatures: they have free will and can make their own choices, but they often do so on the basis of imperfect knowledge (for example, of the future), and they sometimes attempt to extend the range of their freedom well beyond their own bodily limitations. (We are, for example, "free" to drink alcohol to excess, but our bodily limitations may lead to certain results that are physically painful, emotionally scarring, or even fatal.) One of the obvious implications of being free but limited is that we are very likely to make mistakes—sometimes out of ignorance or an inability to see into the future, and sometimes out of sheer malice. When we combine our ability to make mistakes with our ability to focus on our own self-interest at the expense of others, we quickly learn that we are capable of extraordinary wickedness. One only need read the newspaper headlines to know just how many horrific ways human beings have discovered for using their freedom for their own self-promotion, regardless of how much injury they thereby inflict—on other people, on the whole created order, and on God.

Toward the end of the last century, the concept of "sin" began to get a bad reputation; it was deemed too negative, too pessimistic a view of human nature. A heavy emphasis on sin, and on the guilt that is often produced by human sinfulness, was thought to be a distraction from Jesus' message of love. But what the detractors of the concept of sin failed to realize was that, without it, the core claims of Christianity made no sense—including its central message of redemption, its emphasis on forgiveness, and its ethical injunctions. All these grew out of a belief that human beings are capable of doing quite nasty things to one another, and that they bear some responsibility for this, even when it results from an error in the calculations or even a simple lack of adequate information. By sidelining the concept of sin, we were also sidelining the concept of responsibility for our misdeeds—so much so, that almost any accusation of bad behavior these days is responded to with an attempt to assign the blame elsewhere. In his introduction to a recording by *The Hopeful Gospel Quartet*, Garrison Keillor pokes gentle fun at this common response:

> We want to sing you some Gospel music tonight, because some of you look as if you could use it. This is music that says that God loves us, and we live in a universe of love; and yet we're capable of doing *rotten* things. And not all of these things are the result of poor communication. Some of them are the result of *rottenness!* People do bad, horrible, things. And they cheat and they lie, and they corrupt the government, and they poison the world around us. And then when they're caught, they don't feel remorse—they just go into treatment! They had a *nutritional* problem or something. They *explain* what they did; they don't feel *bad* about it. There's no guilt, there's just psychology. That's why we need Gospel music. Guilt is a gift that keeps on giving! And it's all that holds some people in line.

By sidelining the concepts of sin, guilt, and responsibility, we have done away with the idea of forgiveness: if no one has really done anything wrong, why would anyone need to be forgiven?

Of course, some people have not been so willing to abandon the concepts of sin and guilt. But at the other end of the spectrum, another misunderstanding of the Christian message has grown in popularity over the past few decades: the idea that "Christians expect people to be perfect" or "Christians always condemn people for making mistakes." Admittedly, such expectations of "perfect" or "error-free" human behavior have been part of certain strands of Christianity through its history, and particularly a part of certain blends of Christianity and the politics of Empire, such as the so-called "religious right." But please note: these perfectionistic expectations are *not* part of the Apostles' Creed or of any other common creed of the Christian faith. They are, rather, a result of the (often extremely judgmental) statements and actions of certain individuals claiming to speak in the name of Christ. I would argue, however, that if these judgmental statements do not carry with them the central message of the forgiveness of sins, they misrepresent Christianity to an extraordinary degree—for Christians believe in the forgiveness of sins.

The Christian belief in forgiveness is subject to a number of significant misconceptions. I want to examine three of the most common of these in the paragraphs that follow. Briefly, they are: first, the assumption that forgiveness is a one-way activity; second, that forgiveness demonstrates a weakness of character or an inadequate concept of justice; and finally, that forgiveness encourages bad behavior by not holding people to account for their actions. I will address each of these assumptions in turn.

One of the most common misunderstandings of forgiveness is that it is a one-way activity—the burden falls on the person who has been hurt to offer forgiveness. But forgiveness is meaningless if it is offered to someone who doesn't want it or does not see the need for it. Its whole purpose is to bring about reconciliation, to mend the breach that has opened up between two human beings. The completion of the process of forgiveness requires not only a willingness to forgive others but also a recognition on the part of the wrongdoer that a wrong has been done, and a sincere desire on the part of that person to *receive* forgiveness.

Second, forgiveness is sometimes associated with weakness of character—"if you forgive them, you're just letting them walk all over you" or "forgiveness makes it looks like you approve of their actions." Statements such as these are a reminder of how thoroughly we have been shaped by our criminal justice system, which metes out punishment as a deterrent and as a form of retribution against those who have done wrongful deeds. We think that forgiveness implies a tacit approval of the misdeed or a willingness to pretend that it never happened. True forgiveness does no such thing; in fact, the act of asking for forgiveness, and the granting of it, is a clear acknowledgment by *both* parties that a wrong has been done and that reconciliation needs to take place. Perhaps the reason that we imagine forgiveness to be a "weak" response is due to the first misconception: if we think of it as a one-way dispensation, given to the wrongdoer by the victim, then it does indeed appear weak, and sets aside the demand for justice. But if it is true forgiveness, in which wrongdoing is admitted and understood as such, the forgiveness and reconciliation are the only possible paths to true healing.

Finally, forgiveness is sometimes thought to encourage bad behavior by suggesting to potential perpetrators that their wicked deeds will be overlooked or set aside. I would suggest that this could only be true if forgiveness were the *only* thing being taught—that is, if we simply told people that they are free to do any awful thing they'd like, as long as they ask for forgiveness after doing it. But the Christian faith says no such thing. It teaches us a great deal about what kinds of behaviors are good and right, and what are not; it teaches us what a good human life should look like, and what it means to live in response to God's grace. Christian claims about forgiveness do not in any way dilute these teachings.

Perhaps all three of these misconceptions are fueled by the common practice of setting aside the minor slights that we receive by saying "don't worry about it" or "forget it, it's nothing." We sometimes describe such phrases as "forgiveness," but this is something of a misnomer. If some-one bumps into me while I'm carrying a lunch tray, and my lunch spills all over the floor and makes an enormous mess, my reaction will depend on my guesses and intuition about why the collision occurred. If I believe that it was unintentional (or, less likely, necessary—perhaps to avoid something worse), then I really will be willing to say "it's nothing." No real misdeed has been committed; no one has sinned. It was just a mat-ter of two physical objects trying to be in the same place at the same time. The laws of physics take over, and the result is "just an accident." But if the person *deliberately* caused my tray to tumble—out of hostil-ity, revenge, or as a practical joke—then it would be wrong for me to say, "never mind, it's nothing." In this second case, there would have been an actual misdeed committed, and one for which the perpetrator would need to accept responsibility. I should be *willing* to forgive, but the act of forgiveness is not complete unless the wrongdoer admits guilt and is genuinely sorry for the act.

In fact, if I were on the receiving end of an intentional act of cruelty such as this one, the other two options that are open to me would dem-onstrate much weaker character. I could strike back in some way; this is, in some sense, the "expected" response in our culture, but experience teaches us that it is counterproductive. Each vengeful action is met with an equal (or greater) and opposite reaction, and the situation escalates into all-out war. Moreover, the response of revenge runs directly counter to what Jesus and the entire Christian tradition teaches us to do when we are wronged (Matt. 5:38–48; Luke 23:34; Rom. 12:12–21; Eph. 4:32). Despite our culture's approval of "striking back" against an enemy, this is precisely the response that Christians must avoid.

On the other hand, I could respond by acting as though nothing had happened, or I might say something like "don't worry about it, never mind." But if I do this, I will simply encourage the other person's bad behavior, and I will probably harbor secret resentments against that person because of this uncharitable act. This is why Jesus teaches us not to ignore bad behavior, nor to strike back against it, but to work toward reconciliation and forgiveness. To be willing to offer forgiveness when it is asked for is to conform to the kind of character to which Jesus calls us.

The examples that I have used so far are, in some sense, "easy" ones; they are small acts of unkindness and meanness. If the offender admits wrongdoing and asks for forgiveness, we find ourselves relatively will-ing to offer it in such circumstances. But what about the more difficult cases? What about someone who has committed a grievous wrong against us—a slanderous lie that ruined a career, an act of arson that destroyed one's home, or the rape or murder of a loved one? We know that we would have a much more difficult time offering forgiveness in such cases, no matter how much contrition was shown by the perpetrator. Precisely because of their difficulty, these are the cases that we need to examine. This is why I have chosen Sister Helen Prejean's book *Dead Man Walking* to develop this chapter's discussion of the forgiveness of sins.

*  *  *  *  *

The accumulation of arguments in *Dead Man Walking*, when taken together, present one of the most compelling cases against capital punishment that I have ever read. The book is all the more powerful for having been written from a specifically Christian point of view. Even though it is thoroughly comprehensible to those outside that tradition, it will be most meaningful to Christians, who simply cannot avoid the biblical and theological arguments that Prejean offers. But for the purposes of this chapter, my interest in her book concerns what it has to say about the idea of forgiveness.

In this respect, the book is useful in a number of ways. First, it concentrates on the most difficult case of forgiveness: Is it possible to forgive someone who has taken the life of a loved one? If we can create a space in which such forgiveness might be possible, then other moments of forgiveness will seem easy by comparison. Second, it demonstrates that the kinds of books that can be helpful in thinking through the questions of Christian belief need not be limited to the novels and short stories that we have examined thus far. A nonfiction narrative can work in the same way; it can present us with real characters, human beings whom we can get to know and come to understand. In fact, the book itself suggests that our ability to forgive another human being may have a great deal to do with whether we can come to see that person as truly human—capable of doing right as well as wrong, capable of asking for forgiveness and offering it as well. Finally, it regularly reminds us of the two-way nature of forgiveness: it is not just about the offering of forgiveness by the victims (and on their behalf); it is also about helping perpetrators to accept responsibility for their misdeeds and to recognize their need to ask for and receive forgiveness. As such, the book helps to overcome the common misconceptions that I discussed above, and offers a new path toward reconciliation and true justice.

*Dead Man Walking* tells the story of Sister Helen Prejean's involvement with two death-row inmates who were eventually executed by electrocution at the state prison at Angola, Louisiana. It begins as a simple correspondence, but it leads to face-to-face visits, a great deal of self-education about the criminal justice system and the death penalty, and finally, a decision to serve as spiritual advisor to the condemned men, which involves counseling them right up to the moment of their deaths. Because of her lengthy conversations with these men, she gets to know them; and while she remains horrified by their crimes, she is able to recognize them as human beings. She is also able to help them to understand the importance of forgiveness—of recognizing their need for it and asking for it. Of course, this also means that they must come to acknowledge and take responsibility for their crimes.

In addition, the book has been made into an excellent film of the same title, adapted and directed by Tim Robbins and starring Susan Sarandon (for which she won an Academy Award for best actress) and Sean Penn. Of course, any film treatment of a full-length book involves the creation of composite characters and some rearrangement of the details. As always, I recommend that people read the book first, then see the film; but for those who have already seen the film, it's still worthwhile to go back and read the book, which provides a much more detailed account of the events—as well as addressing a number of issues that the film omits.

Most important, the book is about *two different* death-row inmates who were counseled by Sister Helen—Elmo Patrick Sonnier and Robert Lee Willie. A certain amount of the book's power and persuasiveness comes from the author's careful nuancing of the differences between the two men—one is clearly guilty, full of bravado, and has neo-Nazi sympathies; the other, who seems not to have actually committed the murder (though he clearly was an accomplice), is much quieter and more reserved, and, largely because of the work that Sister Helen has done with him on death row, he does actually ask for forgiveness in the end. In the film, these two men are merged into a single man, Matthew Poncelet, who has some of the characteristics of both criminals. This was wholly appropriate for reasons of the economy of characters in the film version, but again, the book has more to offer in its differentiation of the two.

Of course, the film necessarily excludes a great many of the book's detailed criticisms of the criminal justice system and the disparities related to capital punishment in particular, and some of the edge is taken off by the fact that the film documents an execution by lethal injection (as is now the case in Louisiana) rather than the much more horrifying electric chair (as was the case with the actual men whom Sister Helen counseled). In his directorial commentary on the film, Tim Robbins offers a very wise justification of this change: he didn't want viewers to assume that the only thing morally troublesome about the death penalty was that the means of execution seemed barbaric. He wanted to show that even the most "humane" form of killing a convicted criminal could raise serious ethical questions.

Part of the power of both the book and the film is that they are not just about the humanity of the condemned criminals; they are also about the humanity of their victims, and of the families of their victims. When Sister Helen appeared at the pardon board hearing for the first death-row inmate whom she counseled, she was accosted by Lloyd LeBlanc, the father of one of murder victims (the approximately equivalent character in the film is called Earl Delacroix). He asks Sister Helen how she could spend all her time and energy with the criminal, and stand up for his rights, when she had not even come to visit the families of his victims. She reveals that she had not done so because she couldn't imagine that they would want to see her, but she now realizes the importance of this step. In the minds of the victims' families, she was "taking sides" with the murderer and against the murdered, whereas in her own mind, she was attempting to see the true humanity of all the people involved, and working toward forgiveness and reconciliation. She decided at that point that visiting with the families of the victims would need to be an essential part of her ministry, and Lloyd LeBlanc eventually comes to teach *her* something about the depths of forgiveness.

The parents of Loretta Bourque, the other of Sonnier's victims, are much less direct with Sister Helen but equally repulsed by her work with the murderer. Still more hostile is the stepfather of Faith Hathaway, the victim of another death-row inmate that Sister Helen eventually befriends. (In the film, the two female victims are merged into one, who is called Hope Percy). The stepfather, Vernon Harvey (Clyde Percy in the film), has been an outspoken advocate of capital punishment, relishing the upcoming execution and saying that "he can't wait to see Robert Willie 'fry,' that he can't wait to see the 'smoke fly off his body'" (p. 118). Sister Helen finds it very difficult to visit him and to explain to him why she is counseling the murderer of his stepdaughter. But this is her second death-row case, and she has learned that she must always involve the families of the victims from the very outset. Her ongoing arguments with Vernon Harvey help prevent the book from becoming a one-sided diatribe about capital punishment. Because both of them are Christians, they have to face their very different interpretations of the gospel, and must come to some conclusion about how to best respond to horrific acts of depravity.

One of the glories of the book is its exposure of the radical misperceptions about the Christian faith that have become so much a part of our culture. This is a faith in which the most explicit claim we make about how we should treat one another is that we should forgive sins; but this is not the public image of Christianity. We see this first in the book when the first of Sister Helen's charges, Pat Sonnier, expresses surprise at the return address on the letter that he received from her:

> Sister Helen? A nun? He didn't like the nuns who had taught him catechism in grade school. Plenty of hits with a ruler on young hands and knuckles.
> The fierce irony makes me smile.
> "Who is God?"
> *Whack, whack, whack.*
> "God is love. Remember that." *Whack, whack. . . .*
> He asks, "Can we just talk to each other in regular words?" He had a spiritual adviser who had spoken to him in "scriptures" from the Bible. He couldn't hold up his end of the conversation and the relationship soon ended.
> Sure, we can just talk regular, I tell him. It's the only way I know how to talk (pp. 12–13).

The first barrier that she must break down is the one that has been thrown up, not by radical enemies of the faith, but by other *Christians*. Indeed, the most insurmountable barriers are often erected by officially sanctioned Christians, by people who are "Christians by profession": teachers who express love through corporal punishment or pastors who can't communicate with those under their care.

In a similar way, the Catholic Archbishop of New Orleans is not of particular help. Despite the general Roman Catholic teaching that capital punishment should be used extremely sparingly, and despite the clear statement of the U.S. Conference of Catholic Bishops opposing capital punishment, the local Archbishop did not seem to have a strong sense of collegiality with his brother bishops. He had sent priests to testify at a death-penalty trial to argue for execution, and he assured local Catholics that they could, in good conscience, endorse the death penalty; yet in particular cases he agreed to argue for clemency. Sister Helen wryly comments: "Archbishop Hannan is a perplexing man" (p. 55). We have witnessed a real failure of the official spokespeople of the church to be clear about the priority that Christians are asked to place on forgiveness and reconciliation, along with a failure to emphasize the church's official rejection of revenge and bloodletting in the administration of justice.

Fortunately, not all members of the local church hierarchy are quite so perplexing. After Pat Sonnier's execution, Sister Helen and some fellow nuns arrange for his funeral; the officiant will be Stanley Ott, the Bishop of Baton Rouge. "In his homily the bishop says that Jesus has revealed God to us and that God is a God of compassion and love, not a God of retribution. He prays for Pat and for all families who have lost

loved ones to violence—the Bourques, the LeBlancs, and the Sonniers"
(p. 99). Here, I think, is a bishop who has truly understood the centrality of these elements of the Christian faith.

Nor does the general public seem to have much patience for theological arguments about forgiveness and reconciliation. People like to
quote their favorite Bible verses—the ones that favor the position that
they already fully accept—and ignore everything else. In cases of capital punishment, the all-around favorite is from the book of Leviticus
(24:17–20): "Anyone who kills a human being shall be put to death. . . .
Anyone who maims another shall suffer the same injury in return: fracture for fracture, eye for eye, tooth for tooth; the injury inflicted is the
injury to be suffered."

Of course, we do not actually mete out punishment in this way for
anything except murder, and then only in select cases (perpetrators are
*much* more likely to receive the death penalty if they happen to be
African-American, poor, and/or living in a southern state). Nor do Christians follow the laws of Leviticus on almost any other matter (dietary
restrictions, giving to the poor, personal grooming habits—all are
addressed in the same set of laws, but again, we only pick out our favorite
passages). Nor do Christians often note that Jesus directly and explicitly rejects the "eye for an eye" principle, substituting for it the principle of "turning the other cheek" (Matt. 5:38–40). These nuances are lost
on most believers. Once the argument gets more complicated than the
quotation of one's favorite Bible verse, people tend to throw up their
hands in disgust.

The clearest example of this tendency in *Dead Man Walking* comes
during a conversation with a Captain who has jurisdiction over the death
house at Angola:

> "You know how the Bible says 'an eye for an eye,'" he says to me, but
> it's like a gentle pitch in softball, slow and big and easy.
> "And you know," I say back to him, "that Jesus called us to go beyond
> that kind of vengeance, not to pay back an 'eye for an eye,' not to return
> hate for hate."
> He smiles, puts up his hand. "I ain't gonna get into all this Bible quotin'
> with no nun, 'cuz I'm gonna lose" (p. 77).

In the film, Sister Helen smiles at this response; her interlocutor is a
likeable character, and, as she notes, the question was a softball. Nevertheless, I could not smile when I read this passage in her book. It seems
to me symptomatic of the use of the Bible by many Christians: people
quote their favorite verse, and then, when someone points out how that
verse might be interpreted differently, how it is nuanced by other parts

of the Bible, or how Jesus directly overturned it, they don't have to respond to these arguments; they just walk away. In other words, they had already made up their minds how they felt about the issue, and they didn't really care *what* the Bible said about it. They were just quoting it because they had heard a verse that seemed to support their position.

Most people, in fact, don't think about the implications of their Christian faith in such matters. The warden at Angola prison is an example; he's a Methodist minister, but he can't imagine how his decision to carry out the death penalty could possibly test his allegiance to his faith. Sister Helen certainly tries to help him see the problem:

> I challenge him: "But you're a Christian, a minister in your church, a man who professes to follow the way of life that Jesus taught. Yet you are the one who, with a nod of your head, signals the executioner to kill a man. Do you really believe that Jesus, who taught us not to return hate for hate and evil for evil and whose dying words were, 'Father, forgive them,' would participate in these executions? Would Jesus pull the switch?"
>
> The blue-gray smoke from his cigar is intensifying around Blackburn in a cloud. I am beginning to feel as if I'm talking to the Wizard of Oz.
>
> "Nope," he says, "I don't experience any contradiction with my Christianity. Never thought about it too much, really. Executions are the law, and Christians are supposed to observe the law, and that's that" (pp. 122–23).

Sister Helen does not say so at this point, but my thought in reading this passage was how very well this warden would have performed in Nazi Germany. Does he really think that if genocide, for example, is the law, that Christians should carry it out? No, he probably doesn't think so; it's easy, with the advantage of hindsight, to look back on another culture and to recognize the moral blindness among those who claim to be "just following orders." But we ought to realize the degree to which others look to us and see the same blindness that we see in the Nazis. Elsewhere in the book, Sister Helen does lament the degree to which everyone in the process claims to be "just following orders," and she does explicitly connect this to the patterns of human behavior in Nazi Germany and other repressive regimes (p. 103). She also asks: "How is it, I wonder, that the mandate and example of Jesus, so clearly urging compassion and nonviolence, could so quickly become *accommodated?*" (p. 123).

Part of the point of a document like the Apostles' Creed is to point out that the message and example of Jesus may look different from the prevailing assumptions of our day. Another part of its point is to discourage people from quoting random verses of the Bible to support their own predispositions. This is not to say that the creed and the Bible are in tension with each other; rather, as I have suggested throughout this book, the creeds attempt to encapsulate and summarize what the Scriptures say at length. In doing so, they attempt to take account of the differing strands of the biblical narrative, and to direct our attention to the broad themes that arise over and over again—rather than to the occasional verse that might, in a very particular context, suggest something different. So rather than point to an ancient law, conceived under a particular cultural context and eventually rejected in the teachings of Jesus, the creeds point to the broad, overarching direction of the biblical narratives, which emphasize the importance of forgiveness and reconciliation.

The importance of forgiveness is inextricably, but somewhat obscurely, linked to our belief in the church. As I noted in the previous chapter, the Christian belief in the church is related to our conviction that we are not, first and foremost, a sea of scattered individuals, all fending for ourselves, pulling ourselves up by our own bootstraps. We are, rather, members of a larger body, in communion with one another, closely bound to one another through our adoption as children of God through Christ. This means, in turn, that the things we do are never merely our individual actions, separable from the rest of the human community. When people make mistakes or do terrible misdeeds, we need to remember that they are not acting as solitary individuals. They are what they are because, in part, their communities have formed them in that way. This does not excuse them from responsibility; on the contrary, it widens the net of responsibility, reminding us of how we are all, in part, responsible for everything that happens in the world. The character of Father Zosima in Dostoyevsky's *The Brothers Karamazov* believes this to be the secret of the Christian life: a willingness to take on responsibility for everyone and for all things. By doing so, we come to see the whole universe as interwoven and interconnected, and we come to see ourselves as part of the great web of love that God has woven throughout the entire created order.

In a particularly moving passage in her book (pp. 177–78), Sister Helen reflects on how the differences between actions of the murderer and the nun are related to the differences in the lives of their families. Unlike her, Robert Willie

> never really had a father. His own father spent twenty-seven of his fifty-three years in Angola. . . . It makes me think of my own daddy. It has to be one of life's most special feelings to know that your father is proud of you. I was my daddy's scholar, his public speaker, his "pretty little girl," his scribe who kept the travel diary on family vacations. He always had a special tone in his voice when he introduced me to friends and colleagues.

*And this is my little daughter, Helen. . . .* A kid can sail to the moon with that feeling of security from a father.

But Robert Willie . . . Did Vernon Harvey have the facts right? Hadn't he said that Robert's father said his son deserved the chair and he'd be willing to pull the switch himself?

I look across at Robert through the heavy mesh screen. I remember from his juvenile record that he once asked to be kept in jail because he had nowhere else to go.

One of the reasons that we believe in forgiveness is that we know that "no man is an island." We are all, in part, the products of our upbringing, our schooling, and all kinds of other formative influences within our culture. The above-quoted passage is not in the film, but the director makes the point in a careful and subtle way: when Sister Helen is visiting her parents' home, we see images of mutual support everywhere—warm colors, friendly conversation, children playing games, a baby being lovingly held. The members of *this* family, we suspect, will not end up on death row.

At least one man in the prison sees this clearly: Major Kendall Coody, the man in charge of all the operations on death row. He seems to be the only one on the inside of the system who hasn't found it so easy to square his work with his conscience.

> "I'm not sure how long I'm going to be able to keep doing this," he says. "I've been through five of these executions and I can't eat, I can't sleep. I'm dreaming about executions. I don't condone these guys' crimes. I know they've done terrible things. I don't excuse what they've done, but I talk to them when I make my rounds. I talk to them and many of them are just little boys inside big men's bodies, little boys who never had much chance to grow up" (p. 180).

Unfortunately, a scene in which one of the officers expresses such sentiments was cut from the final version of the film because it seemed to interrupt the narrative path that the story had taken by that point.

Also missing from the film are the book's two most important scenes that confirm the importance of the Christian belief in forgiveness. One is positive and one is negative; they are both experiences of the parents of the victims after their children's murderers have been executed. The first scene concerns Vernon Harvey, the man so eager to see his stepdaughter's murderer "fry." Sister Helen visits him two years after the execution. He and his wife have channeled some of their energy into organizing victims' families and working for their rights, but forgiveness has never been on their agenda. As a result, they simply cannot find closure. Sister Helen writes:

I tell them about Robert's last hours and his struggle to formulate his last words. I tell them that I believe he was sincere when he said that he hoped his death would relieve their suffering.

Vernon begins to cry. He just can't get over Faith's death, he says. It happened six years ago but for him it's like yesterday, and I realize that now, with Robert Willie dead, he doesn't have an object for his rage. He's been deprived of that, too. I know that he could watch Robert killed a thousand times and it could never assuage his grief. . . .

I reach over and put my hand on his arm. My heart aches for him. I sympathize with his rage. Reason and logic are useless here. In time, I hope Robert's final wish comes true: that Vernon and Elizabeth find peace. But I know that it will not be Robert's death which brings peace. Only reconciliation: accepting Faith's death—can finally release them to leave the past and join the present, to venture love, to rejoin the ranks of the living (p. 226).

In the end, forgiveness is the only thing that really "works." It is the only vehicle for both judgment and release.

Nowhere is that point made more clearly than in the life of another victim's parent, Lloyd LeBlanc. The book ends with this story, and it is hinted at in the final scene of the film as well—Earl Delacroix appears at the executed man's funeral and later prays beside Sister Helen in a chapel. But the film makes him much more reluctant to move into the realm of forgiveness; he tells Sister Helen that he doubts his own ability to set aside the hatred that he feels. The book, on the other hand, conveys the true Christian heroism of the victim's loving father in its description of Lloyd LeBlanc:

Lloyd has told me how he prays for "everyone, especially the poor and suffering." . . . Now, Lloyd LeBlanc prays for the Sonniers—for Pat and for Eddie [his daughter's murderers] and for Gladys, their mother. "What grief for this mother's heart," he once said to me in a letter. Yes, for the Sonniers, too, he prays. He knows I visit Eddie [serving a life sentence in prison], and in his letter he sometimes includes a ten-dollar bill with the note: "For your prison ministry to God's children." . . .

Lloyd LeBlanc has told me that he would have been content with imprisonment for Patrick Sonnier. He went to the execution, he said, not for revenge, but hoping for an apology. Patrick Sonnier had not disappointed him. Before sitting in the electric chair he had said, "Mr. LeBlanc, I want to ask your forgiveness for what me and Eddie done," and Lloyd LeBlanc had nodded his head, signaling a forgiveness he had already given. He says that when he arrived with sheriff's deputies there in the cane field to identify his son, he had knelt by his boy—"laying down there with his two little eyes sticking out like bullets"—and prayed the Our Father. And when he came to the words: "Forgive us our trespasses as we forgive those who trespass against us," he had not halted or equivocated, and he said, "Whoever did this, I forgive them" (p. 244).

I have read this passage of text perhaps a hundred times as I have read and reread the book, used it in my ethics classes, and quoted it in my own writings; yet I still cannot read it without tears in my eyes.

It's a constant refrain that talk about forgiveness is cheap; we don't really know the extent of our ability to forgive until we are faced with a really difficult case. It's hard to imagine a more difficult case than the cold-blooded murder of one's own child. It's not surprising that the parents of victims say things to Sister Helen like "You haven't lost a child. You don't understand anything" (p. 228). I suspect that, in a very real sense, this charge is false—though Sister Helen is too modest to say so. I expect that she has lost many of her many "adopted children" in the St. Thomas projects of New Orleans, where murder is too often the talk of the neighborhood. But if that same charge were directed at me, the charge would be true. I have never lost a child, not even a godchild or the child of a friend. I have two beautiful daughters—daughters who, I hope, could sail to the moon on the pride of their parents. The question for me is: could I forgive a person who took their lives?

Of course, I don't know the answer to that. I don't think any of us can know until it happens. But I do know that, as a Christian, I am called to do so. I believe that I have been forgiven much, by God and by other people; it would be the height of hypocrisy for me not to do the same for others. But I don't know. I cannot measure or even imagine the wideness of the grief that I would feel, and I cannot imagine retracing Lloyd LeBlanc's footsteps and his prayer and his extraordinary act of forgiveness. But I know that following Jesus means doing precisely that. I pray every day that I might forgive those who sin against me, and every day I confess that "I believe in the forgiveness of sins." For if the day ever comes when I have to do what Lloyd LeBlanc did, I will need every bit of formation and habituation that I can muster, in order to do so. And I will need it, as does he, from that point onward (pp. 244–45):

> He acknowledges that it's a struggle to overcome the feelings of bitterness and revenge that well up, especially as he remembers David's birthday year by year and loses him all over again: David at twenty, David at twenty-five, David getting married, David standing at the back door with his little ones clustered around his knees, grown-up David, a man like himself, whom he will never know. Forgiveness is never going to be easy. Each day it must be prayed for and struggled for and won.

## Questions For Discussion

1. Do you understand your own sins as forgiven by God? If so, what conditions (if any) do you believe are necessary in order for this to take place? How is God's forgiveness of our sins related to our willingness to forgive others?

2. Describe some of the common features of contemporary culture that make forgiveness difficult—both in terms of asking for it and giving it.

3. Think of the most grievous wrong that you have ever had committed against you. (Pick something for which you can actually name one or more individuals as the perpetrators.) Did you communicate your experience of having been wronged to that person? Did the person ask for forgiveness? Were you able to grant it?

4. Now think of the worst thing that you can remember doing to someone else. (Caution: give this one more thought—we often store such memories very far away!) Were you able to ask for forgiveness for the wrong, and was forgiveness granted by the person who felt wronged by you?

5. Do you believe that there are any sins or wrongdoings that God would want us *not* to forgive? Provide some examples. How does this relate to traditional Christian teachings about forgiveness? (You may want to examine some of the biblical texts cited in this chapter, such as Matt. 5:38–48, Matt. 18:23–35, Luke 15:11–32, Luke 23:34, Rom. 12:12–21, and Eph. 4:32.)

## For Further Reading

Countryman, L. William. *Forgiven and Forgiving.* Harrisburg, Pa.: Morehouse, 1998. (Introductory)

Donnelley, Doris. *Learning to Forgive.* New York: Macmillan, 1979. (Introductory)

Hunter, Robert Grams. *Shakespeare and the Comedy of Forgiveness.* New York: Columbia University Press, 1965. (Advanced/Specialized)

Jones, L. Gregory. *Embodying Forgiveness: A Theological Analysis.* Grand Rapids: Eerdmans, 1995. (Advanced)

Nelson, Susan L. *Healing the Broken Heart: Sin, Alienation, and the Gift of Grace.* St. Louis: Chalice Press, 1997. (Introductory/Advanced)

Oliver, Gordon. *Living Forgiveness: Hospitality and Reconciliation.* Cambridge: Grove Books, 2000. (Introductory)

Shriver, Donald W., Jr., *An Ethic for Enemies: Forgiveness in Politics.* New York: Oxford University Press, 1995. (Advanced)

Tutu, Desmond. *No Future Without Forgiveness.* New York: Macmillan, 1999. (Introductory)

Weaver, Andrew, and Monica Furlong. *Reflections on Forgiveness and Spiritual Growth.* Nashville: Abingdon Press, 2000. (Introductory)

Williams, Charles. *The Forgiveness of Sins.* Grand Rapids: Eerdmans, 1984. (Introductory/Advanced)

Williams, Rowan. *Writing in the Dust.* Grand Rapids: Eerdmans, 2002. (Introductory)

## Other Works Examining the Forgiveness of Sins

Edward Albee, *Who's Afraid of Virginia Woolf?*

Charles Dickens, *A Christmas Carol in Prose*

Fyodor Dostoyevsky, *The Brothers Karamazov; Crime and Punishment*

Graham Greene, *The Heart of the Matter*

Victor Hugo, *Les Misérables*

Barbara Kingsolver, *Animal Dreams* (discussed in chapter 9)

William Shakespeare, almost every play he wrote, but in particular, *All's Well that Ends Well, Cymbeline, Measure for Measure, The Merchant of Venice, Much Ado About Nothing, The Tempest,* and *The Winter's Tale* (discussed in chapter 6)

# eleven

# "The Resurrection of the Flesh"

Earlier in this book, I spoke about the phrase "he ascended into heaven" as the element in the creed about which Christians are likely to be most uncertain. Many believers are quite willing to affirm this element of the faith, but it's not always clear what we're being asked to believe, nor why it should be so important for Christians to believe this. Now, we turn to an element of Christian belief with an even more problematic status. Here, the difficulty is not that most Christians fail to understand its meaning and significance; rather, the problem is that most Christians simply do not believe it at all!

If we were to ask a randomly selected sample of Christians the question "What happens to you after you die?" we would rightly expect to hear a variety of answers. I suspect, however, that we would find a number of responses clustering around something like the following: "When you die, your soul is separated from your body and it goes to heaven to be with God. Your body is buried in the ground or cremated; you no longer need it, and it is no longer relevant." We might press the point a bit further, asking a follow-up question such as "But what about at the end of time? Won't your body the reunited with your soul?" If our respondent is a well-catechized Roman Catholic, she or he might respond by saying that yes, this reunification does occur, but that how this is possible remains a mystery, since the physical body obviously decomposes in the ground or in fire. Other Christians might answer by saying that no, there is no final reunification of the body with the soul; the soul is what is really "important," and that it is really all one needs in one's life with God. We're done with our bodies when we die.

All this simply goes to show how thoroughly Christianity has failed to convey its traditional teachings about life after death. According to some translations of the Apostles' Creed, we believe in "the resurrection of the body," but the original language is yet more stark: according to

201

the Latin text of the creed, we believe in *carnis resurrectionem:* the resurrection of the *flesh.* Unfortunately, the belief that is espoused by most Christians concerning the disposition of the flesh after death is not a properly Christian belief at all; rather, it is a modified version of the ancient Platonic story of "the immortality of the soul." According to Plato (and ancient Greek thought in general), the body was essentially excess baggage that weighed the soul down and prevented it from ascending to its proper place. The Greeks even appreciated a word-play between their words for *body* and *tomb: sōma* and *sēma.* The body was indeed like a tomb: it was a space in which something that should properly be alive was improperly confined. The moment of death was understood as a sort of release, in which the excess baggage of the body was put away and the soul could rise to its proper place. This is why, at his death, Socrates suggests that his followers should offer a sacrifice to the gods in thanksgiving for this moment of release.

The rest of the Platonic myth was more complex: it involved a transmigration of the soul through a period of forgetting and possible reincarnation in a new earthly body, within which it would need to relearn what it had known in a previous life (but had now forgotten). Most Christians would not continue to embrace this aspect of the ancient Greek understanding of life after death, but this does not prevent them from being quite enthusiastic about the notion that death brings with it the release from the burden of embodiment. It is the story that we tell our children from the moment of their first encounter with death: the dead person's body is cast aside, and the soul goes up to be with God.

The reasons for our enthusiasm for this particular ancient myth are extraordinarily complicated. Here, I will oversimplify things considerably and name only three of the factors that seem to be of particular significance. First, the dominance of the natural sciences on our modes of thinking has encouraged us to understand what happens to our flesh after death through primarily empirical categories. This is not to say that we have made such great scientific advances in our understanding of the decomposition of the body since the time of the earliest Christians; they too knew precisely what happened to flesh after death. (They even had a name for the coffin that brought this knowledge home: they called it a *sarcophagus*—a "flesh-eater.") But unlike us, they did not necessarily assume that empirical judgments about a physical reality were always the most important things that one could say about them. Flesh in a tomb does indeed decay, but this does not mean that decay is its proper or final destiny. We, on the other hand, assume that this empirical fact is the most important thing that we can say about the disposition of the flesh.

Second, as I have noted at several points in this book, our culture encourages a certain love-hate relationship with our own bodies. On the one hand, we love our bodies, and we work very hard—probably harder than any other culture of the past or present—to improve them and to preserve them for as long as possible. On the other hand, our culture's projected ideal about the body is something that most of us can never actually achieve—at least not without devoting our entire lives to the production of that particular sort of body. And so, disillusioned by our inability to achieve the body that our culture considers ideal, we feel somewhat relieved by the opportunity to finally put it away—to be dis-embodied and therefore no longer subject to the impossible standards that are so often described to us as essential.

Finally, despite Christian teachings to the contrary, most of us still believe in a certain kind of dualism of body versus soul, flesh versus spirit. We have come to see the body as the cause of most of our trou-bles. Our sicknesses, our temptations, the various forms of difficulty that we get ourselves into—all are problems of the body, the physical flesh. If we didn't have our bodies to worry about, we would not be tempted by our appetites, nor would we be limited by the need to be in a particular physical space. To be fair, there are a number of New Tes-tament passages that can be read as supporting this sort of dualism. Jesus' claim that "it is the spirit that gives life; the flesh is useless" (John 6:63)—although originally directed against an excessively physical understanding of nourishment—has often been employed in support of a claim that our bodies are irrelevant at best, and perhaps even gen-uinely harmful to us. Similarly, many of Paul's offhand remarks con-cerning flesh, spirit, body, and soul are often read as propounding a cer-tain kind of dualism—attributing temptation and trouble primarily to the flesh, and salvation primarily to the soul.

Against all of these readings, of course, we have the Christian doc-trine of creation—the world is created good, and the creation of humankind in our physical, embodied state is declared by God to be "very good" (Gen. 1:31). We have injunctions from Paul and other early writers urging us to treat our bodies with the utmost respect:

> Do you not know that your bodies are members of Christ? . . . Do you not know that your body is a temple of the Holy Spirit within you, which you have from God, and that you are not your own? For you were bought with a price; therefore glorify God in your body (1 Cor. 6:15, 19–20).

Finally, we have the most important thing of all: the incarnation, in which we are reminded that God considered our bodies to be such an important part of who we are that God was willing to take on our flesh in order to redeem it.

Nevertheless, our tendency to lapse back into a body-soul dualism—along with our love-hate relationship with our bodies and our enthusiasm for the empirical sciences—have led to great challenges in any attempt to reclaim the traditional Christian belief in "the resurrection of the flesh." It will not do simply to *assert* this claim; the factors that I have mentioned here have far too powerful a grip on our collective conscience for us to imagine that they can be set aside in an instant. Instead, we need to offer concrete demonstrations of the significance of the body—and why it remains important to us, even in death.

Perhaps the most important thing that we can say is that our bodies are part of our identity; they make us who we are. If we want to identify a person to someone else, we usually begin with the body: she is tall, has blond hair, blue eyes . . . or we can simply offer to show someone a picture. In doing so, we're not pretending to claim that a person's physical features provide an exhaustive description of "who she is," but on the other hand, we wouldn't be inclined to leave such features out altogether. Authors who write fiction are well aware of our need for physical description; while they don't usually offer a list of statistical details of the sort one might find on a driver's license, they do provide enough information to enable their readers to see the character in their mind's eye. In many stories, it *matters* what the person's physical body looks like. In the fiction that I have used in this book, for example, it is important to their respective stories that Codi Noline is tall, Asbury Fox is thin, Sethe is black, and Peter Chance has a blond braid of hair.

We are also reminded of the importance of the flesh when we speak about those who have died. When we remember our dead, we remember them body and soul; we show pictures, we tell stories, we place them in their embodied, physical context. The dead are never merely disembodied spirits. If we truly believed that, we wouldn't show each other pictures and say "this is my great-grandmother." As I noted in chapter 6, the flesh may sometimes seem to be a difficult, troublesome, and even dangerous thing, but it is the necessary medium through which our most meaningful relationships must transpire. Therefore, we ought not to forget bodies at the moment of a person's death; we ought not to treat them as irrelevant, as something to be sloughed off. Rather, they await their resurrection, destined to carry on the person's identity *beyond* this world, just as they did *in* this world.

The most detailed biblical discussion of this question comes in Paul's first letter to the Corinthians. There, the Apostle suggests that, in the resurrection of the body, there is both continuity and change; what is

raised up will be bodily, but it will be a different kind of body than that
to which we are accustomed.

> But someone will ask, "How are the dead raised? With what kind of body
> do they come?" . . . There are both heavenly bodies and earthly bodies,
> but the glory of the heavenly is one thing, and that of the earthly is another.
> There is one glory of the sun, and another glory of the moon, and another
> glory of the stars; indeed, star differs from star in glory. So it is with the
> resurrection of the dead. What is sown is perishable, what is raised is
> imperishable. It is sown in dishonor, it is raised in glory. It is sown in
> weakness, it is raised in power. It is sown a physical body, it is raised a
> spiritual body. If there is a physical body, there is also a spiritual body. . . .
> Listen, I will tell you a mystery! We will not all die, but we will all be
> changed, in a moment, in the twinkling of an eye, at the last trumpet. For
> the trumpet will sound, and the dead will be raised imperishable, and we
> will be changed. For this perishable body must put on imperishability,
> and this mortal body must put on immortality (1 Cor. 15:35, 40–44, 51–53).

So the resurrection body will be imperishable, glorious, powerful, and
immortal—that is, it will not die. Most intriguingly, Paul says that the
resurrection body will be "a spiritual body," offering an interesting paradox to those who would like to maintain a strict dichotomy of flesh
and body on one side and soul and spirit on the other. Paul admits that
the resurrection body will not be physical in the sense that we normally
assume (it cannot, after all, be perishable or weak); but it will, nevertheless, be a body. In making this claim, Paul reminds us once again
that the Christian faith considers bodies important; they are not merely
dispensed with at death, but continue to bear the identity of every human
person, suggesting that that identity continues beyond death.

In sum, then, the Christian belief in the resurrection of the flesh is
our way of emphasizing the importance of the physical body, its extraordinary role in giving us an identity as a particular human being, and the
endurance of this identity beyond the boundary between life and death.
As an illustration of all three of these points, one would be hard-pressed
to find a better example than Graham Greene's novel *The End of the
Affair*. In this novel, the characters contemplate the significance of the
body, its role in shaping our identity, and its continuity from life into
death.

\*  \*  \*  \*  \*

I have taught this novel in theology courses longer and more often
than perhaps any other work of fiction. In fact, it may be my favorite
novel of all time: a perfectly executed piece of literature, with sharply

drawn characters and a startling revelation at its core. William Faulkner, who was not easily impressed, called it "one of the most true and moving novels of my time, in anybody's language." We are also blessed with a very fine recent film treatment of the novel, adapted for the screen and directed by Neil Jordan. (The film has one major flaw, to which I will return in a moment; but any writer is fortunate to receive as appreciative a treatment of a novel as this film offers.) In fact, the film and the book are so strikingly parallel that I will interweave my discussion of the two and only mention a few points where the book provides detail that the film leaves out.

*The End of the Affair* is Graham Greene's semiautobiographical novel about a love affair between a successful writer, Maurice Bendrix (played in the film by Ralph Fiennes), and Sarah Miles (Julianne Moore), the wife of a British civil servant. Several years before the novel begins, they had fallen in love. All in all, their affair had been a rather conventional one; its only remarkable feature was the depth of jealousy that Bendrix felt toward every entity that spent more time with Sarah than he did (including not only her husband and her social acquaintances, but even her clothing—and the rain).

Then, quite suddenly and without a clear explanation, Sarah ended their affair. Bendrix could only guess at the reasons for this abrupt cessation; perhaps he had bored her with his insistent jealousy. In any case, he now finds himself unable to believe the promises that she had made to him: namely, that she would always love him, and that she would love no other man. Two years after their affair ended, a chance meeting with Sarah's husband Henry (deftly portrayed in the film version by Stephen Rea) leads Bendrix to believe that she is now having another affair, and Bendrix's smoldering jealousy is fanned into an all-consuming fire.

The entire story is told through a flashback: Bendrix is now writing an account of the whole affair, and the novel (and the film) open with the words, "This is a diary of hate." He knows as he writes how the story will end; but we, his audience, do not. The book and the film are carefully constructed so that the truth is revealed to us slowly; we are misled down several false paths, just as Bendrix had been when he was experiencing his own jealousy and Sarah's apparent promiscuity.

When Henry intimates that he has considered hiring a private investigator, Bendrix takes up the cause for him. The investigator, whose name is Parkis (brilliantly played in the film by Ian Hart), appears to bumble things at first, which provides some useful comic relief. But eventually he uncovers several clues, including several unexplained visits to another man's house, and the following scrap from a love letter:

I have no need to write to you or talk to you, you know everything before I can speak, but when one loves, one feels the need to use the same old ways one has always used. I know I am only beginning to love, but already I want to abandon everything, everybody but you: only fear and habit prevent me. Dear . . .

Although the letter breaks off before mentioning a name, it is clear to Bendrix that someone new has entered Sarah's life. He presents the evidence to her husband, who angrily destroys it without a glance. But in their exchange, Henry does allow himself one discovery: the only explanation for the fervor with which Bendrix was here accusing Sarah of infidelity is that Bendrix himself had once been Sarah's lover.

Henry is devastated by this news, but not particularly angry at Bendrix; he knows he has been a poor husband. Nevertheless, the revelation drives him home to beg Sarah to hold their marriage together. Unbeknownst to both men, Henry's plea comes just as Sarah had been writing a letter to her husband telling him that she was leaving him for Bendrix. In that moment, she recalls the promises of her marriage, and destroys the farewell letter. Sarah is left with Henry, and Bendrix is left alone with his seething jealousy.

Up to this point, in both the novel and the film, we have seen everything from Bendrix's point of view. This seems the only possible viewpoint, because the story is being narrated by Bendrix himself. But here, Greene effects a brilliant literary coup, which is nicely mirrored in the film. Bendrix comes into the possession of Sarah's diary, and suddenly we begin to understand the events of the last several years from the woman's point of view. As Bendrix turns the pages of the diary, he discovers just how misdirected his jealousy has been. He also realizes just how devoted Sarah has remained to him—and realizes that her love for him exceeded all the bounds that he could imagine.

Hate and suspicion and envy had driven me so far away that I read her words like a declaration of love from a stranger. I had expected plenty of evidence against her—hadn't I so often caught her out in lies?—and now here in writing that I could believe, as I couldn't believe her voice, was the complete answer. For it was the last couple of pages I read first, and then I read them again at the end to make sure. It's a strange thing to discover and to believe that you are loved, when you know that there is nothing in you for anybody but a parent or a God to love (p. 88).

Moreover, in reading Sarah's diary, Bendrix also discovers just how wrong he has been about her "new lover." Here the theological significance of this story comes into full prominence.

It turns out that Sarah had ended the affair because of a bargain that she had made with God. In a moment of desperation, she had promised God that she would end their affair, that she would never see Bendrix again, in exchange for a profound act of divine intervention. She gets her wish, and then realizes that her "happiness" must come to an end. Ever since that moment, she has continued to love Bendrix and to be wholly devoted to him; she has never loved any other man. But she has also kept her promise never to see him again, and in the process, she has come to believe in God. Indeed, she has fallen in love with God. God, it turns out, was the intended recipient of the love letter that the private detective discovered. For the reader of the novel (or the viewer of the film), Sarah is transformed from a wanton prodigal into a faithful keeper of promises—even when those promises impinge upon (what she had believed to be) her greatest happiness.

Not that keeping those promises has come easily. In fact, she has attempted to find ways to get out of the vows she has made, with respect both to her husband (that is, her marriage vows) and to Bendrix (her bargain with God). She has, in fact, gone to another man's house; the novel and the film provide different explanations for this, but in neither case is Sarah having another affair, as Bendrix supposes. In the film, the "other man's house" that she is visiting is the home of her priest. She is arguing with him about how she might get a divorce so that she can marry Bendrix and put their relationship on stable ground. Of course, the priest argues against this course of action. In the novel, she is visiting the home of a local atheist, Richard Smythe, hoping that he will be able convince her that God doesn't exist so she can toss her vows to the wind and return to the happiness that she has known with Bendrix. Not only does Richard fail to convert her to atheism; she actually converts him to belief!

Of course, when Bendrix discovers that Sarah still loves him, he immediately takes steps to win her back. He tries to convince her that God doesn't exist, and that the promises that she has made to her husband and to God are worthless. He wants her to get a divorce, take up with him, and live happily ever after. He even chases her into a church in order to make his case. But just as soon as Bendrix imagines that he has won Sarah back and that they will live happily ever after, something happens to interrupt their plans: Sarah dies.

But that is not the end of the story, and this is what makes the novel so appropriate for thinking about the question of the bodily resurrection. Even after Sarah's death, she seems to bring about several amazing moments of healing and reconciliation; these miraculous events are all related somehow to her material body, her physicality. I will return to these events at the end of the chapter.

One of the many fine features of this story is its depiction of a strong woman of extraordinary character. Like all of us, she is a sinner, but she comes to recognize her sin and to turn away from it. She has done the right thing, even if for the wrong reasons, and it has made her a better person. Indeed, because of certain events that take place after her death, she almost seems to have become a saint. But at this point, my one serious complaint about the novel's adaptation to film needs to be highlighted. In the novel, Bendrix's efforts to woo Sarah to break her promise are completely fruitless. He chases her from one place to another, making impassioned pleas on behalf of the sexually charged form of love that he so ardently desires, but he is unable to break the strength of her resolve; her belief in God is stronger than his attempts at seduction. ("I've caught belief like a disease," she eventually tells him [p. 147].) All he manages to do is to pursue her from her home to a church to a movie theater, and so on— forcing her to spend more time out in the rain, and thereby weakening her already fragile health. In fact, the reader suspects that Bendrix's actions have actually been instrumental in bringing about Sarah's death.

But in the film, his conquest succeeds—at least temporarily. The two lovers leave the church together, return to Bendrix's apartment, have sex, and begin to glimpse a rather more conventional form of happiness as they plan a future life together. This imagined happiness still slips from their grasp; but in the film, the cause is a chronic disease that has been diagnosed, leaving Sarah only a few months to live. Unfortunately, this now seems more like divine revenge against Sarah for breaking her promises rather than (as the novel has it) a direct consequence of Bendrix's self-absorbed pursuit of his own desire. In the film, Sarah emerges as a person of weaker character—a woman willing to give up her passionate relationship with God for a mere man, and not a very admirable one at that. Consequently, her miraculous interventions at the end of the film are much less credible.

Nevertheless, the film's director kept a great deal of Greene's very fine dialogue firmly in place, and the film still works very well as a representation of some of the challenges of the relationship between flesh and spirit, and between life and death. After her prayer for divine intervention is answered affirmatively, Sarah prepares to walk away from the only man she has ever really loved. Like Leontes in *The Winter's Tale*, she will have to go on believing in that love, even in the physical absence of the other. But she tries to prepare herself and her lover for this reality by making it clear that their very physical love has something about it that can endure physical absence:

"Love doesn't end, does it, just because we don't see each other?"
"Doesn't it?"

"People go on loving God, don't they, even though they don't see Him?"
"That's not our kind of love."
"Perhaps there isn't any other kind."

In a way, this exchange helps to prepare them both for the even greater
degree of faith that will be necessary for their love to continue beyond
death.

All in all, the novel's theological achievements are really quite remarkable. It offers an implicit critique of a spiritualized Christianity; in other
words, it provides an argument against any theology in which bodies
don't matter. It emphasizes the beauty, the significance, and the essential goodness of materiality in general, and the physical human body in
particular. And it vividly demonstrates how the body's significance and
goodness transcends our experiences of its absence, its suffering, and
even its death. In the remainder of this chapter, I will try to outline how
these themes are orchestrated in the novel.

One of the most important passages in the novel occurs in Sarah's
diary entry for 2 October 1945—more than a year after she ended the
affair. This is where we first see her moving from a vague belief in an
immaterial God to a quite specific belief in the material, incarnate God
of Christianity. She wanders into a church to escape the rain:

> When I came in and sat down and looked around I realized it was a Roman
> church, full of plaster statues and bad art, realistic art. I hated the stat-
> ues, the crucifix, all the emphasis on the human body. I was trying to
> escape from the human body and all it needed. I thought I could believe
> in some kind of a God that bore no relation to ourselves, something vague,
> amorphous, cosmic, to which I had promised something and which had
> given me something in return—stretching out of the vague into the con-
> crete human life, like a powerful vapor moving among the chairs and walls.
> One day I too would become part of that vapor—I would escape myself
> forever (p. 109).

The story she tells here is very much the story that many non-Christians
(and indeed many Christians) would tell: God is an impersonal force,
out there somewhere. God does not have a body and is incapable of
experiencing life in the embodied state in which we experience it. Such
a portrait of God is really much safer, much more predictable, and has
much less direct impact on most of our lives. But suddenly Sarah realizes what many lifelong Christians fail to realize: that Christianity does
not believe in "God the vapor." Christianity believes that God became
incarnate for our salvation, thereby reminding us of the essential goodness of our material bodies—created as they are by God, in God's own
image and likeness. She continues:

And then I came into that dark church in Park Road and saw the bodies standing around me on all the altars—the hideous plaster statues with their complacent faces, and I remembered that they believed in the resurrection of the body, the body I wanted destroyed for ever. I had done so much injury with this body. How could I want to preserve any of it for eternity, and suddenly I remembered a phrase of Richard's—about human beings inventing doctrines to satisfy their desires, and I thought: *how wrong he is*. If I were to invent a doctrine it would be that the body was never born again, that it rotted with last year's vermin (pp. 109–10, emphasis added).

Sarah cannot believe that anyone would just "make up" a doctrine like the resurrection of the body. Why would anyone want to extend the life of something that has to bear—and cause—so much pain and anguish? This particular belief seems so much more credible to her precisely because it is so counterintuitive. Only God could think up such an idea.

The above-quoted passage suggests that Sarah holds a very negative attitude toward human bodies in general and toward her own body in particular, but this is not the last word; it cannot overshadow the much more positive evaluation that she has of the body of another:

I thought, instead of my own body, of Maurice's. I thought of certain lines life had put on his face as personal as a line of his writing: I thought of a new scar on his shoulder that wouldn't have been there if once he hadn't tried to protect another man's body from a falling wall. He didn't tell me why he was in hospital those three days: Henry told me. That scar was part of his character as much as his jealousy. And so I thought, do I want that body to be vapor (mine yes, but his?), and I knew I wanted that scar to exist through all eternity (p. 110).

And of course, if we hope to go on knowing others, even in death—if we want to maintain a relationship with them—we need to imagine the resurrection not only of *their* bodies, but our own as well. Sarah continues:

But could my vapor love that scar? Then I began to want my body that I hated, but only because it could love that scar. We can love with our minds, but can we love only with our minds? Love extends itself all the time, so that we can even love with our senseless nails: we love even with our clothes, so that a sleeve can feel a sleeve (p. 110).

This is a very rich passage of text, and I daresay there may be a great deal for Christians to learn from it—not only about the importance of the body and of its resurrection, but also about our understanding of human sexuality (so important because it is such a clear expression of our embod-

iment), and, in fact, of all of the physical dimensions of love (even in a
nonsexual sense). I cannot unpack these claims here, but I would venture to say that a more detailed investigation into questions about the
resurrection of the flesh would probably lead naturally into some of these
areas of conversation.

Meanwhile, we should note that Sarah's musings on her own body
and its relationship to other bodies has led her full circle, back around
to God. She realizes now that deeply embedded in the Christian account
of reality is a strong material element (something that her husband also
emphasized to her when they were visiting a similarly "materialist"
church in Spain). God becomes a body in the incarnation and dies on
a cross. God becomes a body in the Eucharist. Our own identity as
human beings, created in God's image, is wrapped up in our bodies—
so much so that this identity remains with us even in death, even in spite
of the body's empirical decomposition. Sarah finally sees how all the
pieces fit together:

> So today I looked at that material body on that material cross and I won-
> dered, how could the world have nailed a vapor there? A vapor of course
> felt no pain and no pleasure. It was only my superstition that imagined [a
> vapor] could answer my prayers. Dear God, I had said. I should have said,
> Dear Vapor. I said I hate you, but can one hate a vapor? I could hate that
> figure on the Cross with its claim to my gratitude—'I've suffered this for
> you', but a vapor . . . I looked up at that over-familiar body, stretched in
> imaginary pain, the head drooping like a man asleep. I thought, some-
> times I've hated Maurice, but would I have hated him if I hadn't loved him
> too? Oh God, if I could really hate you, what would that mean? (pp.
> 111–12).

Now she understands that Christianity's positive assessment of the
material created order is another way of stressing its emphasis on *love*.
People find it very difficult to love a vapor, a great cosmic force, or any
other indefinable something that exists "out there in the great beyond."
They can fear such a force, they can seek to evade it, but they can't really
love or hate it—and they can't imagine being loved *by* it. Only because we
can imagine both God and ourselves in fully material, fully bodily terms
can we imagine what it means for God to love us and for us to love God.

As Sarah adopts this belief as her own, we see her take her own first
step toward embracing Christianity:

> Suppose God did exist, suppose he was a body like that, what's wrong in
> believing that his body existed as much as mine? Could anybody love him
> or hate him if he hadn't got a body? I can't love a vapor that was Maurice.
> That's coarse, that's beastly, that's materialist, I know, but why shouldn't

I be beastly and coarse and materialist. I walked out of the church in a flaming rage, and in defiance of Henry and all the reasonable and the detached I did what I had seen people do in Spanish churches: I dipped my finger in the so-called holy water and made a kind of cross on my forehead (p. 112).

Perhaps on the day that Sarah walked out of that church, a tiny mustardseed of faith was present in her decision to dip her finger into the "socalled holy water"—a seed that later grew into a green plant that was able to nourish her and sustain her into a new life.

But that faith would never have been able to offer her personal sustenance had it not been, at its very core, a faith that embraced material reality; no one can love a mere vapor. The Christian God, who became incarnate and dwelt among us, creates for us the possibility of as personal and loving a relationship with God as we have with one another. We have these relationships by means of our bodies; our bodies are part of who we are. They are not to be despised, not to be sloughed off at the end of our lives, not to be considered of marginal relevance in comparison with the high-flying soul. On the Christian account, our bodies are part of who we are; they are part of our identity, and this also means that, according to the Christian faith, we cannot be permanently separated from them at death. If they are necessary to our loving relationship with God, then they must transcend the barrier of death—for as we will observe in the following chapter, our relationship with God transcends death.

It would be impossible, of course, for a realistic novel to portray "the resurrection of the flesh" in any ordinary sense; it's simply not a part of our experience. But by continuing the story after Sarah's death, the author is able to show how she continues to affect people in bodily ways, as though the boundary between life and death were no obstacle. In the film, only a few of these elements are present, but the entire last quarter of the novel is filled with references to Sarah's continuing bodily presence.

The first thing we notice is that Bendrix, who of course does not believe in the bodily resurrection, starts to lose certain elements of her identity—and of his own. "She had lost all our memories for ever, and it was as though by dying she had robbed me of part of myself. I was losing my individuality. It was the first stage of my own death, the memories dropping off like gangrened limbs" (p. 138). If he could believe in the continuing significance of Sarah's body, he would not be feeling the loss of identity that washes over him so strongly. "I couldn't imitate her voice. I couldn't even caricature it: when I tried to remember it, it was anonymous—just any woman's voice. The process of forgetting her had set in" (pp. 144–45).

But the forgetting will not be as easy as he thinks, because her death has not changed the fact that he is still intertwined with her. For example, the whole affair has brought him into ever-increasing contact with Sarah's husband, Henry; and now that Sarah has died, Henry begins to rely on Bendrix as the closest thing he has to a friend. Henry is troubled by the fact that Sarah had called out for a priest before she died; he had planned on a nonreligious cremation service, but he hesitates. (At the time the novel was written, Roman Catholics insisted on burial as a more visible sign of faith in the bodily resurrection.) Since Bendrix has been privy to Sarah's love for God as recorded in her journal, he knows that a Christian burial service would have been appropriate for her, but he keeps this information to himself as a form of revenge on Sarah's "other lover"—God. Henry says that he will have a burial service if that's what she would have wanted, but Bendrix stamps out the idea, lying to her husband about her faith:

> "Oh no, Henry. She didn't believe in anything, any more than you or me."
> I wanted her burnt up, I wanted to be able to say, Resurrect that body if you can. My jealousy had not finished, like Henry's, with her death. It was as if she were alive still, in the company of a lover she had preferred to me. How I wished I could send Parkis after her to interrupt their eternity (p. 137).

Later, Bendrix is told by Sarah's atheist friend, Richard Smythe, that she was in the process of becoming a Catholic, and he believes that Sarah should be buried rather than cremated; but Bendrix refuses to make any effort to encourage Henry to change the arrangements. Finally, he goes home and discovers a letter written by Sarah, which had been delayed in the mail. In this final letter, which seems to come to Bendrix from beyond the grave, she says quite explicitly that she is a full-fledged believer and that she is in the process of becoming a Catholic. For a third time, Bendrix denies her: a Catholic priest visits Henry to try to persuade him in favor of burial, but Bendrix argues viciously against any change of plans (pp. 152–55).

Bendrix is still thinking in empirical terms: he believes that if Sarah is cremated, that will put her beyond the reach of God, will somehow wipe out the reality of her devotion. Of course, it has no such effect. At the funeral, he tries to arrange a rendezvous with a woman that he has just met, planning to initiate a new affair (and thereby to get revenge on Sarah for dying on him). "Are you there? I said to Sarah. Are you watching me? See how I can get on without you" (pp. 158–59). But this is a slip on his part; he has, he admits, allowed his hatred to believe in her continuing survival, in the future resurrection of her body. And as Sarah had discovered before him, once we let our hatred believe in something, that opens the door for our love to follow it. Soon, after having second thoughts about the negative effects that his planned tryst might have on the girl he is seducing, he utters a little prayer to the dead woman whom he *thought* he believed to be extinct: "I implored Sarah, Get me out of this. . . . I don't want to begin it all again and injure her. I'm incapable of love. Except of you, except of you" (p. 159). As soon as he has uttered his prayer, Sarah's mother appears out of nowhere, introduces herself, and makes it nearly impossible for him not to ask her to dinner. Sarah has answered his prayer in the surviving earthly form closest to her own body: her mother.

But Sarah is not done. A lock of her hair, placed on Richard Smythe's deformed cheek, seems to have healed the ugly strawberry marks with which he was born. (In the film, the strawberry marks are given to the private detective's son, but the same point is made; in the book, the boy is healed of a different ailment, apparently through the intervention of a book in which Sarah had written a blessing.) And she is still present in the house, somehow, in all of the physical items that came into contact with her. Henry points out to Bendrix how, in one of his earlier novels, he had accidently displayed his misunderstanding of death:

> You described a house after a woman in it had died. . . . It seemed all right at the time. I thought it very plausible, but you got it all wrong, Bendrix. You described how the husband found the house terribly empty: he moved about the rooms, shifting chairs, trying to give an effect of movement, of another being there. . . . But now the house never seems empty like that. I don't know how to express it. Because she's always away, she's never away (p. 169).

Bendrix has noticed it too, though he doesn't like to admit it: the house is filled with little mementos from their affair, and he is reminded of her every time he hears a particular stair creak—it had been their warning that someone was on the way upstairs.

Sarah's death also brings about a reconciliation between Bendrix and Sarah's husband. Henry asks him to move in with him, in order to fight off the loneliness; but this only brings Bendrix into more and more contact with Sarah's enduring presence. After Parkis returns Sarah's book (the one that, according to the novel, inspired Parkis's boy to claim that Sarah came to him in the night and healed him), Bendrix can barely fight off the urge to believe:

Oh, I'm as capable of belief as the next man. I would only have to shut the eyes of my mind for a long enough time, and I could believe that you came to Parkis's boy in the night with your touch that brings peace. Last month in the crematorium I asked you to save the girl from me and you pushed your mother between us—or so they might say. But if I start believing that, then I have to believe in your God. I'd have to love your God (p. 181).

After an attempt to reassure himself back into disbelief, Bendrix summons up Sarah's bodily presence once again:

From the drawer of my bedside table I took her journal and opening it at random, under a date last January, I read: "O God, if I could really hate you, what would that mean?" And I thought, hating Sarah is only loving Sarah and hating myself is only loving myself. . . . Nothing—not even Sarah—is worth our hatred if You exist, except You. And, I thought, sometimes I've hated Maurice, but would I have hated him if I hadn't loved him too? O God, if I could really hate you . . . (p. 182).

As the chapter ends, Bendrix demonstrates the depth of his conversion by a small act of kindness toward Henry—a very small act, "putting two biscuits by his bed in case he woke"—but few could have imagined Maurice Bendrix undertaking such an act of kindness when they met him at the novel's opening.

Even after her death, Sarah Miles has somehow led Bendrix to think seriously about God. He had once laughed at those who believed in God, and believed that Sarah was his co-conspirator in this effort: "We had agreed so happily to eliminate God from our world" (p. 69). But by the end of the novel he is speaking of God as an active agent and addressing God as "you" and even as "You." Admittedly, he has not yet fallen in love with God, as Sarah did; the final line of the novel (and the film) is an admission of pain and anger, but it is also a prayer:

I wrote at the start that this was a record of hate, and walking there beside Henry toward the evening glass of beer, I found the one prayer that seemed to serve the winter mood: O God, You've done enough. You've robbed me of enough. I'm too tired and old to learn to love, leave me alone forever (p. 192).

But I, for one, have never been convinced that Maurice Bendrix would be able to resist God forever. Like the character of Asbury Fox in "The Enduring Chill" (see chapter 8), he will discover that God is not placated so easily. Such is the power held over us by the people we love; their bodies continue to press up against our minds, even after they have died.

And yet, as I have suggested, the pull of our everyday cultural assumptions is very strong. We are somehow convinced that the dead are really gone; they couldn't possibly continue to speak, to touch, or to hear us. I have given a lot of thought to the Christian belief in the resurrection of the flesh and have taught it in countless theology courses, but I too am subject to the undercurrent of our culture. As I was doing the final revision of this chapter, I searched through the novel for the page number of a particular quotation—Sarah's line about catching faith like a disease. I had written it in from memory, but now needed to provide a citation. I knew I had marked it in the book, but although I thumbed through it page by page, I couldn't locate it. Of course, when I was thumbing through, I always stopped at the point where Sarah died. She couldn't possibly have said anything after that. But of course she could. The quotation was in the letter to Bendrix that arrived two days after she died.

I should have known. After all, Christians believe in the resurrection of the flesh.

## Questions For Discussion

1. Describe some of our standard cultural assumptions about death. How do we treat the bodies of those who have died? What practices surrounding death suggest that we think that the bodies of the dead still "matter"? What practices suggest otherwise?

2. Name some additional reasons, other than those suggested in the chapter, as to why Christians might often tend to think of life after death in terms of "the immortality of the soul" rather than "the resurrection of the flesh."

3. Think of what you know about a person, personally known to you during his or her lifetime, who is now dead. When you think of this person, do you still mentally connect him or her with a physical body? What factors affect how we think of the bodies of the dead?

4. Describe your own experiences of how the dead continue to be present to us. Concentrate especially on examples of presence that seems bodily in one sense or another: photographs, items that the person might have touched, and so on. Why do these objects have such power to recall the dead person to our minds?

5. Do you think that it is possible for a dead person to affect people who are still alive, as Sarah seems to have done at the end of the

novel? What factors do you think may have contributed to your belief (or disbelief) in such effects?

## For Further Reading

Aukerman, Dale. *Reckoning with Apocalypse: Terminal Politics and Christian Hope.* New York: Crossroad, 1993. (Advanced)

Bynum, Caroline Walker. *The Resurrection of the Body in Western Christianity, 200–1336.* New York: Columbia University Press, 1995. (Advanced/Specialized)

Jüngel, Eberhard. *Death: The Riddle and the Mystery.* Translated by Iain Nicol and Ute Nicol. Philadelphia: Westminster Press, 1974. (Advanced)

McClendon, James Wm., Jr. *Systematic Theology.* Vol. 1, *Ethics.* Nashville: Abingdon Press, 1986. (Advanced)

Schmemann, Alexander. *For the Life of the World: Sacraments and Orthodoxy.* 2d ed. Crestwood, N.Y.: St. Vladimir's Seminary Press, 1973. (Introductory/Advanced)

## Other Works Dealing with "The Resurrection of the Flesh"

Denys Arcand, *Jesus of Montreal* (film)

Richard Matheson, *What Dreams May Come* (book and film)

Frank McCourt, *Angela's Ashes*

Toni Morrison, *Beloved* (discussed in chapter 7)

Flannery O'Connor, *The Violent Bear It Away*

Walker Percy, *The Thanatos Syndrome*

Wim Wenders, *Wings of Desire* (film)

William Shakespeare, *Hamlet, Prince of Denmark; The Winter's Tale* (discussed in chapter 6)

## twelve

# "And the Life Everlasting"

We conclude our reflections on the basic elements of Christian belief with a question that has entranced humankind for all of its recorded history. In every realm of life and every discipline of study, in every time and place, human beings have had to face the reality of death. We live out our days, some in happiness and some in suffering; but no matter how long or short our time on earth may be, we know that "our little life is rounded with a sleep." And every time a human being dies, others are left to ponder the questions: What now? Where is this person, whom I saw and heard and touched just a few minutes ago? Where will she go? What is he experiencing at this moment, as I gaze upon his lifeless body? These questions must be faced and responded to at some point by every philosophy of life, every system of faith, every account of human existence, and every reflective human being.

As I suggested in the previous chapter, Christians have always claimed that human persons do not cease to be persons once they have died. Nevertheless, their relationship with other human beings is changed dramatically at the moment of death. Is their relationship with God changed as well? What is this new state into which they have been transformed? Will I be able to see this person again, to know her again, when I die? We are often told that life after death brings us to a state of happiness and perfect peace; yet if I am so convinced that my dying friend is going to such a good place, why do I find myself still crying?

Christian reflection on life after death begins with a number of strongly worded sayings of Jesus—sayings that promise life beyond the boundary of death. The promise of "eternal life" is present in all the Gospels, but in the Gospel of John it becomes a prominent and recurrent theme. Its best-known instance is in a verse that is sometimes called a summary of the Christian faith: "For God so loved the world that he gave his only Son, so that everyone who believes in him may not perish

219

but may have eternal life" (John 3:16). The claim that belief in God and in Christ leads to eternal life is repeated at John 3:36, 5:24, 6:40, 6:47, and 17:3, as well as 1 John 5:13. The promise of life everlasting seems to depend primarily on our willingness to receive the nourishment and the words that Jesus offers us (John 6:54, 6:68, 10:28, and 17:2, as well as 1 John 2:25 and 5:11).

Frequently, the promise of eternal life and eternal happiness is understood as inversely related to human happiness on earth. At several points in the biblical text, future happiness is specifically keyed to earthly sorrow, and earthly happiness seems more likely to lead to sorrow in the afterlife. "Those who love their life lose it, and those who hate their life in this world will keep it for eternal life" (John 12:25). Similar sentiments are expressed, less directly, in the portion of the sayings of Jesus known as the Beatitudes (Matt. 5:1–12; Luke 6:17–26). In these passages, those who suffer in this life—the poor, the hungry, the persecuted—are said to be blessed, for their "reward is great in heaven" (Matt. 5:12; Luke 6:23). And in Matthew 25, Jesus tells the story of a scene of judgment, in which those who have helped others during their lifetimes "inherit the kingdom prepared for [them] from the foundation of the world," whereas those who have failed to help others are sent "into the eternal fire prepared for the devil and his angels" (Matt. 25: 34, 41).

But with such passages of text, we must tread very carefully. Throughout its history, Christianity has too often been portrayed as a faith that is concerned primarily about preparation for life after death—so much so, in fact, that life in the here-and-now is transformed into something marginal or irrelevant. And worse still, as I noted in chapter 4 when discussing the problem of suffering, Christians have too often used the promise of future reward to justify the sufferings (of others!) in the present. Even when we have the power to relieve suffering right now, we too quickly substitute the promise of a greater reward in the afterlife.

In fact, language about the afterlife has frequently been used to repudiate one of Christianity's most central claims: the claim that we can't bribe God. We cannot win God's favor just by doing the required number of good deeds. God loves us unconditionally; God doesn't wait, like some kind of cosmic Santa Claus, to see whether we've been good little boys and girls before deciding whether to give us a present. Rather, God gives freely: God brings us into existence out of nothing, pursues us when we go astray, and takes on human flesh to redeem us. God brings all of this about, not because we've been particularly good and have therefore earned God's favor; quite the contrary, in fact. Rather, even though we have done nothing to deserve it (and quite a lot to suggest that we are not worthy of it), we are offered a free gift of grace, and we are invited to respond to that gift in freedom and gratitude.

This basic pattern is repeated throughout the story of the faith. When God writes the Ten Commandments on tablets of stone, they are not conditions through which we might earn God's favor. In fact, the Commandments begin with a statement of what God has already done for the people of Israel, without any good works on their part, but only because God has chosen them: "I am the Lord your God, who brought you out of the land of Egypt, out of the house of slavery" (Exod. 20:2). In the Psalms and the writings of the prophets, God is described as returning to the people and calling them back into a right relationship, not because of their great achievements and pious deeds, but *in spite of* their ignoble acts. And Paul never ceases to remind the recipients of his letters that their good deeds and their efforts to obey the law will not save them; rather, we are justified by God's gracious gift, through redemption in Christ (Rom. 3:24).

The church has often gone astray on this point. We find it very convenient to use the promise of a future reward or punishment to enforce good behavior in the present. The device is known to anyone who has felt frustration when trying to encourage a child to develop certain good habits: by promising a wonderful dessert after the meal (or threatening to withhold it), we can persuade children to eat their vegetables. In a similar way, we improve our employees' performance by promising them promotions or threatening them with downsizing, and we motivate students by reminding them that at the end of the course they will receive a grade. But it is a serious theological mistake for us to project this human behavior—motivated as it is by the imperfections in our own relationships—onto God, thereby implying that it characterizes God's attitude toward us. Each time the church has attempted this kind of projection, someone has come along to offer a correction. Against a theologian named Pelagius, who suggested that God could only save us if we undertook good works, St. Augustine reemphasized the importance of God's grace and our utter dependence upon that grace for our salvation. Against some abusive fundraising practices of the medieval church, Martin Luther preached the importance of justification through faith, not works. And contrary to popular opinion, this need *not* be an issue of significant ongoing theological difference between Protestant and Roman Catholic Christians. At the Council of Trent, which formulated the Catholic Church's response to the Reformation, the "Decree on Justification" begins with a clear and solemn rejection of any suggestion that we can bring about our own salvation by doing good works.

Quite consistently, the Christian faith has officially proclaimed that God's love for us is unconditional; we should be grateful for this love and respond by doing good, but our good works do not cause or earn God's love for us. Of course, as I have often noted in this book, official proclamations are one thing, and popular belief is quite another. Our culture encourages us to use the threat of future rewards and punishments as a means of coercing certain attitudes and behaviors, and claims about the afterlife seem to be the ultimate example of just such a system. My own view is that Christianity would be a much more widely embraced faith, if it could only convince people that it did *not* believe in a God who withheld favor from us until we behaved rightly.

I am not trying to suggest that the promise of future rewards has no role whatsoever to play in Christian belief—only that this promise should not be used as a replacement for concrete ethical claims about how we are to live our lives in the present, as though the next life were the only one that really mattered, and the present one were irrelevant. Nor should we use the promise of a good life beyond death (or the threat of a bad one) as our primary means of motivating certain kinds of behavior in the present. For one thing, this account distorts our understanding of God's freely given grace, making God dependent on our good works for the dispensation of divine love. Moreover, if we are motivated to act rightly only through fear of future punishment, our lives are not thereby transformed; we are simply subordinating ourselves to the more powerful will of another. It's rather like the case of citizens who salute their nation's flag only because someone is holding a gun to their heads: we see an outward show of patriotism, but nothing has been done to win the hearts and minds of those whose loyalty is being forced upon them. In fact, very often, the opposite result comes about: people feel so frustrated and patronized at being forced to display a feeling that they do not really feel that they turn against those who are forcing them to do so—planting their feet ever more firmly in opposition.

If the Christian belief in eternal life is not primarily a threat that God uses to coerce us into good behavior, what *is* its meaning and significance? As I suggested in the previous chapter, Christian beliefs about death have important implications for other aspects of life, some of which may not be obvious at first glance. To speak of "eternal life" is to claim that our relationship with God and with other people is not terminated by the event of death. Death *does* represent a significant change in our existence, but it does not mean our annihilation.

We often describe the dead as "going to" heaven or to hell, but to describe these realms as "places" in any ordinary sense is somewhat problematic. As I suggested in chapter 6, the ancient world was quite comfortable with the picture of a three-tiered universe with heaven above and hell below. But we don't tend to think in these terms anymore (though as I observed at that point, our language still bears many symbolic markers of the claims that "up" is good and "down" is bad!). In any case, the description of heaven and hell as "places" leads us to ask a lot of distracting and irrelevant questions about these realms—Where are they? How big are they? What do they look like? I describe these questions as "distracting" because they miss the point that Christians are trying to make when they speak about heaven and hell.

The classical theological definition of heaven is "dwelling in the complete and utter presence of God," whereas hell is "the complete and utter absence of God." Heaven and hell are attempts to describe our ongoing relationship with God (or lack thereof) after our deaths. Of course, we believe that dwelling in the complete presence of God would be absolute bliss, and so we tend to depict heaven as a place of peace and happiness, with fluffy clouds and angelic harps. Conversely, since the utter absence of God is the worst thing imaginable, we tend to depict hell as a place of true horror, with reference from everything to "weeping and gnashing of teeth" (a common biblical phrase) to medieval depictions of cackling demons equipped with various instruments of torture. I'm not suggesting that these depictions are "wrong" (How could I? I don't know what heaven and hell look like!); I'm just suggesting that they need to be treated as precisely what they are. They are speculative attempts to describe the glory of God's eternal presence and the horror of God's eternal absence in the most vivid terms imaginable.

Many people are troubled about the idea of the existence of hell. Why would God create a place or a state of being that was so horrible? How could God possibly allow any of us to end up there, if divine love is as powerful and all-encompassing as we have been told? The usual answer to this question is that the existence of hell, of a place of God's utter absence, is necessary because of God's decision to endow human creatures with free will. If we are truly free, we must have the power to say "no" to God—not only in our present lives, but for all eternity. Hell is that place where people end up for as long as they continue to turn away from God. But precisely because God's love is so strong, many people believe that no one will ever manage to refuse it forever. As I noted in chapter 8, the Christian belief in the Holy Spirit is an expression of our conviction that God pursues us relentlessly, never flagging in the effort to woo us back into a right relationship. If this is true, it seems unlikely that anyone would ultimately choose to turn away from God. As some theologians have put it: our free will means that hell must exist for those who choose it, but the wideness of God's love and mercy makes it quite possible that hell will ultimately be empty.

Regardless of their final resting place, the dead do not cease to be persons; their existence is as real as that of the living. In chapter 9, I quoted one of Barbara Kingsolver's characters in *Animal Dreams* concerning the rituals surrounding the Day of the Dead: "In these families you would never stop being loved." To believe in eternal life is to believe that, even after a person dies, there is still a person who needs to be loved and cared for as we loved and cared for that person in life. This, in turn, has a number of concrete implications—three of which I would like to explore here.

First, because Christians claim that the dead are still *persons* who have ongoing relationships with God and with other persons, this recasts our understanding of the significance of time and space as categories of distinction and separation. In the normal course of life, we assume that we are closest to the people who live at roughly the same time and in the same place that we live. But as I suggested in chapter 9, Christians believe in the communion of saints: the connectedness of all Christians, of all times and places, is of greater significance than the accidental closeness that we feel with those of our own time and place.

This belief in the communion of saints is reinforced by our belief in eternal life: those who have gone before us, because they continue to exist (as the dead rather than the living, but still continuing to exist), are as much a part of this communion of saints as are those who are with us today. The beliefs and commitments that bind us to other Christians are more important, more central to our lives, than are the factors that bind us to randomly selected individuals that happen to live in our own time and place. This is related to my comment in the introduction to this book, to the effect that we should be able to recognize certain similarities of belief between ourselves and Christians who lived in a previous era. If we take seriously our belief in eternal life, we know that those "Christians of the past" are not really "past," but are in some sense still present to us. This is why Christians have traditionally prayed for the dead. We believe that, although they are dead, they are still persons, and they continue to deserve the active support of our prayers.

Second, our belief in eternal life is a reminder that our experience of a human being's life is not a complete experience of who that human being is. Even before we are born, we are tied into a network of relationships that involve our parents, our larger communities, and God. After we die, these relationships continue, though of course in a profoundly altered way. This means that the brief glimpse that we have of a person during his or her life is never a complete picture: people are always more complex, more multifaceted, than our experiences of them. This should give us pause about rendering any ultimate judgments about people based on what we have experienced of them during their lifetime. We have no idea whether, and to what extent, their character might be changed by the dramatic alteration of their relationships that is brought about by death. Perhaps death brings a clear, unclouded perspective on questions and issues that seemed obscure to us in life. Perhaps in death, we are able to experience a love and care that is purer than anything we have known in life. Perhaps the experience of such love and care can have a transformative power, helping us move away from whatever obstructed our relationships in life.

Of course, we cannot know whether such experiences await us in death. This is, ultimately, the case with any and every claim about the specific elements of eternal life: we simply don't know. Everything is speculative; all that we can say for certain is that the believer's life transcends the boundary of death. When we imagine what heaven looks like, or whether we will recognize people when we get there, or any other such question, we are in the realm of guesswork and imagination. (Sadly, these kinds of reflections seem to dominate the discourse of most people who write about these questions!) Precisely because all discussion of the afterlife is necessarily speculative, we should exercise a good deal of caution about pronouncing a final verdict on anyone's humanity on the basis of his or her life.

One of the ways this problem has manifested itself over the course of Christian history is with the church's attitude toward suicide. Given the very positive picture that Christians have sometimes painted of the afterlife, it is understandable that some people—particularly those who experience a great deal of pain in their earthly lives—would want to hasten their own move to that "better place." But we also believe that we are created and placed on the earth for a purpose, and that our earthly lives are not to be ended prematurely. Unfortunately, in the church's justifiable effort to dissuade people from suicide, it has sometimes claimed that those who commit suicide put themselves beyond the reach of God's salvation. I think that this was an unfortunate development; it reminds me of the withholding of dessert from children who don't eat their vegetables. In fact, no one knows the extent of God's mercy, and every other aspect of the Christian faith leads me to believe that God is both able and willing save a confused and lonely person who commits suicide. In saying this, I am *not* suggesting that suicide is acceptable; at some level, it is always, as the saying goes, "a permanent solution to a temporary problem," and I don't believe that anyone should commit suicide under any circumstances. But the church's claims about the lack of salvation for suicides has not prevented Christians from taking their own lives; it has only increased the anguish of the victim's friends and relatives, who fear for the salvation of the dead person and thereby magnify their own feelings of guilt and shame. In any case, given the fact that we cannot see beyond the boundaries of a person's earthly life, I would not want to put myself in the position of making any final proclamation about that person's ultimate fate. I am happy to leave that in God's merciful hands.

Third and finally, the belief in eternal life is a way of encouraging ourselves to be honest with ourselves and to live authentic lives. The Christian claim about eternal life suggests that our lives are seen by God in a broader perspective and against a wider backdrop. This means that we cannot ultimately hide anything; our self-deceptive words and deeds cannot be closeted away. If we thought that our humanity were narrowly bounded by our birth and death, then we might be able to accept the notion that "all our secrets die with us." But the belief in eternal life means that our existence is exposed to a much greater degree of scrutiny; in order to keep a secret forever, we would have to "hide" for all of eternity!

Even though ancient Judaism did not have a well-developed notion of the afterlife, the people of Israel certainly understood that God had no difficulties seeing into the hearts of human beings. This is well expressed in Psalm 139:

> O LORD, you have searched me and known me.
> You know when I sit down and when I rise up;
>     you discern my thoughts from far away.
> You search out my path and my lying down,
>     and are acquainted with all my ways.
> Even before a word is on my tongue,
>     O Lord, you know it completely.
> You hem me in, behind and before,
>     and lay your hand upon me. . . .
> Where can I go from your spirit?
>     Or where can I flee from your presence?
> If I ascend to heaven, you are there;
>     if I make my bed in Sheol, you are there.
> If I take the wings of the morning
>     and settle at the farthest limits of the sea,
> even there your hand shall lead me,
>     and your right hand shall hold me fast.
> If I say, "Surely the darkness shall cover me,
>     and the light around me become night,
> even the darkness is not dark to you;
>     the night is as bright as the day,
>     for darkness is as light to you.
> For it was you who formed my inward parts;
>     you knit me together in my mother's womb.

The later Christian interpretation of this Psalm has, if anything, extended and strengthened its claims about the wide range of God's insight into our character. For Christians, God's perception extends not only to every conceivable place and back to the time before our birth, but also into the infinite future.

Perhaps this is why people who face an impending death so often feel compelled to make a final confession of sin or to reveal some secret that they had harbored all their lives. Such behavior would seem irrational if we really believed that we carry such secrets with us to the grave. But as I have already observed, we don't really have much specific information what lies beyond death; so when it is approaching, we tend to want to settle our accounts.

Of course, some accounts can't be settled before death. Some people die very suddenly or in a state of estrangement from God or from other human beings, or they die without an opportunity to seek reconciliation and absolution (as in the case of suicide). What happens to such people? Are they condemned to the complete and utter absence of God for all eternity simply because they never heard the message in a persuasive enough form, or because they were too weak or too distracted to respond to it? Such a situation would hardly seem consistent with the love and mercy that is so characteristic of the God in whom we place our trust. Because of the difficulty of this question, Christianity developed a doctrine of purgatory—a realm of the dead that is neither heaven nor hell, but a place where the dead can continue to "work out their salvation" beyond the grave.

The belief in purgatory is not universal among all Christians. Many Protestants believe that it is inadequately attested in Scripture (though there are some passages that are thought to imply its existence), but the main source of the rejection of the teaching were the abusive medieval practices associated with the purchasing of indulgences for the dead. Long before that time, purgatory had been a standard feature of Christian teaching. Both in the Eastern and Western church, it is attested from the earliest centuries. Sometimes it is described as a place of purifying punishment for lesser sins, but it might be better understood as a place where we come to a clearer understanding of God's love for us and our love for God. It is also a place where that love is allowed to break down our resistance so that we can ultimately respond positively to God's gracious initiative toward us.

As I suggested with respect to the discussion of "the resurrection of the flesh" in the previous chapter, no work of realistic fiction or film can adequately portray this belief. Since we have no concrete, physical experience of death until after we die, we cannot depict it in a way that can be "recognized" by anyone, as we might be able to portray a foreign city or a familiar room. Therefore, writers have had to be more creative in addressing how we might better understand these beliefs and what they might possibly mean. As an illustration of how this might be done, I have chosen an obscure but absolutely brilliant film by the talented Italian director Guiseppe Tornatore. He is known to some American audiences as the Academy-Award-winning director of *Cinema Paradisio* (1989). In 1995 he wrote, directed, and even edited this wonderful gem of a film, entitled *A Pure Formality*. It stars two giants of the international film world, Gérard Depardieu and Roman Polanski. See it soon—it has a wonderful twist that I'm going to have to reveal later in this chapter, and I'd hate for you to miss the experience of it while watching the film.

*  *  *  *  *

From the opening gunshot, we suspect that Depardieu's character has committed some kind of horrible crime, but we are not privy to the details. The ensuing investigation does not help us much. It takes place at a remote and rustic police station (location unknown), in the midst of a torrential storm; water drips incessantly through cracks in the roof. The place is a bit eerie; the clock has no hands, the telephones don't work, and the guards seem uncannily calm. The setting evokes Kafka's *The Trial* even before the suspect has a chance to remark on the absurdity of his situation. Even the man's *name* is a matter of debate. He claims to be the famous French novelist, Onoff—a claim that draws smirks from the police and is disputed by the Inspector (Polanski), who happens to have read all of Onoff's works. Eventually the author is able to quote enough of his own material to convince everyone of his identity.

Onoff's celebrity status gets him better treatment from the police, but we are still suspicious. Despite the suspect's acknowledged genius, he is still put through the usual interrogation: name, date and place of birth, details of his activities during the day. He does not seem particularly reassured by the inspector's claim that the whole process is "just a formality."

Before the questioning gets underway, the doors of an old cupboard accidentally come open, revealing—among other things—a mousetrap. It is not one of the typical "killer" mousetraps to which we are accustomed; it is a European model, more complicated and potentially more humane (it simply closes a door when the mouse takes the bait, allowing the animal to be released elsewhere). Despite its less-than-fatal nature, however, the trap quickly becomes a metaphor for Onoff's view of his circumstances: this must be a trap.

And as the interrogation begins, it soon looks like one. After a while, we begin to believe that perhaps Onoff *deserves* to get caught in a trap. The film's expert editing splices visual images of Onoff's activities of the day into his report, such that we see when he is telling the truth, when he is lying, and when he is shading his comments in his own favor. Of course, the inspector does not get to view these scenes, but his subtle method of investigation slowly allows him to piece together the day's events.

The inspector's technique is partially drawn from standard police procedures, but he is also an expert "confessor" in the old sense of the word (the one who hears confessions and guides people to remember and accept their own wrongdoings). The inspector develops a rapport with Onoff, frequently quoting from his works and reassuring him. He casually notes the inconsistencies in Onoff's account of his recent activities, occasionally starting the whole process over when the suspect is caught in his own intricately constructed network of lies and half-truths. We are not sure whether Onoff is deliberately concealing certain details of his life, whether he has repressed them, or whether he simply can't remember. His recollections are shown as a series of rapid-fire scenes; the audience thus comes to experience both the clarity and the sketchiness of the suspect's memory.

As the interrogation becomes more intense, Onoff finally demands to know the reason for his detention. The inspector provides it: a murder has taken place nearby. The police have a corpse, but its face is mutilated and they cannot identify it. They believe that Onoff will eventually reveal the identity of the body, because they believe that he committed the crime.

Onoff dramatically insists that he did no such thing. In fact, he claims that he has never even held a gun. The inspector throws doubt on this claim by noting that, according to the details of his own biography, Onoff served in the military. This leads Onoff to make the first of many confessions that he will make before the investigation is over: that he fabricated the details of his own biography, even changed his name, so that the reading public would be more likely to "accept" him as a novelist.

But did Onoff really commit the crime? Our suspicions continue because he is quickly frustrated by the questioning; he often explodes in anger. At one point he even attempts to escape; but as he runs through the nearby forest, his leg is caught in a steel jaw trap (reminding us again of the mousetrap). Throughout the interrogation, the weather outside reflects Onoff's own inner turmoil: whenever he is able to admit to one of his many misdemeanors, the continuing downpour seems to weaken a bit, but when he returns to the devices of deception, the storm rages. When his most profound deceit is discovered, we hear, from inside the cupboard, the mechanism of the trap and chatters of protest from the apprehended mouse.

Eventually, the inspector confronts Onoff with more and more evidence of his own past, such that he is forced to remember the events of his life and of that day with clarity. He is confronted with a large sackload of photographs, the product of a long-term hobby of his. In viewing them, he begins to put the pieces of his own life together again. He is particularly entranced by one photograph—a man he describes as his inspiration for writing. The inspector is incredulous; the photograph is clearly of an old tramp, a bum who lives on the streets. Onoff explains that the man produced pages and pages of nonsensical writing; after his death, Onoff took the writing home and tried to decode it. Finally, he broke the code and published the tramp's beautiful writing as his book *The Palace of Nine Frontiers*. He tells the inspector that this shouldn't come as a surprise to him because the book is dedicated to the man. The inspector denies this: "You've never dedicated a book to anyone. It's well known." He then produces a copy of the book to prove it.

Onoff has in fact published another man's writing under his own name without any form of acknowledgment. He has committed the writer's greatest sin—plagiarism. As Onoff admits his guilt, we see him understand that he must be accountable for his actions. He needs to admit *who he really is*—even if the picture is not a particularly pretty one. Once he has begun to admit this, to allow himself to be judged for his faults, he is able to accept and embrace the whole of his life. This leads to the film's dramatic final revelation.

As Onoff finally reconstructs the events of the day in a complete and truthful manner, he has to admit many things that he has not been able to admit. His friend Paula did in fact come to see him and depart again; he did search his attic looking for a gun; he did write a long note of farewell, urging its future reader to "Forget me often; forget Onoff," and he did in fact kill someone. The surprise is that the person he killed was *himself*.

Onoff has committed suicide; the police station, it turns out, is a stop along the way in the journey of the afterlife. It is neither heaven nor hell; it most resembles purgatory insofar as it seems to be a place where lives are purified in the refiner's fire. But the point of the film is an important one, whether or not we accept the existence of purgatory: it suggests that life and death are not so easily distinguished from one another. The accused man cannot tell the difference. He is, of course, separated from the living; but even in death he continues to have an ongoing existence within which he must come to terms with himself. He must acknowledge who he really is, confess his sins, and ask for forgiveness from those whom he has injured.

When he is successfully led to admit to his own act of suicide, he is finally able to remember everything with clarity. He breaks down, weeps, admits his fault, and asks to call Paula to ask her forgiveness. At that moment, the incessant rain stops, the storm clears, the handcuffs come off. He is even allowed to make his phone call, and he tries to tell Paula of the terrible deed that he has done. Of course, she cannot hear him; the boundary between the living and the dead, though wafer thin, is absolute. (For the same reason, all the scraps of evidence that the police have accumulated from his house cannot be kept; "We have to put everything back," Onoff is told. But these artifacts of his life also remind us of his physicality, his fleshliness. In fact, they were carried into the police station in a body-bag—which Onoff thinks is the body of whomever he is accused of murdering!) Through a painful (but ultimately victorious) process of slow, consistent revelation, Onoff has been brought to realize the importance of forgiveness and reconciliation. The "formality" he has undergone turns out to be "pure," but not just in the sense of "merely a formality." It is also *purifying:* it has prepared him for the possibility of salvation.

At this point, Onoff looks around the room at all the evidence that has been amassed against him, and begins to discover some odd things—things that help to explain why his phone call didn't go through, why the inspector knew all his writings by heart, and why he was not able to write (and not allowed to use the typewriter). In fact, he discovers that the typewriter has no ribbon; he has only been led to think that the details of the proceedings were being recorded for posterity. None of his "confession" has been saved to use against him; after all, its purpose was not retributive. Its only purpose was to bring him to an authentic assessment of his own humanity.

At the end of his look around the room, Onoff spies the mousetrap. He discovers that the cheese has been taken, and that the doors are shut—but that the mouse is not there. Like the mouse, Onoff finally took the bait—only to find himself not imprisoned, but set free. The handcuffs are off; dawn is approaching, and he will soon leave the police station. We are not told exactly where he is headed, but the inspector observes the dramatic change in the weather and comments that this is "a good sign." As Onoff leaves, another man is brought in, treated with the same kindness that he was treated when he arrived (a blanket and warm milk). At this point he realizes that no one knows, when they arrive in the afterlife, where they are; they first have to be brought to accept responsibility for themselves and to ask for forgiveness. "Mr. Inspector," says Onoff, "you have a good job. Difficult, but . . ."—and the inspector nods in agreement. His job is to help people grasp the salvation that is freely on offer.

"This must be a trap," we think—and in a way, it is. God draws us in, offering us salvation, and asking only that we confess our sins and ask for forgiveness. Once we have done so, we are "caught"—but then, in an act of pure grace, God sets us free. Like the clump of cheese in the mousetrap, the bait is ours to keep. In this sense, the film provides a commentary, not just on the Christian belief in life everlasting, but on the whole structure of the faith: the grace of God, the goodness of creation, our sinful condition, God's intention to save us, God's ongoing and relentless pursuit of our souls (and our bodies!), the importance of forgiveness, and the resurrection of the flesh.

Admittedly, the process by which we are led to this salvation is difficult and even dangerous. We are resistant creatures, and it sometimes takes a great deal of time and effort for God to lead us to the place that has been prepared for us. But that does not make the outcome any less inevitable. The long, slow process is, from God's perspective at least, a pure—and purifying—formality.

## Questions For Discussion

1. How have you usually imagined heaven, hell, and (if you've thought about it) purgatory? What stories, images, and concepts most influenced these perceptions? What do you think of the theological claim, mentioned in this chapter, that "there is a hell, but it will ultimately be empty"?

2. Do you think that Christian claims about the afterlife are frequently used to persuade or coerce people into certain kinds of behavior? Do you think this is acceptable? Why or why not?

3. Think about the degree to which our culture continues to think of the dead as *persons*. Offer some examples and illustrations, both for the claim that we *do* continue to honor the dead as having some kind of continuing personal existence, and for the claim that we treat the dead as extinct, as having no further existence.

4. As suggested both in the present chapter and in chapter 7 (on the return of Christ to judge the living and the dead), the experience of judgment encourages us to live more authentic lives by owning up to our thoughts and our deeds. Think about the experience of having one's life or one's character formally judged by another. Do you think that this would only be frightening and demeaning? Could it provide the opportunity for coming to terms with one's own life, and for reconciliation?

## For Further Reading

Cohn-Sherbok, Dan, and Christopher Lewis, eds. *Beyond Death: Theological and Philosophical Reflections on Life after Death.* London: Macmillan, 1995. (Advanced)

DeWolf, L. Harold. *Eternal Life: Why We Believe.* Philadelphia: Westminster Press, 1980. (Introductory)

Maloney, George A. *Death, Where Is Your Sting?* New York: Alba House, 1984. (Introductory)

Zaleski, Carol. *The Life of the World to Come: Near-death Experience and Christian Hope.* New York : Oxford University Press, 1996. (Advanced)

## Other Works Relating to "Everlasting Life"

Richard Matheson, *What Dreams May Come* (book and film)

# Conclusion

# "Amen"

When the creeds are used in a service of worship, they end with the word "Amen": "so be it." This provides yet another reminder that, as I noted in the introduction to this book, the creeds are not mere laundry lists of statements about the Christian faith. In fact, they are really much more like *prayers*. When we say them, we are not merely announcing what we think or describing the state in which we find ourselves; we are also asking God for help and guidance in living into the faith that the creeds attempt to articulate. We are confessing our faith, but we are also confessing our *unfaith*. We know that, in various ways, we have failed to orient our lives entirely toward God; we have failed to make God the one true object of our allegiance. When Christians say "I believe," we are also saying, "please help me to believe." It is therefore entirely appropriate that we *pray* the creeds, and that we end our prayer—and this book—with a request that God might make it so: Amen, so be it.

Our tendency to inhabit the borderlands between faith and unfaith is not new. It is not merely a recent development brought on by life in an increasingly secular age. In fact, it has been rather typical of the way that people have responded to the gospel of Jesus Christ through the ages. Many of the greatest Christian writers, looking back over the course their lives, have tried to understand why they had so adamantly resisted God's claim upon their lives and why unbelief remained their regular companion, even as they came to believe. In his *Confessions*, Augustine offers a wonderful description of the long and arduous path that he wandered through the equally attractive lands of faith and of doubt until he finally came to realize that "our hearts are restless until they rest in God." And what Christian has not been beguiled by the beautiful story in the Gospel of Mark, in which the father of a sick child is told that all power and possibility is dependent upon his ability to believe? He cries out to Jesus, as would we all: "I believe; help my unbelief!" (Mark 9:24).

The tension between belief and unbelief is a common theme in works of narrative fiction, and it may help to explain why such fiction is so helpful for understanding the nuances of the Christian faith. If the creeds (and similar statements of Christian belief) were merely collections of logical propositions that Christians were asked to affirm, it would make sense to examine them only by means of detailed philosophical arguments and similar forms of finely tuned analysis. But if statements about Christian belief (such as the creeds) are actually *prayers*—assertions of belief and acknowledgments of unbelief—then matters are different. The explication of these statements will depend much more on our ability to immerse ourselves in a world in which we are caught up into the space between faith and doubt, between reality and imagination, between commitment and reserve. Within this unstable, uncertain space, we discover the depths and breadth of the Christian life—not only its joys and hopes but also its occasions of sorrow and despair. A complex, rich, and fully-lived human life will always experience tragedy as well as comedy. Those who have experienced the depths of both will usually prefer either one rather than a steady drone of rational, dull, and passionless thought.

Many writers and literary critics have spilt limitless ink in an attempt to define the terms *comedy* and *tragedy,* and to distinguish the two. Still more energy has gone into the effort to sort various works of fiction and drama into one category or the other. But such efforts eventually founder on the essential point that all great works of literature have their comic and their tragic elements. In fact, this is one of the most obvious ways in which literature mirrors life: it gathers our greatest joys and our deepest sorrows into one circumscribed space and invites us to recognize that both sorrow and joy are essential elements of *who we are*. Every work of literature that is examined in this book includes both comic and tragic aspects, and critics could probably generate good arguments, in almost every case, for classifying the work as a comedy or a tragedy. But part of what makes a work of literature *great* is its ability to outstrip the categories that we have constructed to try to contain it. Every time we return to one of these great pieces of fiction, drama, or film, we see something new. We find ourselves resonating in new ways with the imaginative world that these stories present to us.

The Christian life is similarly complex. It is rich and poignant and deep. It cannot be sorted neatly into the categories that we have constructed for it. It is certainly much more than a "religion," as social scientists have narrowly defined that term. Nor can it be adequately encompassed by labels such as *comedy* and *tragedy*. Christians know that the world is headed toward a gloriously redemptive conclusion, which is surely not tragic; and yet, in this "time between the times," we meet with far too many occasions of separation, loneliness, and despair to be comfortable describing our lives in the classic terms of comedy. Consequently, the Christian life cannot be well explicated by simplistic stories in which good conquers evil, love wins again, and everyone goes home whistling a happy tune. Nor, conversely, can it be adequately represented by narratives in which the whole cosmic order is portrayed as shot through with meaningless pain, or in which injustice carries the day. Only complex, multifaceted, and somewhat inconclusive stories will adequately reflect the life that we are called to live as Christians: a life of waiting and watching, confident in God's final victory, yet aware that the journey will involve much suffering with those who suffer, as well as rejoicing with those who rejoice.

Thus, when choosing works of narrative fiction to employ in explicating the central elements of Christian belief, I tended to gravitate toward precisely such complex, multifaceted, and somewhat inconclusive works of literature. I believe that such works are most likely to accomplish the goals that I mentioned at the outset of this book. They create an imaginative world within which we can dwell, thereby directing our attention away from a focus on ourselves alone and urging us to attend to the lives of others. They lead us into a relationship of sympathy and empathy with other human beings—helping us to recognize, in the lives of fictional characters, our own lives and indeed the whole human condition. They help us to see and appreciate the *whole* of a human life, thereby better demonstrating the relationship between belief and action and providing realistic circumstances within which we can begin to understand what our own beliefs might mean in practice.

These are the kinds of effects that these stories have had on my own life, and I hope they have had a similar effect on yours. In the process, they may begin to transform statements of Christian belief from dry, logical propositions into a passionate, fully engaged way of life. I also hope that these imaginative stories will help transform the unfortunate reputation of theology from an esoteric discipline that has little or nothing to do with the Christian faith into a worthwhile occupation for every Christian believer. Perhaps these stories can even help transform our perception of the Apostles' Creed (and other statements of Christian belief) from a suspiciously antiquated checklist of beliefs into a heartfelt and life-transforming prayer—a prayer that we can utter in the spirit of a bereaved parent who cries out, "I believe; help my unbelief!" and a prayer to which we can, with confidence and joy, say "Amen."